THE INNER EDGE

THE INNER EDGE

The 10 Practices of Personal Leadership

JOELLE K. JAY

Foreword by Howard J. Morgan

PRAEGER
An Imprint of ABC-CLIO, LLC

A B C 🌑 C L I O

Santa Barbara, California • Denver, Colorado • Oxford, England

Library of Congress Cataloging-in-Publication Data

Jay, Joelle.
  The inner edge : the 10 practices of personal leadership / Joelle K. Jay.
       p. cm.
  Includes bibliographical references and index.
  ISBN 978-0-313-37805-8 (alk. paper)   ISBN 978-0-313-37806-5 (ebook)
1. Leadership.   2. Success in business.   3. Success.   I. Title.
  HD57.7.J39   2009
  650.1—dc22   2009012775

13   12   11   10   9   1   2   3   4   5

This book is also available on the World Wide Web as an eBook.
Visit www.abc-clio.com for details.

ABC-CLIO, LLC
130 Cremona Drive, P.O. Box 1911
Santa Barbara, California 93116-1911

This book is printed on acid-free paper (∞)

Manufactured in the United States of America

Graphic art: Shawn Sariti

For Tim, who keeps me grounded while I reach for the moon,
and
for TSC.
This one's for you.

Contents

Foreword

Leadership: one word with powerful, multidimensional meanings. Although countless books and articles have been written on leadership, few have focused on the internalization of the concept. Most efforts have focused on models and techniques that build skills to help us lead others more effectively. We have spent most of our time trying to figure out the differences between managing and leading—with most leadership analysis being focused on interaction with others. Indeed, many would argue that engagement with other people is inherent in the word *leadership*. But few give us insight into how leadership fundamentally impacts us as individuals. What is our role in the process?

A perspective that has not been fully explored, until now, is the notion that we cannot become more effective leaders of others without first becoming more effective at leading ourselves. We must better understand our personal role within the leadership process. By exploring ways to improve self-leadership, we will build clarity and confidence to more successfully influence and lead others.

When I met Joelle Jay several years ago, I soon discovered that she possesses the characteristic that I value more than any other when assessing the effectiveness of people with whom I interact—the willingness and commitment to learning. The closer we come to thinking we have all the answers, the further we stray from the knowledge and answers that we seek. Joelle intuitively knows this and remains open and curious. She is less focused on what she knows than on what she can learn. The people that can have the most impact on our lives are the ones that share life's lessons with us. It is the learning from their continuous journey that allow us the luxury of enhanced clarity—those wonderful "ah hah" moments.

In this book, Joelle shares such insights and provides us with practical, simple steps that help us all to be more effective. And most importantly, she teaches us to acknowledge our role in leading ourselves in order to more effectively impact others. Put a different way, she walks the talk—living the counsel that she shares. Who better to provide thoughts and insights to guide us through these turbulent times? Treat this book as a guide that will allow you to be a better person and a better leader. The worksheets and practical approach will leave you wanting more.

Welcome to personal leadership.

Howard J. Morgan
Managing Director,
Leadership Research Institute & 50 Top Coaches

Acknowledgments

You who have helped create this book, you have my deepest gratitude.

Whether you helped with a word, a line, an idea, or a phrase—or whether you helped by reading a chapter, taking care of my kids, giving me a break, giving me a chance, helping me think, or loving me for who I am—you gave me a part of your self, so that I could find mine.

Thank you.

Tim

Morgan and Jackson

Karen McRae

Shannon O'Brien

Jeff Olson

Kevin Smokler

Amy Kovarick

Stan Wakefield

Heidi McKenna

Howard Morgan

Michelle Nichols

David Stipech

John Breternitz

Anne-Marie Hoppe

Kathleen Conaboy

Rayleen Cudworth

Judy Irving

Erin Mecseji

Ali Dugan

Rich Whitney

Chris Cox

Meggin McIntosh

Bradley Charbonneau

Clive Chafer

Lesley Means

Karen Grupe

Chris Lehr

Tony Manfredi

Shawn Sariti

and of course, Mom and Dad

The Inner Edge:
What Is Personal Leadership?

Most true happiness comes from one's inner life.

—*William L. Shirer*

LEAH

Leah Zellner, the president of a national resort group, dashed into her office, throwing off her coat.

"I'm sorry I'm late!" she gasped. "It's been a crazy day!"

For the next five minutes, she raced through a litany of concerns: leading her company as its first female president, finalizing a merger, launching a new global strategy, moving into a new office, speaking at a client conference, throwing her daughter's wedding, and expecting her first grandson.

"You certainly are busy!" I commented.

"You have no idea," she wheezed. "Meetings, calls, invitations, a trip to New York . . ."

I watched Leah rush about her office. Here was a woman who seemed to have everything she wanted: a glamorous, high-paying job; exciting travel; and a happy, growing family. But today everything that made up her charmed life seemed to be getting in the way.

I wondered, *Is this what our busy lives have come to? That our momentous life events have become items to check off a list?*

Leah flopped into the chair beside me. "You know, it used to be that it was Ready, Aim, Fire. Then it became Ready, Fire, Aim. Now it's just FIRE! FIRE! FIRE!"

Leah's life as a leader mirrors many I've seen in my years as an executive coach. Every day, I see talented, accomplished leaders struggling because they're too stressed, too stretched, or too tired of sacrificing. As a result, many businesses are losing their leaders, and many leaders are losing themselves. It's become a stubborn predicament: how to achieve success without sacrificing your quality of life.

There's another way to be successful as a leader in today's world that is more thoughtful. More strategic. More reflective. You can learn to lead in a way that preserves your talent while enhancing your quality of life. You can succeed without the sacrifice. Leading well and living well, both at the same time. In the pages of this book, you will discover a new way to be a better leader . . . and lead a better life.

But be aware that this book isn't about leading your organization or leading your team. It's about leading yourself.

WHO ARE YOU AS A LEADER?

Everyone is a leader in some way. Throughout this book, I will be referring to leaders, and I do *not* just mean presidents and CEOs. I mean you.

A business or corporate leader. Corporate leaders often hold leadership positions in their organizations: president, vice president, director, manager, or supervisor. You may even own the company. But you can also serve as a leader in your company even without the fancy title by the way you act and interact.

A professional leader. You can be a leader in your profession whether you are a consultant, an entrepreneur, or an independent professional like an attorney, speaker, or physician.

A community leader. You may have a leadership role in public service, as a nonprofit board member, in your church, with the Girl or Boy Scouts, or in your neighborhood.

A family leader. As a mother, father, sister, brother, son, daughter, grandparent, or cousin, you may take an active part in creating your family environment.

An inspirational leader. You may be a leader among your friends, family, and fans by the way you conduct yourself—as reflected by your character, your choices, and your demeanor.

A thought leader. You could be leading change with original ideas and new ways of thinking.

An action leader. Maybe you're the one with the energy to make things happen and the charisma to get others to do the same.

The leader of your own life. No matter who you are or what you do, you get to take the lead in your life. No one else will do that for you. No one else *can.* You may or may not have a fancy suit, a nameplate on the door, and an assistant just outside. But every single one of us is leading a life, which may be the most exciting kind of leadership of all.

In what ways are *you* a leader?

LIVING AND LEADING ON THE EDGE

Every leader has an inner and an outer edge. Your *inner edge* is the you behind the scenes: your thoughts and motivations, your aspirations, your plans, your decisions, your strengths and weaknesses, your values, and your way of becoming a success. Your *outer edge* is the you that you show the world: your words, your actions, and your interactions with the people around you. Your inner and outer edges are intimately related. The way you feel influences the way you act. Your actions affect your results. Your results determine the way you experience life. In order to be effective as a leader and in your life, you need to spend time on both your outer and inner edge.

Most leaders, like Leah, often concentrate on their outer edge. They focus on the company vision, mission, results, customers, and clients. All of that is appropriate and productive, and you will continue to do this work as a leader. But leaders must also learn to think about their inner edge.

- Who are you as a leader?
- Who do you want to be?
- What do you want to achieve, why, and how?

Questions like these are the inner work of a leader, and they shape your ability to lead and live well.

The Möbius Strip

Parker Palmer, author of *A Hidden Wholeness* and *Let Your Life Speak,* illustrates the relationship between our inner and outer selves using a geometric shape called the Möbius strip (see Figure 1). The Möbius strip is a seamless circle twisted so that as you trace your finger around the loop, the inner side becomes the outer side, and outer turns to inner.

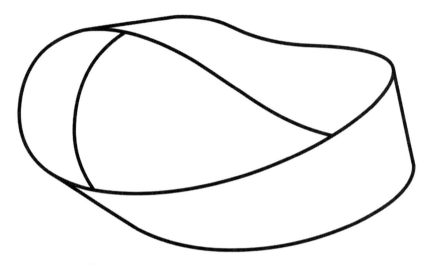

FIGURE 1   A Möbius strip

Palmer writes,

> The mechanics of the Möbius strip are mysterious, but its message is clear: whatever is inside us continually flows outward to help form, or deform, the world—and whatever is outside us continually flows inward to help form, or deform, our lives. The Möbius strip is like life itself: here, ultimately, there is only one reality.[1]

Your thoughts and feelings (your inner edge) influence your effectiveness as a leader, and your actions and interactions (your outer edge) in turn shape your life. As you start to integrate your life and leadership, your inner edge becomes your outer edge and your outer edge becomes your inner, just as on a Möbius strip. Distinct parts and priorities start to disappear as life becomes one harmonious whole.

In the same way that your inner and outer edges are intimately related, so are your life and your leadership. The way you lead helps shape your life. The life you live will help you lead. Become a better leader, and lead a better life.

If you don't pay attention to both outer and inner aspects of leadership, you may suffer a fate common to many leaders: you'll lose your edge.

LOSING YOUR EDGE

> In a few hundred years, when the history of our time is written . . . the most important event historians will see is not technology, nor the Internet, not e-commerce. It is an unprecedented change in the human condition. For the

first time—literally—substantial and rapidly growing numbers of people have choices. For the first time, they will have to manage themselves. And society is totally unprepared for it.

—Peter Drucker, "Managing Knowledge Means Managing Oneself,"
Leader to Leader

We live in a time of extraordinary choice and change. It requires every one of us to take responsibility for our own lives. You may want to achieve—even overachieve—and you've got the talent, drive, and chutzpah to do it. But it's not always easy. In my work coaching, speaking, and teaching across the country, leaders tell me what it is like to lead in the 21st century. This is what they say.

Our customers are impatient. Our competitors are going fast. And so we just have to have this incredible sense of urgency to beat our competitors and to overachieve on their expectations.
—Charlene T. Begley, President and CEO Enterprise Solutions, GE

We Are Overwhelmed. Assuming the responsibilities of leadership creates a struggle between professional ambitions and quality of life. Just juggling your workload fills every day. Add in children, home ownership, personal finances, and the rest of your life, and you can feel like you're ready to collapse. But there seems to be little option in a society that equates working hard with being good. You still get the gold star for staying late, and busyness has become a badge of honor. In recent years, organizations have made a nod to this issue in the form of flex time, telecommuting, and other creative options for doing business. Unfortunately, many of these ideas come with a stigma. Colleagues frown on counterparts who work less or leave early. It's difficult to retain a decent quality of life when the weakest member of the team is perceived to be the one who gets home in time for dinner.

We Are Discouraged. The realities of leadership can be discouraging. For many, the glamour is gone. Unscrupulous CEOs are paid as heroes but behave like villains, and the results are abysmal. In fiascos like the housing mortgage crisis and numerous Wall Street investment scandals, industry leaders have brought huge companies to disgrace and jeopardized the savings and livelihoods of thousands of people. Loyalty and good performance no longer buy the long-term security they once did. Layoffs, wage cuts, outsourcing, offshoring, automation, and reduced benefits are crippling our spirits. No matter how hard we work, no matter how fast we go, there always seems to be more, more, more to do. It's starting to feel like more is *never* enough.

We Are Disengaged. Engagement is the degree to which you feel committed to your job, and it is a critical aspect of performance. Yet in 2005, 72 percent of the U.S. working population described itself as disengaged from its work.[2] Does this sound familiar? You're bored in your meetings. You can't rally to stay late or come in early. You spend more time at the coffee stand than you should. Your work is mediocre, and you know it. Stripped of the opportunity to do what you do well, you don't really feel like doing it at all. Instead of a sense of meaning, sometimes we just feel unmoved.

We Are Needed. As leaders we don't always get what we need, but our businesses desperately need us. As baby boomers retire in droves and global business continues to grow, the need for new leaders grows, too. Those needs can't be met by just anyone. Experts are calling for leaders who are authentic, creative, innovative, resilient, self-initiating, and trusted.[3]

Most of the leaders we know are, or want to be, these kinds of leaders. But it's hard to be so thoughtful and present in such a frenzied climate. Nevertheless, we live in the information age, and business is driven by our knowledge. As leaders, we are needed to compete.

We Are Talented. The good news is that despite these challenges, it turns out we're really talented. Years of Gallup research have proven that we are at our best when we are most ourselves.[4] Unfortunately, we don't all capitalize on our strengths. Less than 20 percent of us believe we have the opportunity to be our best every day,[5] and only 17 percent of us play to our strengths most of the time.[6] Compare that to the reports of people on high-performance teams who say they rely on their strengths 75 percent of the time,[7] and it's clear there's a lot more potential to be tapped.

We Are Leaving. Crowded by the pressures of modern leadership, we can't seem to make it all work. We may want to lead with our strengths, but our jobs demand that we just go, go, go. We may want to be strategic, but every day we just need to get things done. At some point, it just becomes too much. That's why so many leaders are responding in a quiet, decisive way: They're taking their marbles and going home. Literally. The business world is facing a collective brain drain as educated, talented leaders opt out of the business world for more alluring alternatives, including full-time parenting, home-based businesses, and start-up companies. With low set-up costs and instant access to global markets, we no longer need corporate infrastructure to fulfill our ambitions. We can do it on our own. We live in a free agent nation.[8] Going out on our own is flexible, it's freeing, and it's fun.

But having the opportunity to leave one's job isn't always the win it might seem. Businesses lose highly talented leaders, and leaders lose their home in the world of work. Many leaders don't feel like they have a choice: They either live with the stress and busyness, or they leave for another way of life whether they want to or not. For both you and your organization, your leaving is really a loss. You can end up living a "less-than" life.

Less-Than Lives

What does it look like to lead a less-than life? Perhaps you'll relate to some of these leaders:

- Ali, a systems administrator for a global network, works around the clock. With clients in California, India, and China, he works in three time zones. Business hours span 24 hours a day. It is not uncommon for Ali to sleep with his PDA under his pillow or answer his phone in the middle of the night.
- Dean just can't seem to get ahead. A software engineer in the Silicon Valley, he makes what would be considered an enviable salary in most parts of the world. But his bills—for his children's private school tuition and his trophy house, among other things—are even bigger than his income, and he has become one of the new "working-class millionaires" who are trapped by their success.[9] His life might seem luxurious, if only he could pay his bills.
- Molly is trying to hold her life together. After the birth of her son Alex, she hired a housekeeper, a cook, a gardener, and a nanny so that she could juggle her home life with her job as a corporate attorney. Now instead of feeling more relaxed, she spends her time chasing after her staff at home and at work. She runs back and forth between her home and office all day, trying to sneak a few moments with her baby before rushing off to reassure clients that she's still committed. One rueful moment, she looked into her son's face as she handed him to his nanny and thought, "I will regret this for the rest of my life."

Of course, not every leader is affected to this extreme. Yet the signs of losing one's edge show up in common, everyday ways. See if you've felt any of the following symptoms.

Frustration. It can be enormously stressful to want success and quality of life and somehow not be able to attain it. It becomes a daily values clash between the life you're living and the life you want.

Confusion. When life gets busy, you can lose your focus. You end up doing whatever's most pressing, because you can't see past it to what matters more.

Frenzy. With so much to think about, you can start to feel buried in your to-do list. The demands are steady, the e-mails keep coming, and you have a thousand places to be. You fly through things as fast as you can just to stay afloat.

Sacrifice. When you separate success from quality of life, you face a dilemma. You end up making decisions you don't want to make: to work or stay home, to take a promotion or preserve your sanity, to follow your heart or stick to the security of a so-so job.

Dissatisfaction. When you aren't able to pinpoint your contribution and live a life of meaning, your achievements can feel hollow. You might feel discontented, bored, isolated, unmotivated, stagnant, or burned-out. You might even start to wonder what it's all for.

Mediocrity. When you become disconnected from the grander vision of your life and leadership, you end up tinkering in the minutiae instead of increasing your value. Forget about high expectations. You're just shooting for "good enough" and "done."

To some degree, everyone experiences these signals now and then, sometimes without much concern. But for leaders who ignore the warning signs, the effects can be grave. Failed marriages, estranged children, heart attacks, midlife crises, and career abandonment aren't uncommon for the most accomplished leaders, who've let go of their personal lives to hang on to their careers.

But it's not just a personal problem. No business can survive for long on the backs of tired, stressed-out leaders, because the leaders themselves can't last. Talk about a loss: employee depletion, disengagement, and attrition cost the business world dearly. As Gallup researchers Rath and Clifton report,

> This rampant negativity is not only disheartening, it's *expensive:* It costs the U.S. economy between $250 and $300 billion every year in lost productivity alone. When you add workplace injury, illness, turnover, absences, and fraud, the cost could surpass $1 trillion per year, or nearly 10% of the U.S. Gross Domestic Product (GDP). These costs are not specific to the United States; they exist to varying degrees in every country, industry, and organization we have studied.[10]

Even though businesses go to incredible lengths to figure out how to attract and retain talent, those efforts are wasted when they fail to nurture the talent they've got.

In a society characterized by independence and self-reliance, it makes sense that we would sacrifice a bit of ourselves for our work. If you work hard, you'll get ahead. It's the American Dream. But somehow over the course of several generations that ethic has been distorted. Now, we know that if you work *too* hard you may or may not get ahead, but one thing is sure: You'll still be working.

It's time to upgrade that way of thinking. You don't just need to work hard. It serves no one for you to be at work at all hours, eking out shoddy deliverables through squinty eyes, powered by fast food and triple lattes. Getting ahead has less to do with time and effort than it does thoughtful, reflective consideration—the kind of inner work that allows you to choose who and how you want to be. You get to work in a way that supports your life.

We need a remedy for leaders who lose their edge. Only when leaders are able to sustain their motivation and talent in a way that works for their organizations and for themselves will they truly succeed. We need a new way of leading—one that leads to a new way of life.

You are far too talented to lose your edge. You can choose the quality of your life *and* improve your effectiveness both at the same time, benefiting both yourself and your business at once. Then you won't lose your edge. You'll gain an edge because you will truly be at your best. In order to lead for a lifetime, you'll need to spend some time on your inner edge. You'll need to take personal leadership.

PERSONAL LEADERSHIP

All around us, a few exceptional individuals and teams are accomplishing the seemingly impossible. . . They're hitting higher-than-expected targets and making it look easy, doing it with more ingenuity and fewer resources, more speed and less stress, more trust and less time—while still managing to have rich and full lives.

—*Robert Cooper, Get Out of Your Own Way*

Personal leadership is your commitment to take the lead in your own life. You take the opportunity to design, create, and achieve your ideal ways of living and leading. In a positive, unselfish way, personal leadership means putting yourself first. Literally speaking, personal means "about you"; leadership means "coming first." A definition:

Personal leadership is the self-confident ability to crystallize your thinking and establish an exact direction for your own life, to commit yourself to moving in that direction, and then to take determined action to acquire, accomplish, or become whatever you identify as the ultimate goal in your life.[11]

When you practice personal leadership, you lead from the inside out. The process involves asking yourself, "How do I need to be and act and think in order to be my best?"—a kind of self-driven style well-suited to dedicated leaders like you who will carry business into the future. In order to do that, you must periodically turn away from the concerns of the day—the people, the problems, and the pressure—to explore and discover your inner edge.

To practice personal leadership, you apply the principles of leadership that make businesses a success . . . to yourself. For example, leading in business involves having a compelling vision, developing strategies, and inspiring people to use their talents to meet a goal for improved business results. Leading yourself means applying these same principles of leadership to your role as a leader and your life. You, too, need a compelling vision and a strategy for reaching it. You need a team supporting you. You need results, as well as a sense of contribution and purpose. The difference is that personal leadership doesn't just make for better business, it makes for better leadership. It makes for a better you.

As a leader, you must learn to lead yourself to stay effective. When you practice personal leadership, you use every ounce of your potential with inspiration instead of perspiration, synergy instead of sacrifice, and wisdom instead of work. Personal leadership is so important, in fact, that renowned management expert Peter Drucker once called it "the only leadership that's going to matter in the 21st century."[12]

Characteristics of Personal Leadership

Personal leadership is distinguished by its focus on the individual and an appreciation for who you are. Here are some defining characteristics:

Respectful. Personal leadership respects the extraordinary value of each human being. It does not, as so many models do, tell you to be like someone else.

Reflective. Personal leadership means thinking about what you're doing, in a spirit of wholeheartedness, openness, and responsibility.[13]

Renewing. A 2000 report from McKinsey and the Society for Organizational Development reported that "the most important tool for leading 21st century change is the leader's *self.*"[14] Unlike a take-no-prisoners approach to leadership, personal leadership offers an element of renewal—a way for leaders to slow down and advance in a powerful yet sustainable way. When you are overworked, overtaxed, and overtired, you burn out. When you are rested, rewarded, and renewed, you excel.

Rewarding. No matter what you do for a living, your work can be rewarding. Personal leadership offers you the chance to create true prosperity—the kind of happiness that comes not just from financial gain but also from the richness of life.

Raising the Bar. A focus on slowing down and thinking about oneself might seem at odds with traditional business goals of speed, profitability, and results. On the contrary, there is no correlation between success and hours worked.[15] There is, however, a strong correlation between your ability to produce and the joy you take in your work.[16] Those who practice personal leadership don't just meet expectations; they exceed them.

When you invest in your own growth and potential, you and your organization reap the rewards (see Figure 2).

Benefits for You

Personal leadership gives you a host of ways to do more, faster, and better.

You Are More Efficient and Productive. You learn to do things the way they come naturally so you can be productive without being so busy. You learn to use your mind well. You manage your focus instead of your time, and your energy instead of your effort. The result? You achieve more with less. You experience quality work and quality time at once.

You Feel Motivated and Inspired. Practicing personal leadership means you not only know what you do well, you know why you're doing it in the first place.

Living with Life	to	Leading a Life
Frustration	⟶	Peace of mind
Confusion	⟶	Clarity
Overwhelm	⟶	Balance
Stress	⟶	Choice
Sacrifice	⟶	Sustainability
Dissatisfaction	⟶	Fulfillment
Ineffectiveness	⟶	Focus/Productivity

FIGURE 2   **From living with life to leading a life**

Work isn't just work anymore. It's your chance to contribute your talents to people and ideas in which you believe.

You Experience a Life of Joy and Fulfillment. One important aspect of personal leadership is the ability to connect, not separate, the different parts of your life. You can still be committed to your work, but your commitment supports your personal life. You can still devote yourself to your personal interests, but your devotion is integrated with your work. You don't have to trade one for the other, and so you move from *distress* to *de-stress.*

Reconnecting with your sense of self does more than enliven your work. It makes life more rewarding. You see through the well-documented myth that money alone can buy happiness. Don't worry—you don't have to give up the gains of success. You just get to experience the rewards of joy and fulfillment as well.

You Get Your Life Back. When you learn to lead yourself, you find more free time, choice, and control. Practicing personal leadership, you learn that you can have it all without doing it all. You learn to put first things first and to let things happen instead of making them happen. Then at last you can achieve your ambitions while still saving something for yourself.

You Get Better Results. It may seem that personal leadership has an awful lot to do with *you.* Indeed it does. But your success as a leader also produces better results for the business. As you focus on your inner edge, you become more effective on your outer edge. As you improve yourself, you improve your team, your organization, your company, and your results.

Benefits for Business

In a time when leaders are gasping for breath, personal leadership breathes in new life. Businesses that honor the development and well-being of their leaders experience the following:

- higher customer satisfaction
- lower turnover
- higher productivity
- increased creativity
- integrity
- resilience
- speed
- quality
- innovation[17]

Study after study show the importance of high-performance leadership in business. Engagement alone, just one result of personal leadership, accounts for an 18 percent advantage in earnings-per-share for organizations over their competitors.[18] A study of the top 20 companies for leadership development showed that companies that emphasize leadership development gain higher profitability long-term.[19] The bottom line: Personal leadership is smart business.

It is good for business for business to be good to you. But you've also got to be good to yourself. When you feel your best, you can give your best to your company, your clients, and your team. That's not just a win. It's a triumph.

THE 10 PRACTICES

In the chapters of this book, you are going to learn 10 practices of personal leadership you can use to lead well and live well. We call these *practices* because you practice them the way one might practice yoga or sports or medicine. You engage in each practice over and over again, each time getting a little better until eventually, you've mastered the skill.

1. *Get Clarity.* Connect clearly and instantly to your long- and short-term visions of success.
2. *Find Focus.* Focus your attention on top priorities even when the world around you is pulling you away.
3. *Take Action.* Stop spinning your wheels and start driving with direction—easily, swiftly, and in less time.
4. *Tap into Your Brilliance.* Identify what's exceptional about you, both positive and negative, and use your uniqueness to your advantage.
5. *Feel Fulfillment.* Discover what drives you—your values, meaning, and purpose.
6. *Maximize Your Time.* Think differently about time and learn to do more with less.
7. *Build Your Team.* Develop your own private team of supporters—not just fans, but advocates who will help you succeed.
8. *Keep Learning.* Keep adapting and improving in this world of unending change.
9. *See Possibility.* Take advantage of the hidden opportunities all around you—the ones most people miss.
10. *All . . . All at Once.* Align and integrate your life so you can enjoy and excel in every moment of being a leader and leading your life.

The 10 practices are not like a ladder; you do not have to do step one to get to step two. But nor are they a collection, a basket of separate, distinct concepts and ideas. They are more like stones in a river. Depending on where you are, you may only need one stepping stone, helpfully placed, to make the jump from where you are to where you want to be. On another day, you might need two or three. And if you want to go through a very systematic process of growth and change to truly maximize your potential, you can step on stones one, two, three, four, five, and so on for a straight, secure path to a whole new place.

Throughout the book, you will find everything you need to master personal leadership:

- insights
- questions
- exercises
- worksheets
- resources

Every chapter ends with a section titled "Your *Inner Edge* Coaching Assignment" that can be used to advance your practice of personal leadership and help you refine your inner edge.

You will also find examples of leaders who are practicing personal leadership. Their stories come from leaders I have coached, interviewed, and worked with over the years. These leaders aren't famous. You've never heard of them, and you probably never will again. They are composite illustrations of everyday leaders doing extraordinary things—just like you. Although names and details have been changed in consideration of their privacy, these descriptions reflect the experiences of real leaders.

As your coach, I'm here to help. You can even call. Just go to the website, www.theinneredge.com, and you'll find all the support you need to help you be as successful with the practices as you intend to be with your life.

STARTING YOUR PRACTICE

> There is only one corner of the universe you can be certain of improving, and that's yourself.
>
> —*Aldous Huxley*

Most business books try to help leaders by changing who they are. Not here. This one shows you how to become more of who you are. In this book, you will do that by practicing personal leadership. Not just reading about it, but actually thinking, writing, reflecting, and taking action using the principles of leadership that can help you be a better leader, and lead a better life.

You got where you are today by being good at what you do. My guess is that you are energetic, committed, and sharp. You apply yourself. You get involved. You set high goals and challenge yourself to exceed them.

But sustaining that level of excellence over long periods of time can be tough. You need to be able to maintain your excellence without becoming jaded or worn-out.

And that's a challenge. You have more to do than ever before. There's more pressure to perform, and higher expectations to meet. You feel like you are going as fast as you can, and you feel pressure to go even faster. Running, running, running through every day, you feel as though you need to catch your breath—if you could only find a smarter way, if you could only find some shortcut to get you where you need to go, maybe you'd be. . . .What? More successful? Happier? Less stressed?

There *is* another way. It's a way that has you still succeeding, still achieving, and still leading the way toward the results you want. But it does so in a way that comes easily and naturally. You save time, reach your goals, and enjoy yourself by taking an approach that is aligned with who you truly are. You reach higher than you ever knew you could and expand your results. You get a better return on your efforts, and you do it by investing in yourself.

Then, you find out what's *really* possible.

You will accelerate your achievements and exceed your own expectations. You will amaze yourself with the results. You will learn how to make the most of all you've been given and all that you've gained—to not just fulfill your potential but to blow past it, to not just learn but to be transformed, to not just grow but to be rewarded with the greatest possible return.

Personal leadership is not just a conceptual ideal. It is a practical strategy for continuously renewing yourself and your leadership so you can reach your greatest potential and make your biggest, most powerful, positive impact, all while enhancing your quality of life. You can be an effective leader who adds more value to the business, and yes, you can still be home in time for dinner.

YOUR *INNER EDGE*: A SELF-ASSESSMENT

To get started, take a few minutes now to answer a few questions for reflection using the worksheet "Preparing for Practice." At the end of this chapter, you will also find a self-assessment titled Your Inner Edge to test your skills in personal leadership. Take that survey, then use the rest of this book to improve your effectiveness in leading yourself.

Leadership is not just for corner offices anymore. You don't become a leader because someone else says you are. You become a leader because you embrace leadership for yourself. When you practice personal leadership, leader is not just a label; it is a way of life.

PREPARING FOR PRACTICE

Why are you reading this book? What are you hoping to gain?

- A new perspective, clarity of thoughts.
- Comfort that I can succeed at a high level while
  maintaining perseverance.
- To learn a better way of going about work-life satisfaction/balance
- Develop personally so operating at high level is more natural.

What will happen if you achieve what you want?

- Greater satisfaction at work & home
- Better relationships with family & friends
- Financial progress - better investment, & savings
- Fitness, energy, confidence
- Spiritual toughness & clarity

What will happen if you don't?

- Burn out
- Won't be able to sustain level of effort
- Sickness, lack of health both physically & mentally

At the back of the chapter you will find a survey to test your skills in personal leadership. Take that survey now. What does it tell you?

- That there is a lot of insight to be gained
  And improvements to look forward to

I learned to explore my own personal leadership and personal mastery. It was transformational to me. It transformed the way I felt about my work. I started to think more purposefully about what I was about, what I brought, why I did what I did and how it connected to my work. It really changed a lot about how I thought about leadership. It became more personal.
—Cheryl Scott, Senior Advisor, Global Health, Bill and Melinda Gates Foundation

CHAPTER SUMMARY

Key Points

- As a leader, you must learn to lead yourself to stay effective.
- Personal leadership means applying the principles of leadership to yourself for success at work and in life.
- The way you lead helps shape your life. The life you live will help you lead. Become a better leader, and lead a better life.
- Personal leadership is smart business. Even though businesses go to incredible lengths to figure out how to attract and retain talent, those efforts are wasted when they fail to nurture the talent they've got.
- Personal leadership offers you the chance to create true prosperity—the kind of happiness that comes not just from financial gain but also the richness of life.

YOUR INNER EDGE: A SELF-ASSESSMENT

ARE YOU PRACTICING PERSONAL LEADERSHIP?

This survey will give you a sense of where you are just living your life and where you are actually leading it. Ask yourself to what extent you agree with each statement. Mark the corresponding number and give yourself an average score. Be sure to actually mark up your survey so you can revisit it later. A blank survey is available on the website, www.theinneredge.com, for you to download anytime. Check in again every six to eight weeks. Is your score improving?

Strongly Disagree		Agree		Strongly Agree

Clarity

1. I am clear on what I want and know how to get it—for the big things and the small.

1   2   3   4   5   6   7   8   9   10

2. I practice a strategic, reflective approach to leadership.

1   2   3   4   5   6   7   8   9   10

Focus

3. I know where to focus my attention on a daily basis.

1   2   3   4   5   6   7   8   9   10

Action

4. I am able to maintain peak performance at all times.

1   2   3   4   5   6   7   8   9   10

5. I maintain my sense of stability and equilibrium in times of change.

1   2   3   4   5   6   7   8   9   10

Brilliance

6. I have identified my talents, strengths, skills, and weaknesses.

1   2   3   4   5   6   7   8   9   10

7. I know how to maximize and leverage my unique talents and abilities.

1   2   3   4   5   6   7   8   9   10

Fulfillment

8. I am delighted with my quality of life both on and off the job.

1   2   3   4   5   6   7   8   9   10

9. I feel very little stress in my life. I am not overwhelmed.

1   2   3   4   5   6   7   8   9   10

10. I make a meaningful contribution every day.

1   2   3   4   5   6   7   8   9   10

Time

11. I have plenty of time for people, activities, and events that are most important to me.

1   2   3   4   5   6   7   8   9   10

12. I take regular action toward my most important goals—not just what's most pressing.

1   2   3   4   5   6   7   8   9   10

Team

13. I have a wide network of people who support me, and whom I support in return.

1   2   3   4   5   6   7   8   9   10

Learning

14. I am constantly learning and improving myself.

1   2   3   4   5   6   7   8   9   10

Possibility

15. I intuitively recognize and take opportunities.

1   2   3   4   5   6   7   8   9   10

16. I am often astounded by the way the opportunities I want and the solutions I need present themselves at just the right moment.

1   2   3   4   5   6   7   8   9   10

Alignment and Integration

17. I achieve a sense of renewal and restoration on a daily basis.

1   2   3   4   5   6   7   8   9   10

18. I am proud of my ability to maintain my values and the essence of who I am, even when life gets hectic and/or as I get more and more responsibility.

1   2   3   4   5   6   7   8   9   10

Success with Quality of Life

19. I have achieved success as I define it.

1   2   3   4   5   6   7   8   9   10

20. I can say with confidence that every day I am at my very best.

1   2   3   4   5   6   7   8   9   10

The First Practice

Get Clarity: *What Do You Want?*

We are what we think. With our thoughts, we make the world.

—*Buddha*

WILLIAM

In the heart of the Silicon Valley, deep in the middle of an office park, a lone light shone in an office on the 17th floor. Inside, William sat alone at his desk. He looked at the clock. Ten at night

You've got to be kidding me, he thought to himself. *This is ridiculous.* He'd started his day at four in the morning. Another 18-hour day.

He turned back to his computer. Staring back at him was the report he'd been working on since six. After 17 years at this high-tech firm, William had become a regional general manager for product development. At his company, he had both power and prestige. Most days William had an enviable job: flying the company jet from coast to coast, dining with powerful people in fancy restaurants, and trying out flashy new gadgets. But tonight, all of that seemed empty. He thought regretfully of his 10-year-old soccer player at home and the game he'd missed that evening. He loved his job, but at the end of the day, he felt like just another suit working his life away.

ELIZABETH

Elizabeth, the new head of her accounting division for a pharmaceutical company, dashed into her office. The 9:30 meeting she'd just left had been exciting, but it had left her with plenty to do. Since she'd just gotten this promotion, she felt eager to impress, but suddenly she felt like she'd overcommitted. She wished she could just sit down for half an hour and collect her thoughts, organize her notes, and make sure she hadn't missed anything. But no time for that. She dumped the stack of papers she was carrying onto the desk.

Ugh, she thought. *The pile grows!* She grabbed another stack and hurried out. On to the 10:30 meeting.

GRANT

Grant had a lot to be proud of. The founder and chief cardiologist of the Southwest Center for Heart Health and Wellness, he was totally invested in its success. The heart center had been his idea. He'd dreamed it up, secured the funding, and built the organization from the ground up. Now doctors were seeing patients and the research was underway. Three years after opening its doors, the center was a respected organization for care and research. Grant was as inspired as ever.

What's next for us? Grant wondered, his mind buzzing with ideas. *A bigger grant, a research breakthrough, a new wing? Maybe we need new staff or a high-profile teaching fellow . . .*

With so many possibilities, Grant barely knew where to start. Suddenly he felt overwhelmed. His heart started to race. He could see so much potential, and he wanted to do it all, right now! But he was only one man, and a cardiologist at that, not an organizational expert. He knew he needed to find a way to make the heart center thrive.

But, he asked himself, *how do I do that?* He stopped walking. *Seriously. How do I?*

What William, Elizabeth, and Grant have in common is that, despite their success, they all want something more. William wants something more for his life. Elizabeth wants something more for her job. Grant wants something more for his organization. The problem is none of these leaders exactly know what their more *is*. So they keep doing what so many people do: slog through the work with their heads down, ignoring that vague, unsettled feeling that they are not truly being the leaders they could be or leading the kinds of lives they want to live.

Perhaps you've felt the same way. You can be motivated, driven, and extremely busy and yet still not be as clear as you could be about exactly what it is you want.

What *do* you want? A promotion? Time for yourself? Better relationships with your friends and family? That ever-elusive work/life balance? None of these are possible unless you stop moving long enough to figure out what you're after. Explore your ideas. Envision a different reality. In order to achieve success in your life and as a leader, you need *clarity* about what you really want.

In this chapter, you will learn how to get that clarity. Ultimately, you are not just going to become clearer about what you want. You're actually going to get it.

THE PRACTICE OF GETTING CLARITY

> You can't depend on your eyes when your imagination is out of focus.
>
> —*Mark Twain*

Getting clarity is the first practice of personal leadership.

When you are clear about what you want, you are able to describe it in vivid detail. You know a little something about what it will take to get there and how it will feel to arrive. You connect to an inner source of inspiration that will call you forth and compel you to achieve a powerful new vision.

Clarity versus Vision

In some ways, getting clarity is equivalent to setting a vision. The importance of a vision is widely accepted in the business world. A vision usually refers to a long-term, inspiring description of the future of a business. From big corporations like American Express to small businesses like Zingerman's Deli in Ann Arbor, Michigan, companies around the world spend millions in consulting fees trying to define their corporate vision, because they believe a vision is the starting point for better results. Indeed it is.

A vision is just as important for you as a leader. In his book *Get Out of Your Own Way*, Robert Cooper reports that "people who carefully frame their goals into the meaning and path of their lives are at least twice as likely to achieve their goals."[1] But there's a secret to clarity many leaders *don't* know. You don't just need a clear vision of the future. You need to have the skill of getting clarity again and again.

Vision and clarity are related, but they are not the same.

Vision	Clarity
Analysis	Intuition
End product	Ongoing process
Distant future	Immediate, near, or distant future
Created with experts and input	Created by you, for you
Guides an organization	Shapes your life and leadership
Endures over time	Revised over and over every time

- A *vision* is a process and a product—a particular system for achieving a particular result: the vision statement that can guide progress for years to come.
- *Clarity* is a practice you engage in over and over to move from moment to moment without getting off track from your vision.
- A *vision* involves a finite, involved, analytical process.
- *Clarity* is an ongoing, intuitive, creative experience.
- A *vision* typically focuses on a distant, often ideal image of the future.
- *Clarity* focuses on a practical, realistic image of the immediate, near, or distant future, or even right now.
- A *vision* usually involves bringing together people and ideas, often with the guidance of a trained facilitator, to get all efforts heading in the same direction.
- *Clarity* is a process engaged in by you, for you, shaping your thinking and keeping you sharp and agile as you constantly revise your ideas about what's possible.

As leaders, we don't always make the effort to get this kind of clarity. We get lost in the details. We zero in on the *now*, and if we're really lucky, we look ahead to next week. But that's a shortsighted view. Business needs leaders who can see farther into the future—not just for their organizations but also for themselves.

Throughout this book, we can still use the word *vision* to mean "what you want," but just remember that what you want will change as *you* change. The goal of this chapter is not just to get a vision, although ultimately you will. The goal is for you to learn the skill of getting clarity again and again.

The Benefits of Clarity

When you have clarity, you know what you're doing and why, with benefits for both you and your business:

You're More Strategic. Emotional intelligence expert Daniel Goleman explains that one distinguishing factor between average and star performers is "the 'big-picture' thinking that allows leaders to pick out meaningful trends from a welter of information and think strategically far into the future."[2] Clarifying what you want frees you from today's trivialities and aligns you to tomorrow's potential.

You Make Smarter Decisions. Leaders make decisions constantly—sometimes decisions that affect thousands of lives, and definitely decisions that affect their own. When you practice clear, forward-focused thinking, you slow down enough to see the possibilities. You consciously choose a strategy. Having clarity about what you want ensures that you make the right choice.

You Take Faster Action. Your goals get obscured by foggy thinking. Clarity clears the way. As CEO advisor John Hamm writes, "When a leader defines what he or she really means and sets a clear direction according to that definition . . . action is more efficient and on-strategy, and improved performance follows."[3] No longer slowed by indecision and deliberation, you can act—fast.

You Relax. Perhaps the most exciting result of getting clarity is that you end up creating what you want, whatever that may be.

How to Practice

Three strategies will help you get clarity:

1. The Inner View
2. You and Improved
3. The Path

All three of these strategies will bring you insight on who you are and who you could be as a leader, any time you need it. I've seen it in my coaching practice time and again. When you state with clarity what you want, it actually shows up. You can almost hear the *click* as everything falls into place, just the way you'd imagined.

THE MIND-SET FOR GETTING CLARITY

Relaxed. You think clearly when you are relaxed. Take a few minutes to breathe, release any tension, and close your eyes before you start. Then take another moment or two to get in the right frame of mind.

Spontaneous. Let your right brain—the creative, intuitive side—take charge.

Open-minded. Allow yourself to be surprised. The right mind-set is optimistic, creative, and open to new ideas.

THE INNER VIEW

The first strategy for getting clarity is *exploring*. You ask yourself a range of questions about a variety of topics:

- your hopes
- your fears
- your concerns
- your questions
- your needs

You ask these questions to uncover thoughts and feelings that influence your ability to be successful. Doing this helps you see where you stand now in relation to what you ultimately want—that long-range vision. But you don't just *answer* the questions; you *explore* them. Exploration is not an interview. It's an *inner view*.

Grant used this strategy when he'd lost his vision as a leader.

GRANT

Grant had been grappling for a while with the question of how to evolve the heart center. Even though he was its chairman, he didn't see himself as a leader. He was a doctor. He didn't really know how to ensure that his leadership team was making the best business decisions. So far they had been riding along on enthusiasm, but that seemed like a fickle plan for the future. His lack of experience guiding other leaders seemed painfully clear.

That's when Grant called me. In a rush tumbled out his fears and anxieties.

"We've been working so hard to get the heart center up and running," he explained. "We've just been making it up as we go along! At first that was exciting, but now it just seems scary! All this time I saw myself as the visionary and the rest of the leadership team as the implementers. Now it suddenly seems like none of us know what we're doing!"

Grant laughed ruefully. Somehow in his work with the heart center, he had lost clarity about how to lead it into the future.

You can see from the example above that Grant was grappling with a long-range vision. At the time, he felt what he needed were answers. But before he could decide what to do next, he really needed to take a preliminary step. He needed to explore the questions.

Exploring is a great starting-point strategy you, too, can use to get clarity about what you want. There are three steps to exploring your inner view.

Step 1: Identify the Topic

As your first step to getting clarity, you identify the topic. What do you need to get clear about? What's the issue, challenge, desire, or goal that's worth exploring now? What is your purpose for seeking clarity at this time? For Grant, it was a sense of direction for the heart center. For other leaders, it could be a decision about their own careers, a particular outcome for a project, or a new way to approach a goal. You are going on an exploration; think of this step as defining the territory.

Step 2: Ask Open-Ended Questions

Once you've defined the territory you want to explore, you mentally walk around in it, allowing your mind to wander around as you find out what there is to know. You do this by asking open-ended questions.

Perhaps the most obvious place to start is with the all-powerful question, What do you want? Examples include the following:

- You know you're talented and motivated, and you want to be your best, but somehow you're not getting there fast enough. Ask yourself, what do you want?
- You know you need to get clarity on your plan for the next quarter in your business. Okay, so what do you want?
- You know you need to get clarity on what's happening with a dysfunctional team. Good. Now what do you want?

When I ask leaders this question, the answers are as varied as the leaders themselves. The box "What Leaders Want" will show you some of the wants they've named.

WHAT LEADERS WANT

- I want to add more value to my organization.
- I want to empower my employees.
- I want to get systems in place to use my time better.
- I want to be a loving, giving part of my family.
- I want to feel freer and more restful.
- I want to claim my role as a leader with more confidence and conviction.
- I want to end every day feeling great about what I've done.
- I want to extract myself from the technical day-to-day issues and be more strategic.
- I want to make a graceful exit.

Here are some more questions to help you see what else there is to learn as you explore:

- What are the biggest challenges you face?
- What's the best-case scenario? What's the worst-case scenario?
- How would you like to see this play out?
- What else is there to know?

Open-ended questions like these help you find what else is important for you to keep in mind.

Grant used the process of exploring to develop his ideas for the leadership of the heart center. We started with a very basic question. "What do you want?" For the next 45 minutes, we moved through a series of open-ended questions. "How do you envision the heart center as being different than it is today?" "What's preventing you from having what you want now?" "What role do you want to play in the future of the center? What role do you not want to play?" Sitting back with his hands behind his head, Grant gazed across the room and explored the answers. As he talked, his ideas about the future developed detail and depth.

When Grant explored his intuitive answers to the questions I posed, he was able to move away from his original stress-producing hypothetical worries ("What are we *doing?*") in favor of concrete, clarifying questions he could actually answer ("What do we want for the center?" "What do I want as its leader?" and "What do I want for myself?"). Those questions became the basis for discussions with the center's leadership about how to take the right steps now to create a world-class center in the future.

You may find that asking open-ended questions like these will suffice to make you feel comfortable and clear about the topic you're exploring. You'll figure out where you are, and you'll discover where you want to go next. Excellent. It's equally likely that you'll feel a little lost. That's okay. It takes time to get clarity. Throw off the pressure and just poke around. That's what exploring is for. You may stumble across some enlightening ideas.

Step 3: Explore the Answers

After you have an idea of what you want and some questions to stir your thinking, give yourself time to explore your ideas. Exploration (especially self-exploration) is a process. Give it time. Remember: You don't have to have all the answers. But you do have to ask the questions.

When my business was at a turning point, we found ourselves a little at a loss as to which direction to go next. Our big breakthrough came when we asked ourselves honestly, "What do we want?" Once we had that clarity, we could go out and make it happen. And we did.
—Sue Pipal, Interior Designer and Owner, Dragonfly Designs

YOUR INNER VIEW

Step 1: Identify the Topic

What is your purpose for seeking clarity at this time?

_____

_____

Step 2: Ask Open-Ended Questions

1. What do you want?

_____

_____

_____

2. What do you hope will happen, and why?

_____

_____

_____

3. What challenges are you facing?

_____

_____

_____

4. What questions do you have?

_____

_____

_____

5. What else is vitally important to you at this time?

_____

_____

_____

Step 3: Explore the Answers

- Think
- Talk to a friend
- Meditate

- Write
- Create new questions
- Record your ideas aloud

- Brainstorm
- Work with a coach
- Keep asking questions

Exercise

Use the worksheet "Your Inner View" as a guide to your exploration. A copy of this worksheet is also available at www.theinneredge.com.

YOU AND IMPROVED

The second process for getting clarity is *envisioning the future.* Envisioning means using your imagination to *see* yourself in the future—what Wharton School of Business researchers call "the leadership skill of time travel."[4] You actually close your eyes and get a visual picture of what you want. It's a day-dream with meaning. In your mind, you see yourself succeeding. You . . . and improved.

Envisioning helps you see a more complete picture than you get from answering questions in words. When you envision the future (as opposed to just ruminating on it), you *see* it in the form of vibrant images, alive with details. The pictures serve to amplify important internal messages, explain gut reactions, and reveal intuitive wisdom. They are imbued with meaning, which can help you make decisions and take action.

Envisioning is not fantasizing. Quite the opposite, it's a practical, efficient technique to get clarity instantly by tapping into these rich stores of knowledge that sometimes get obscured in the chaos of daily life.

This strategy worked well for William, who knew he wanted something different in his future. He just didn't know what.

WILLIAM

William seemed like a guy who had direction. Promotion after promotion had landed him in the tech firm's general manager chair, and he was positioned for further advancement. He wanted that. In our very first meeting, he even told me where he saw himself in five years: "In five years, I expect I'll be taking on some of the international work and helping to grow this part of the business worldwide."

The trouble was that William's job title was just one small (if significant) part of his life. The answer to the question "Where do you see yourself in five years?" was this: "Running an international division." But unanswered questions remained. "Is that a life you want to live?" "What's going to sustain you so you can lead without burning out?" "How does this career path fit with your hopes for the rest of your life?" To get to some of those answers, I didn't have to spend all afternoon grilling William. All he had to do was close his eyes.

Like William, when you envision the future, you close your eyes and imagine yourself exactly where you want to be as a leader and in your life.

Prepare. To envision the future, you start by getting prepared. As you did in your exploration earlier, set the context. Is there something specific you want to envision? Or would you rather choose a time frame and just see what's there— say, an hour from now? Six months? A year? Three years? More? You can use the envisioning technique to look far into the future (the traditional notion of "getting a vision") or you can use it to think about an event or a moment in time in the near term, short term, immediate term, or right this moment.

Relax. Envisioning always works best when you are relaxed. Before you rush off to envision your future, *slow down.* Part of the value of this process is the feeling it evokes. You don't get that from catching a peek at a blip on the screen. You get it from engaging in the experience. Save this process until you can give it your undivided attention, then take 15 minutes to do it well. Escape to a quiet café, stop at the park, or wait until you go home. In this exercise, you will be stepping into another reality. You will get more from the process if you start by detaching from the reality you are in right now.

Envision. When I walk leaders through the process of envisioning their future, I use a certain process for envisioning that you may also find helpful. You imagine yourself at the time and place of your choosing—whatever and whenever it was you said you wanted to envision—and really see yourself there. You take it all in, using all of your senses and emotions, observing what it's like to be you . . . then. This creates the detailed images that illustrate what you most want in your life.

Then, to get the bigger picture of a life in which this slice of your vision lives, you take yourself on a tour. As if you were walking the scenes of a movie set, you move from one image to another. Your work. Your career. Your home life. You see it all while you're there, visiting your future.

When William was ready to envision a new-and-improved future for himself, I walked him through this process of envisioning. "Envision a day in your life three years from now. Imagine that everything is just how you want it to be. What do you see?" William envisioned a few of the scenes from his life: at work, at home, in the daytime, in the morning, in the evening. Sitting quietly across from me, William didn't say a word but just watched the scenes flash across the screen of his mind.

After envisioning scenes from his future life, William described what he'd seen: images of himself golfing with clients and celebrating accomplishments with his wife.

I've known leaders who have seen very realistic images of themselves (only happier), and others whose images were so different from their current lives they could hardly understand what they meant. Whatever you see in your mind will take on new meaning when you take the time to debrief.

Debrief and Interpret. Perhaps the most meaningful part of envisioning the future is remembering what you saw.

After William described an image of himself golfing, I suggested that maybe there was something important to learn from the images and encouraged him to think about them further. What followed was a long conversation about what the images symbolized for William. Achievement. Challenge. Fun. As a result, William understood something that changed his approach to his work from then on: He could relax and still do well.

After you've envisioned a few scenes in your mind ask yourself what you saw in the images.

- What had you accomplished that pleased you?
- What about you had changed?
- What surprised you?
- Was there anything missing?
- How did it feel?

Questions like these anchor the images while they're fresh in your mind.

You can get additional insight by interpreting the images you saw. To do this, you recall the details and ascribe them meaning. Maybe you were wearing a golf shirt instead of a tie. Does that mean you're hoping you'll be able to loosen up? Maybe you saw yourself laughing with your colleagues. Does this mean you had a big win? There's no secret answer key anywhere to tell you what the details mean. You get to make it up. But when you do, you will find that those details represent real meaning—meaning that will help you create the future you want.

Finally, to find out how this process has clarified your ideas about what you want, write down the answer to this final question: "When you have achieved what you want to achieve . . . when you have become who you want to be . . . when you have done what you want to do . . . what will be true for you?" Keep what you write. *This* is your vision.

By envisioning himself in the future, William gained a whole new understanding of what it would mean for him to lead and live well—much more than he would have gotten if we'd discussed his future in words. If I had asked William, "Where do you see yourself in five years?" he would have given a different answer— probably an oversimplification including a particular job title and an impressive net worth. When he envisioned the answer instead, he got a complete picture, one that included his financial and professional goals but also incorporated his need for some down time, fresh air, and fun.

DIRECTIONS FOR YOU AND IMPROVED

Preparing for the Process

What do you want to envision? How far into the future do you want to go?

_____

_____

_____

_____

Suggestions for Relaxation

Close your eyes. Tell yourself that everything else will keep. When you open your eyes, your work and your duties will still be there. You are only escaping for a few minutes to clear your head and get connected with your vision. You have plenty of time. You can relax. Breathe.

The Envisioning Script

Get a picture in your mind of the future you want to create. Imagine that you've arrived where you want to be, sometime in the future. Now picture a day in your life. Everything is just how you wanted it to be. Notice the location. See where you are, and notice the details around you. Envision yourself walking around the space, owning it.

Now notice yourself going somewhere. It's a day in the life of the you you wanted to be. Where are you going? Who are you with? Notice the people around you. See yourself interacting with them, and notice how they react to you. How do you hold yourself? What do other people see, hear, and experience when they are with you?

Widen the view. What do you notice about your home and personal life, your health, your downtime, your professional aspirations, your finances, and the ones that you love?

Spend time here. See yourself moving through the day and notice the evidence of your success, however you define it. See how different you are in this vision than you are now. See how your day-to-day life has changed. Walk yourself through the hours of an ideal day, living the life you wanted to live. Take in the scenes with all of your senses—sight, sound, touch, taste, and smell. What emotions are you feeling? How can you tell? Connect with those emotions. Imagine yourself feeling them. Experience them now.

Questions for Reflection

• What was it like for you to envision the future?

_____

_____

_____

_____

- What did you see? Where were you? Who else was there?

_____

_____

_____

_____

- What had you accomplished that you were proud of?

_____

_____

_____

_____

- What about you had changed? What was new, better, or different?

_____

_____

_____

_____

- What were your dominant emotions, and what contributed to you feeling that way?

_____

_____

_____

_____

- When you have achieved what you want to achieve . . . when you have become who you want to be . . . when you have done what you want to do . . . what will be true?

_____

_____

_____

_____

You will have your own reasons for envisioning and your own unique ways of using this practice. Follow the complete directions for envisioning You and Improved whenever you want to get clarity and develop a vision. When you do, you'll find that envisioning brings you clarity and, ultimately, better results.

Exercise

Use the "Directions for You and Improved" worksheet below to envision your future. A copy of the directions along with an audio you can use to guide you through the envisioning process are also available at www.theinneredge.com.

THE PATH

Ironically, the problem with envisioning as we've discussed it so far is that it all happens in the future. Of course, that's the idea, but it can be a little intimidating. You may be able to see how a visit to the future can help you gain confidence, clarity, and practical ideas about where you're headed, but that still doesn't solve the problem of how to get from here to there. And that can be a pretty daunting proposition.

For that reason, I offer you the third strategy for getting clarity: a visualization called The Path. The Path is an organizing metaphor—a scenario that helps you order your thoughts so you get clarity where otherwise there might be darkness or confusion. To get a sense of this, here's a glimpse of Elizabeth's path.

ELIZABETH

Sinking back in her chair with her eyes closed, Elizabeth saw herself running on a trail of soft amber dirt through a mountain wood. She was running a race. As she looked around, though, she noticed there were no other runners. She wasn't even wearing a number. Wait a second, she thought. This isn't a race! It's just me! Elizabeth slowed her pace. She jogged along, taking in the scenery. The birch trees, the dewy ferns. She saw a rise up ahead, and then a long downhill slope. She quickened her step up the hill, panting, until she could see the vista. There, she stopped to take in the view.

Behind her, Elizabeth saw a long, steep path. Before her, the path flattened out and twisted gently along. The scene invited her on. She started jogging again into new territory—this time, relaxed and ready to run the distance.

Elizabeth opened her eyes and smiled. For the last five minutes, she had been visualizing this jog through the woods. Just a few minutes with her eyes closed had brought her a sense of reassuring clarity—not about jogging, but about her growth as a leader.

When Elizabeth visualized herself jogging through the woods, I had been taking her through the visualization I call The Path. Even though what she visualized was a mountain trail through the woods, upon reflection the images helped her better understand who she was as a leader: where she'd been, where she was now, and where she was going. Your path will do the same for you.

When you visualize your path, instead of envisioning the future you want, you engage in a visualization that takes you on an imaginary journey. Later, you interpret the visualization. You will find answers to questions such as these:

- Where am I going?
- What will it be like to go from here to there?
- How does where I am now fit into the bigger picture of my life and goals?

While exploring and envisioning give you clarity about what you want, visualizing The Path encourages you along the way.

Sometimes it's uncomfortable to look at the vision because it seems impossible, or you know that it's going to be costly and difficult to get there. It might feel like there's an insurmountable obstacle in front of you. If you can't visualize what you're working toward it's hard to stay focused and driven. —Patrick Byrne, CEO, Overstock.com

---

To start, picture yourself on some kind of a path—a long path, usually, with occasional changes in terrain. You get to choose the path. You might picture a paved path through a park or a view from a high mountain peak. I've heard about paths winding through a corn maze and one person driving on the Autobahn. My own path is a mountain. I've trudged up one side and skied down the other. You choose the path that suits you best.

Or, if you prefer a more spontaneous, intuitive option, you don't have to choose the path at all. You can just start the process and let the images of a path spontaneously appear as you follow the directions guiding the process. The directions will just ask you to visualize a path, and your intuition will somehow deliver the right image for you.

Once you have a path in mind, you imagine yourself starting somewhere that is meant to symbolize where you are now. Then you see yourself journeying along—past obstacles, through the changes, over time—to a destination that represents where you want to be. As you visualize yourself traveling along this path, you will experience sights and insights that give you direction, reassurance, and ideas about how to reach your actual destination—your vision—down the road.

To visualize yourself moving along your path only takes a few minutes, and it's easy to do. But the real journey starts when you reflect on the experience and interpret what you saw. Analyze the visualization. Ask yourself, If this path were a metaphor for my life, what would there be to learn? If I were to lead myself down a path like this, what would I need to do now? What meaning does that have for me in real life?

Although this process may be new to you, it is actually a version of a technique called "histories of the future" used by organizational development experts, and it helps effective leaders make sense of their realities in a fast-changing world.[5] I have often used this kind of visualization with leaders when they feel overwhelmed about the big decisions they have to make ("I want to leave my job and go out on my own" or "I'm ready to take this business to the next level") or when they feel discouraged about their ability to achieve their goals ("I don't know what I'm doing!" or "I know what I want but I have no idea how to do it!"). I offer The Path to you as one more way to get clarity about what you want . . . and how to get it.

ELIZABETH

For Elizabeth, the time-strapped accountant, The Path was a route out of the chaos that defined her life.

Elizabeth had never done any visualization before, so she was a little nervous before I asked her to visualize her path. But she was also exhausted and it felt good to put her feet up and close her eyes. After a few minutes of relaxation, I led her in some guided imagery.

The scenario of her jog through the woods is what she saw. With her eyes closed, she followed the images that appeared in her mind over the hills along the dirt trail. Later, eyes open, she interpreted the experience not in terms of jogging but in terms of her path as a leader. "For so long I've been running a race—trying to get ahead. I always feel like I'm almost there and can't afford to stop."

But in her visualization on that mountain path, Elizabeth *had* stopped. "When I visualized myself jogging, it was okay to stop. I could look around and get the long view," she explained. "It makes me think that maybe on my career path, it would also be okay to stop and take in the bigger picture. For now, at least, I can stop running so fast. If I keep acting as if I'm in a race, I'm going to miss the important things that need my attention along the way."

By detaching from real life and stepping into her visualization, Elizabeth had gotten a new perspective of herself not as an employee always racing to keep up, but as a leader in the company who was responsible for making every step count.

DIRECTIONS FOR THE PATH

Suggestions for Preparation and Relaxation

Review "The Mind-set for Getting Clarity" a few pages back and refer to the preparation and relaxation processes at the beginning of "The Directions for You and Improved." Make a habit of quieting your mind anytime you start a visualization.

The Visualization Script

Close your eyes. Visualize yourself on a path. Notice what the path looks like. Really take it in. Look left. Look right. Look overhead and all around you. Turn and look behind you.

As you look around this path, see everything that led you to this point. See also what you're moving away from.

Now turn and face the horizon. Start to move toward it, noticing your surroundings as you go. Notice what's in your way as you travel. Notice if there are any other people nearby. Notice suddenly your biggest obstacle. What is it? Study it; understand it. Now see yourself moving past it toward your destination.

Give yourself time to travel, noticing any changes that occur as you move along the path. What do you see?

See yourself arriving at the end of the path. What is this destination? What is the spirit of this place? Notice how you feel as you stand there.

Picture a sign nearby with a message. The message contains advice or wisdom for you now. What does it say?

See yourself sitting down. Take in the view from where you are.

You are going to leave this place in a moment. Stay as long as you wish, then open your eyes.

Take some notes while the experience is still fresh so you can revisit this visualization again.

Questions for Reflection

1. Where does the path lead?
   SERENE PEAK
   _____
   _____

2. What kinds of people are on the path with you?
   NO ONE ON THIS PARTICULAR PATH
   _____
   _____

3. What kind of landscape does it pass through?

Rocky at times, Flowers, trees (Large), views

4. What is the destination like?

High Above mountains views AND VAst valleys & Canyons

5. Is there a message for you, or any other kind of sign?

"FiNiSHing is MorE important than How long it takes"

Questions for Interpretation

1. What does the imagery you visualized mean to you?

_Rocky - times of challenge and difficulty. Flowers - stop And enjoy
High views - the payoff for Rocky climb, but plenty to Be enjoyed along the way._

2. What does your path tell you about your leadership—both where you are now and
   where you are going?

SEEMS a bit Rocky Now, But not excessively. Smoother As the view Appears

3. What does the journey tell you about your process of growth and development—how
   you are going along now and how to continue?

_- Rocky path feels growth & persistance. Am I making it Rocky And I will
Smooth out the next part of the path?_

Exercise

When you feel it would be useful to do this visualization yourself, use the "Directions for The Path" worksheet. Since your eyes will be closed, you won't be able to read the directions as you do the visualization, but you can get help from a friend, from the audio of the visualization script on the website (www. theinneredge.com), or by reading and then visualizing from memory. When you're ready, visualize your path. Take your time. The journey should take 5 to 10 minutes.

Afterwards, reflect back on the experience and see what you can learn. Look for the meaning in surprising images, notice the emotions you've been feeling, and write down any insights you discover. Then interpret what you saw using the questions provided to understand the images better.

PERFECTING THE PRACTICE

> So many of our dreams at first seem impossible, then they seem improbable, and then when we summon the will, they soon become inevitable.
>
> —*Christopher Reeve*

GRANT

After his initial exploration, Grant was buoyant. He carried the answers from his inner view back to the leaders of the heart center and even did a whole-group envisioning session to get their input on what was possible for the future. This step started an important conversation among the leaders about what they wanted and how they could create it that would fuel the leadership team for years to come.

WILLIAM

As soon as William had seen a version of himself as relaxed and confident instead of stressed-out and high-strung, his whole demeanor changed. He made a regular habit of envisioning various scenes from an improved future for his company and for himself. His business goals didn't change, and he was still as productive and ambitious as ever, but his focus shifted from climbing the corporate ladder to being the kind of charismatic, personable leader who would advance the business and help it grow internationally—a more inspiring and sustainable vision.

ELIZABETH

As she had on her path, at work Elizabeth slowed way, way down. She talked to her boss about key challenges (an understaffed department, an underperforming assistant). She proposed solutions (hiring, training, and reallocation of responsibilities). Together, Elizabeth and her boss stopped running long enough to get the bigger picture of the department and how they wanted it to be. Within months, Elizabeth had stopped running herself ragged. She became a leader who was thoughtful and productive instead of just busy.

I chose William, Grant, and Elizabeth as leaders to illustrate the practice of getting clarity because each of them was dramatically changed by the process. The impact wasn't sudden. All three of them emerged from their coaching sessions with some clarity then thought more about the ideas in the weeks that followed. Over time, with patience and persistence, getting clear on what they wanted helped them become the kind of leaders they wanted to be and live the lives they wanted to lead.

Now it's your turn. What do you really want? When you can get clarity on just that one question, you have already gone a long way toward getting your vision.

Your *Inner Edge* Coaching Assignment: Your Vision

At the end of this chapter, you will find a worksheet called "Your Vision" where you can record what you know so far. Over time, the notes you take will evolve into a clear and coherent description of your vision. Turn to that page now and record your ideas about what you want for your life and leadership. A blank copy of this worksheet can be found at www.theinneredge.com.

And remember to update your vision often. Take a break from your work and spend some time exploring, envisioning, and visualizing your future. It will pay off. Remember these wise words, spoken to Time Warner architect Stephen Ross by his father:

> There are those who work all day, and there are those who dream all day, and those who spend an hour daydreaming before setting to work to fulfill those dreams. Go to the third category because there's virtually no competition.[6]

FAQS

Q: How often should I practice the techniques for getting clarity?

A: Fortunately, getting clarity doesn't take a lot of time. As Robert Cooper says, "It only takes a moment, a clear far-forward glimpse, a special 'stretch' toward the future here and there everyday . . . keeping you ahead in a changing world and positioning you to achieve an ever-better future."[7] You can practice getting clarity as you drive to work, jog through the park, or lay on the couch. Anytime you're feeling stuck, tired, frustrated, unsure of your abilities, or unsure of your direction, asking yourself "What do I want?" can be just the thing to restore your energy and commitment.

Q: Once I have a vision, do I also need to have a vision statement?

A: Many leaders want to know if they need to have a personal vision statement.

Yes, you can capture your ideas in a vision statement. Many leaders do this. I use a vision statement myself to maintain clarity on my goals and purpose. You can find directions and samples for writing your own vision statement on the website www.theinneredge.com.

But writing a vision statement is not our mission in this chapter. The goal here isn't just an end-game vision, it's clarity in every moment. In other words, you don't just need to *have* a vision, you need to *envision* ideal outcomes again and again.

Q: What if I still don't know what I want?

A: Your imagination isn't a crystal ball. It can't forecast your future. On the other hand, both your intuition and your imagination are important access points to valuable information—information that you need to surface in order to clarify your vision.

A few suggestions can help if you're still not clear about what you want.

First, remember: You may not know everything, but you know something. You probably know more than you think. You might end up with a sense of what you want instead of a clear answer. You might have some answers but not others. You might even end up with more questions than you had before. That's okay. Concentrate on clarifying what you do know, and write down the questions that remain.

Second, break it down. The question, "What do I want?" is so big that at times it can be difficult to answer. Sometimes you just don't know what you want. You can't say it, you can't see it, and visualizing a path doesn't make it any clearer. If you're really getting nowhere with this process, start small. Instead of asking, "What do I want for my *future*," ask, "What do I want *right now?*" Keep practicing asking this question whenever you can: looking at your task list trying to decide what to do next, debating where to go on vacation, even standing in front of the fridge trying to figure out what to eat. Then grow it bigger. Before you enter into a conversation or meeting, ask yourself, "What do I want from this interaction?" Any time you feel frustrated or held back, ask yourself, "What do I want to have happen instead?" You will be sharpening your clarity skills and preparing to answer the bigger questions about what you want for your life.

And if you're still not clear on your vision, that's okay too. Practice the other skills of personal leadership. Your vision will evolve, and the answers will become more robust. At different times in our lives, we have clarity in different degrees. Know that the more you grow as a leader, the clearer you will become. Return to this chapter at that time and try again.

By seeking clarity, you have boldly gone inward to discover what is really true for you. You have gotten honest about what you want. Literally speaking, you've gotten the picture. You've discovered that getting clarity can move you quickly out of overwhelm, distraction, and confusion into excitement, confidence, and peace. By exploring, envisioning, and visualizing what lies in your heart, you have exposed a very important source of knowledge and insight. Now with a clearer view of what lies ahead, you can truly lead yourself and your business into a more successful future.

Then you go make that vision happen. In the next chapter, you will carry your vision out of your imagination and into your life.

CHAPTER SUMMARY

Key Points

- In order to achieve success in your life and as a leader, you don't just need a clear vision of the future. You need to have the skill of getting clarity again and again.
- Both your intuition and your imagination are important access points to valuable information—information that you need to surface in order to clarify your vision.
- Getting clarity can move you quickly out of overwhelm, distraction, and confusion into excitement, confidence, and peace.

YOUR VISION

What do you want for your life and leadership? What do you still need to know? Describe your long-term vision in a paragraph or jot down some notes. Update your vision often.

_____
_____
_____
_____
_____
_____
_____
_____
_____
_____
_____
_____
_____
_____
_____
_____
_____
_____
_____
_____
_____
_____
_____
_____
_____
_____
_____
_____
_____
_____
_____
_____

The Second Practice

Find Focus: *Where Will You Put Your Attention?*

The main thing is to keep the main thing the main thing.

—*Stephen Covey, First Things First*

YOU

It's three in the afternoon. You're standing in the middle of your office. Hands on your hips, you deliberate about what to do now. Do you sit down and sling out a rash of emails? Do you return a few phone calls? Or do you close your door and somehow try to concentrate on the big project you really need to work on? Frozen, you are immobilized by the possibilities. You drift off for a minute, staring off into space. Then you catch yourself and snap back into action.

The rest of the day you spend busily working. You pull out a project, then the phone rings and sets you off in another direction. You keep on top of your emails and other people's requests as best you can in an attempt to keep the deluge at bay. Head down, you fly through tasks and manage the crises, barely looking up to notice the time until finally, the day comes to an end.

Driving home, you're spent. The day has been intense and full. You take satisfaction in enumerating all you've done. Then you realize even though you've been busy all day, you haven't really done anything. You've been so buried, you've lost sight of your grander vision. You find yourself being haunted by vague, unanswerable questions. Could I be doing better than this? Is this what I wanted for my life? Am I making any difference? Somehow answering these questions never gets to the top of the list. Why is that? Your mind drifts off, hypnotized by the traffic and whirring about what you need to do tomorrow.

Have you ever had this experience? Ironically, even though you may be working all day, you never feel like you get anything done. You're busy but not necessarily productive. Somewhere in the back of your mind, you wonder if you're doing the right things. Not that you have a choice. You're too swamped with what you have to do today to dwell for long on what you want to do or ought to do to be more effective. Still, you know there's something wrong with this picture.

And you're right. There is. What's wrong is that when you bounce along from task to task, you're not choosing where to put your attention. You're living by chance and not by choice. You may be ignoring the most valuable parts of your life—the parts that are going to help you achieve your vision, possibly in the long term and definitely for today. Or, you may be doing many of the right things, but you're not really sure. You haven't stopped moving long enough to check. Plus, there are so many priorities, you find it hard to keep them all straight, much less stay on top of them all at once.

> It's very difficult to move forward at the end of a 12-hour day or a 16-hour day. I look at myself and ask, okay, what did I accomplish today? All I did was react to everyone's e-mails, irate customer calls, and other people's needs. It's very non-fulfilling, because I didn't drive my agenda, my charter, forward. And I have more days like that than I'd like to admit.
> —Wendy Newcastle, Executive Vice President, Bank of America

In order to get what you want, in order to be who you want to be, in order to live the kind of life you want to live and lead the way you want to lead, you need to be more strategic than that. You need to find focus.

In this chapter, you're going to pull your thoughts out of the crowded rabble of your mind and give them the attention they deserve. Get ready to move from chaos to control.

THE PRACTICE OF FINDING FOCUS

Learn enough about your goal that you would recognize it if you saw it.

—*Robert Fritz*

The second practice of personal leadership is *finding focus*. Finding focus means choosing the select few areas that you must prioritize in order to achieve your vision. You decide exactly what deserves your attention at the moment and block out everything else.

FINDING FOCUS

Finding your focus moves you from. . .

- chaos to control
- overwhelming to manageable
- random to strategic
- complex to simple
- abstract to concrete
- general to specific
- inaction to action

The Zoom Lens

Finding focus is about choosing where to put your time, energy, and attention. It's a selection process—something like the steps you go through when you take a photograph. Getting the vision for your life is like using the wide-angle lens. It gives you the opportunity to take in a lot at once. Finding focus, by contrast, is zooming in to take one specific picture, then another, then another. In this section, I will show you how to zoom in to different areas of your vision so you can reach the goals one at a time that ultimately add up to your vision. As a result, you will select the parts of your vision that are most important to you now, stay focused on them, and accomplish more—more quickly—than you can when you do everything at once.

A Leader's Answer to the Strategic Plan

Finding your focus is a little like the strategic-planning process so common in organizations. You break your vision into manageable pieces, which you can shape into concrete goals and, later, specific actions and steps.

Businesses often go through a strategic-planning process to chart a vision for where they want to be in 5 to 10 years. The goal is to build a sound structure for the organization by hammering together a strong, cohesive plan for progress. Once an overarching framework is formed, the vision gets tacked down into goals. Each of those goals then gets attached to specific objectives, and finally, tactics: specific actions that individual people must take to get results. Strategic planning works because it helps companies find focus, but it's not quite what you need when you lead yourself.

As a leader, you do need to be strategic, and you do need to plan. But compared to strategic planning, finding your focus isn't as heavy. Finding focus is less like construction and more like juggling. You may have 20 balls to juggle—leadership goals, career advancement, job responsibilities, health, family, friends, finances, fun, leisure, and so on. But how many priorities can you comfortably juggle at a time? The real trick isn't to figure out how to become a master juggler, but to realize that you can only gracefully manage so much before your life starts to feel like a circus.

Finding your focus means highlighting, combining, minimizing, and even deleting priorities so your choices fit neatly in the greater context of your life. Then you know that the balls in the air are the most important. You can let the rest drop.

Unfortunately, many leaders neglect to take the step of finding focus. Harvard Business School Professor Robert Kaplan notes, "A common pitfall in articulating a vision is a failure to boil it down to a manageable list of initiatives. Culling the list involves thinking through and then making difficult choices and trade-off decisions."[1] By "culling the list," Kaplan means whittling it *way down*. As he points out, "having 15 priorities is the same as not having any at all."[2] There's only so much you can think about at once.

The trick, however, is to make sure you have the right priorities. In *First Things First,* Stephen Covey explains that you need to be sure you're doing "the right thing, for the right reason, in the right way."[3] Your ability to succeed hinges on your ability to find that kind of focus.

What happens if you don't? All of those images of what you want for your future, your intentions for being a better leader, your thoughts for your life in the long run—they all hang just out of reach. You want them but you don't get them. You become your own bottleneck, stopping the flow of progress because you're managing too much. Your personal needs and aspirations become smothered by obligations, and you get feeble results.

On the contrary, when you find your focus, you gain a sense of order that not only makes it easier to attain your vision but allows you to enjoy your life.

The Benefits of Focus

Finding your focus can be helpful in a variety of ways.

You Keep Track of What You're Trying to Achieve. No matter how clear you are about what you want, you can still lose sight of your vision day to day. You have meetings to attend, clients to respond to, relationships to develop. You have presentations to give, reports to finish, teams to organize, people to hire. You have money to make and vacations to take. Life gets in the way. Your focus keeps you tethered to your vision. As you bear in mind what you want, you focus on the areas that will help you get it. The less relevant areas fall away.

You Prevent Dangerous Oversights. Focus is about balancing priorities. Perhaps this has happened to you. You zero in on one concern—think deadlines, pressures, and emergencies—and block out other concerns like relationships, personal renewal, and health. You get tunnel vision. The consequences can range from mildly irritating (an extra-long day, a less-than-perfect product, a missed deadline) to severe (a life filled with overwork, failed relationships, a loss of self).

Finding focus can keep you from overlooking vital elements of your life. When you get the right focus, you are reminded that whatever is most important to you in one area is not the only thing that's important in your life. You realize you can give your attention both to your work and your personal life, to all of the people who matter to you, and to your long-term vision and your short-term goals. Less sacrifice. More satisfaction.

You Keep Pace with Shifting Priorities. Unlike a strategic plan, which locks in the vision, your focus is flexible. If your life changes, your focus changes with it. Your focus can change as fast as your life does. What's important to you will shift as your circumstances change, and even better, as you progress.

Whether your need to find your focus is precipitated by some big event (like a promotion, a momentous decision, or an important project) or grows out of an ongoing goal (like a career objective or a vision for your life), finding your focus can ensure you get into the zone of productivity right from the start.

How to Practice

To get a sense of why focus is so critical, meet Tom.

TOM

Tom was a 42-year-old accountant who had just been promoted from comptroller to vice president of finance for a national auditing firm. He felt exhilarated but anxious. Suddenly instead of practicing accounting, he was managing a team of accountants. He had a new staff, a new boss, new responsibilities, and a new office, which at the time was filled with boxes from floor to ceiling.

Walking down the hall on his first day, Tom was met by an enthusiastic colleague. Slapping Tom on the back as he went by, his friend hailed, "Congratulations on your promotion!"

"Right! Thanks!" replied Tom, thinking, *What have I gotten myself into?*

Tom had a lot to sort out in his new job, and he felt under enormous pressure to succeed. There was so much to do, he could barely think. He needed to find his focus.

The process of finding focus would give Tom a sense of control in a time of great change. He had to let go the need to do everything at once and identify the specific areas that would get his attention now. Finding your focus will help you do the same.

Snapshots

You find your focus by setting *focus areas:* a short list of well-chosen priorities that lead to an important result, designed to be little snapshots of your ultimate vision. To find your focus areas, you take five steps that you can see summarized in the overview of the process for setting your focus areas (see Figure 3).

Think again of that process of taking a picture. First, you survey the scene, taking in the panoramic view before choosing what photos to shoot. Second, you choose your focus. You decide what pictures to take. Third, you study your subject up close through the lens. Fourth, you sharpen your focus for the kind of shot you want. Finally, you take a snapshot, capturing a moment in time to remind you of this special time and place. The process of finding your focus follows similar steps, only instead of snapshots of people or scenery, you end up with snapshots of the vision you're trying to create.

It's better to be able to say, "These are the three things I was able to accomplish" than to have a laundry list of things that are half-done. Your priorities reflect your strategies. If you don't have priorities you don't have a strategy.
—Adam Barnes, Vice President External Affairs, AT&T

The initial process of creating your focus areas may take you an hour or so. Later, the same process will take you 20 minutes, then 10, then eventually finding your focus will happen in a flash—a way of thinking that takes no more time than it does for a practiced photographer to snap that perfect picture.

STEP 1: SURVEY THE SCENE

The first step in finding your focus is to survey the scene. In other words, you step back and take in that panoramic view of your life. To get a clear answer you may have to revisit ideas and images about your vision. Or, for a faster refresher, just ask yourself (once again), "What do I want?"

For Tom, the newly promoted attorney, the answer came intuitively. "What do you want?" I asked him. "I want to be confident in this job," he said. Being confident in his new job was a goal-within-a-goal. Ultimately, Tom wanted to build a strong leadership team that added increased value for the company and help the organization reach key results. Right now, though, Tom just needed

Step 1	Survey the scene	Briefly review your vision so your focus will be aimed in the right direction.	What do you want?
Step 2	Choose your focus	Name three to five specific areas that need your attention if you're going to successfully attain your vision.	What areas do you want to focus on to achieve your vision?
Step 3	Study the subject	Get specific about what each focus area means.	Where are you now? Where do you want to be? How will you know when you get there?
Step 4	Sharpen your focus	Make a commitment.	What will you do and when will you do it?
Step 5	Take a snapshot	Write down your focus areas where they can serve as a reminder of what's important to you now.	What do I want to remember?

FIGURE 3   Setting your focus areas overview

to get on his feet. If he could focus on gaining the confidence he needed to be successful now, he would soon be able to move to the broader vision.

Exercise

1. Remind yourself of the long-term vision you want for your life and leadership in the future.
2. Zoom in on the near-term vision of your life today.
3. Ask yourself, "What do I want?" Get a short answer. One sentence. Write it down.

STEP 2: CHOOSE YOUR FOCUS

After you've reconnected to the bigger vision of your life and leadership, you choose your focus. That is, you identify the aspects of that vision that deserve your time, energy, and attention right now. Choose three to five priorities to focus on in order to achieve your vision. These are your focus areas.

The definition of focus areas is purposefully loose. What you're looking for are the categories—however you define them—that will help you be the leader you want to be and create the life you want to live. Then instead of having a thousand things to do, you have a handful of priorities—few enough to count on one hand.

TOM

Tom had said that what he wanted most now was to feel confident in his new job.

"Let's break it down," I suggested. "What are five areas you want to work on to feel confident?"

He thought of several. First, he wanted to "get settled"—to move through the stage where everything was new and different. Second, Tom also wanted to improve his self-confidence. For someone who had been fairly successful, he secretly felt like a fraud. He knew he was second-guessing himself, and he could see it was contributing to his stress. Third, Tom was feeling anxious about two open positions in his department. He felt the demand to hire his team, and soon. Fourth, Tom added that he'd like to have some semblance of balance. "I work a lot," he told me. "I like to work. I'm good at it. But sometimes it would be nice not to have to." Tom paused. That was pretty much it. He was surprised his list of stressors was so short.

But that was only four categories. I had given Tom room for five. What else was there? He thought. Ah, yes. Personal relationships. His wife deserved to be on the list.

I asked Tom to recap his focus areas into five succinct bullet points, which he did:

1. Get settled in my job
2. Improve self-confidence
3. Hire team
4. Work/life balance
5. Personal relationships

Five bullets. Ten words. That's focus.

Your focus areas might include these elements:

- ambitions
- projects
- learning
- results
- responsibilities

In short, they can include any area of life that you want to highlight at this time.

To choose your focus areas, take your vision—that brief statement of what you want—and chunk it down into three to five categories that will require your attention if you are to attain it. Ask yourself, "If I want what I say I want, what areas will I have to focus on to get it?" Write down your ideas.

Exercise

Ask yourself, "What areas do I want to focus on to achieve my vision?" Choose five and write them down.

[Handwritten notes: LEARN to Enjoy; Go EASY & go tough; Daughter lil's; Positive ENERGY; Strategic clarity; M-F 8-5 schedule]

STEP 3: STUDY THE SUBJECT

Before you take a photograph, you study the subject through the lens to set the shot up right. Just so, you must study each focus area to be sure you've made good decisions about every one. Three questions will help you do this.

Where Are You Now? The question "Where are you now?" provides a reality check. If you have to get to California, it helps to know whether you're starting in New Zealand or New York. The same is true for your focus areas. If you know where you are now in relation to what you want, you increase your chances of getting there quickly.

For instance, one of Tom's focus areas was hiring his team. Asking "Where am I now?" would give him a sense of whether this would be a massive undertaking or a fairly small task. Knowing where you stand with respect to this focus area establishes a starting point.

As you answer the question "Where am I now?" judge your position against a few indicators. Be specific. Sometimes it helps to give yourself a score. Here are a variety of indicators you could choose:

- A percentage—a 30 percent increase in productivity, a 15 percent reduction in costs, a 25 percent rise in customer satisfaction

- A number—1,000 units sold, a million-dollar year, three times a week
- A letter grade—A, B, C, D, E, F
- A score—a scale from 1 to 10, a GPA of 3.8, a 97 out of 100
- An emotion—feeling more in control, feeling more at ease, feeling more content
- A gauge—getting approval on a project, sensing your boss's satisfaction, getting through your work with ease

For instance:

> If you want to beat your sales targets by 10 percent, what are your sales figures now, and what will they be when you succeed?
> If you want to have a highly performing team, what letter grade would you give their performance today? An A+? A C−? An F?
> If what you want is to communicate more effectively, how effectively do you communicate today? Somewhat? Very? Not at all?

For each indicator, explain what you mean using succinct, descriptive words. Back to our example of hiring Tom's team, he might say his team is 75 percent complete, meaning that most of the positions were filled but he had a few gaps. Or he might say it was 35 percent complete, meaning he would essentially be building a new team from scratch. You need both the indicator and an explanation of what it means.

Where Would You Like to Be? The question "Where would you like to be?" describes the ultimate result you want. It shows you how much is enough and keeps you from that common modern trap of always wanting more. To answer this question, compare where you are now to where you want to be for each focus area. Use the same indicators you used before.

Tom wanted a more organized office. As he stood among the piles of files, he gave himself a 0 in organization on a scale of 1–10. Where he wanted to be was a 7. "I don't need to have everything put away in nice little systems. I just need to know where it all is."

Without answering the question "Where do I want to be?" you end up constantly striving for an ever-distant horizon. You can never feel satisfied. Before you leap into the business of trying to get somewhere, you need to figure out where that somewhere is.

How Will You Know When You Get There?. The last question to apply to each focus area is "How will you know when you get there?" Whereas you answered the first two questions, "Where are you now?" and "Where do you want to be?" with indicators you could measure, this question you answer with your gut. You're describing the sense of success. What it will be like when you arrive?

Here are a few examples:

- Everett knew he would have conquered his organizational challenges when he could say, "I feel in control."
- Fran thought she would have been successful with delegation when she could "just give projects away and they get done."
- Jordan would be happier with his presentation style when he could "command the attention of a room."

In each of these examples, the measurement of success that came from the question "How will you know when you get there?" was an intuitive sense, not a number or percentage, yet these leaders sufficiently described what they wanted to achieve.

The three questions you ask to study your focus areas give you a specific starting point for achieving your goals. You can see how Tom answered these questions for his focus area of "improving self-confidence" by looking at the sample in the box, Tom's Focus Area #2.

TOM'S FOCUS AREA #2

Improve Confidence

1. *Now:* Where are you now?
   7/10: I'm new, not sure of responsibilities and expectations
2. *Then:* Where would you like to be?
   9/10: I want to have a handle on the whole job.
3. *When:* How will you know when you get there?
   I'll be confident when I'm not wondering how I'm doing, just doing the job well.

For the record, you can use specific indicators and measurements to answer *any* of the three questions you ask of your focus areas. Some people thrive on specifics. Having some kind of concrete metric against which you can compare your progress can be very helpful. At the other extreme, you can leave measurements out of your focus areas altogether. As statistician Dr. W. Edwards Deming once said, "97% of what matters cannot be measured."[4] In a business initiative, where metrics are king, you probably couldn't get away with this kind of imprecision. But your success is too big to be restricted by statistics. You can use any language you want to describe where you are now, where you want to be, and how you'll know when you've arrived. When you answer the three questions you ask of your focus areas, use the language that makes the most sense to you. Be clear but don't obsess.

Exercise

Study one of the focus areas you chose earlier by answering the following three questions as specifically as possible, using indicators or measurements as you wish. Ultimately, you will want to go through this process for every focus area you set.

LEARN TO ENJOY

1. *Now:* Where are you now? *Low/medium score on "OFF BALANCE")*
2. *Then:* Where would you like to be? *30% increase in score*
3. *When:* How will you know when you get there? *TAKE QUIZ ONCE PER MONTH*

STEP 4: SHARPEN YOUR FOCUS

The fourth step in finding your focus is sharpening your focus. When you set up to take a photograph, you choose the settings to create the exact image you want. In finding your focus, you choose the specific commitments you will make for the results you seek. The questions to ask to make those commitments are "What will you do?" and "When will you do it?"

What Will You Do? When you ask yourself "What will I do?" you're looking for a place to start.

Let's say you have a focus area called "financial growth." Right now you are in debt, and you want to be making money. You'll know you're successful when you've got 12 consecutive reports showing your company to be in the black. The question "What will you do?" forces you to consider how you'll get there. Will you eliminate debt? Make an acquisition? Sell more? Spend less? Invest? Your answer is your commitment.

When Will You Do It? When you ask yourself "When will I do it?" you're setting a time frame. When will each focus area be complete? You can set milestones of any kind. You might describe where you want to be in several days, weeks, months, or years—or by the end of the summer, or by the time the merger goes through, or by your 50th birthday. Long term, short term, it doesn't matter as long as you have a time frame that will keep you motivated and focused.

Tom made this commitment for his focus area of "improving self-confidence" (see box).

IMPROVING SELF-CONFIDENCE

Commitment: Discuss expectations with my boss   *Time Frame:* 2 weeks

Exercise

Look back at the focus area you studied above. What commitment can you make for this one important priority? What will you do and when will you do it?

Commitment:_____Time Frame:_____

STEP 5: TAKE A SNAPSHOT

When you have completed all of the steps for setting a focus area, write it down. Be succinct.

Exercise

Create a snapshot for one focus area, using "The Snapshot" worksheet as a guide.

Ultimately, you will want to create a snapshot of all of your focus areas and collect them in one place. The end result will be a complete list of your complete and final focus areas along with their commitments. You will find an example of Tom's finished focus areas in the box.

TOM'S FOCUS AREAS

Vision: To Become Comfortable and Confident in My Position

Focus Area 1. Get Settled in My Job
- *Now:* 5/10: I still need to set up my office, organize files, and get systems.
- *Then:* 9/10: The logistics of the job will run smoothly.
- *When:* When I'm successful, I will feel settled.

Commitment: Unpack and organize office   *Time Frame:* 1 month

Focus Area 2. Improve Self-Confidence
- *Now:* 7/10: I'm new, not sure of responsibilities and expectations.
- *Then:* 9/10: Ultimately, I want to have a handle on the whole job.
- *When:* When I'm successful, I won't be wondering how I'm doing; just doing the job and knowing what it takes to do it well.

Commitment: Discuss expectations with my boss   *Time Frame:* 2 weeks

Focus Area 3. Hire Team
- *Now:* 7/10: My team is incomplete.
- *Then:* 10/10: Ultimately, I want to have at least another assistant and a paralegal.
- *When:* When I'm successful, I will have made the hiring and promotion decisions.

Commitment: Sketch out desired criteria   *Time Frame:* 2 months

THE SNAPSHOT

Focus Area:_____

_____

_____

1. Now _____

_____

_____

_____

_____

2. Then _____

_____

_____

_____

_____

3. When_____

_____

_____

_____

_____

*Commitment:*_____

_____

_____

*Time Frame:*_____

_____

_____

Focus Area 4. Work/Life Balance
- *Now:* 3/10: Now, I'm working as long as I can every day.
- *Then:* 7/10: I want my job to fit into my life instead of the other way around.
- *When:* When I'm successful, I will have vacations and a reasonable schedule.

Commitment: Schedule gym time 3x/week   *Time Frame:* NOW

Focus Area 5. Personal Relationships
- *Now:* 8/10: Now, I have a very close family. They count on me to be there.
- *Then:* 9/10: I want to make time for the big events and the everyday stuff.
- *When:* When I'm successful, I'll feel "present" even when I'm busy.

Commitment: Spend quality time with my family   *Time Frame:* By Friday

A PERFECT FINISH

If you really want your focus areas to lead you from where you are to where you want to be, polish them off with a few critical questions before you consider them complete.

Do Any of Your Focus Areas Conflict?

It's important to look at your focus areas as a set and see how they interact. This helps you make sure they're not working at odds.

If you're not careful, your focus areas can interfere with each other. Like bumper cars, they can smash into each other in random, counterproductive ways. So your focus on getting ahead knocks against your hope for inner peace, or your commitment to hitting your numbers slams into your intention to help others succeed. Instead, your focus areas should work together like the cars on a train—each distinct, but all of them going in the same direction and pulling each other along.

For instance, let's say you want to spend more time at home on the one hand, and that you want to take on a big high-profile project on the other. Those two focus areas could clash. One is about working more, and the other is about working less. You'll want to give some thought to how you can accomplish both at once. Otherwise you will feel guilty when you go home early and even guiltier when you work all night. Your focus areas should reduce stress, not create it. You need to recognize the effect your different focus areas will have on each other.

Can Any of Your Focus Areas Combine?

It's also possible for your focus areas to interact in a positive way. Looking again at your focus areas, you may be able to see ways to achieve synergy and advance several goals at once. For instance, if you want to spend more time with your friends while also improving your health and fitness, you might plan a weekend biking tour instead of the annual beer fest. If you want to strengthen your leadership skills as well as your financial skills, you might chair a finance committee so you can do both. When you obtain synergy among your focus areas, seemingly competing efforts combine to make the others happen.

Is Anything Missing?

Is anything missing? This is an absolutely critical question to ask, and one many people overlook.

Make a conscious effort to step back from your focus areas and think about the bigger picture of your life. It may be that you started your focus areas thinking about something specific you want—for instance, making a big career jump or succeeding in a new business stream. All of your focus areas logically will be designed to lead you to that end. But focusing on one part of your life to the exclusion of others can lead to disaster, or at least imbalance. Be inclusive. Throw in some personal focus areas along with the professional, and the other way around.

PERFECTING THE PRACTICE

✎ Take the first step in faith. You don't have to see the whole staircase—just the first step.

—*Martin Luther King, Jr.*

YOU

It's three in the afternoon. You stride into your office with a sense of purpose. You have exactly one hour before you need to meet your next appointment and a long list of things to do.

One hour, you think. *What can I accomplish in one hour?* You need focus. You walk over to your desk and pick up a small square of paper: your focus areas, the short list of what's important for you to lead and live well. In one glance, the glut of tasks in your head sorts itself out. You can see, compared to this list, which of these tasks are truly essential and need your undivided attention right now. The rest suddenly seem less worthy. Necessary, ultimately, but comparatively trivial.

Scheming, you look again at the list in your hand.

Ah, yes. I do want to do that, you think, tapping the most compelling item with your finger. To clear your head, you jot down a few of the pressing things you also need to get done today—promises to keep, answers to deliver. You'll get back to them in just a bit. But right now, you know where to put your attention. One golden hour. You're going to devote it to the top thing you need to do. The thing you want to do. You turn around, close the door, and get to work.

Look around you. Chances are that very close by, you have snapshots of the people and events that matter in your life. Memories. Good times. Moments you want to remember. Now that you've created your focus areas, you also have snapshots of the vision you're creating. Priorities. Goals. Commitments. Keep these close by, too. Whenever you're planning your day, scheduling your time, or unexpectedly enjoying free space in your calendar, look at your focus areas. Just a glimpse at the list will trigger your vision and point you back toward the future you want to create. Then as you arrange your time, you will be motivated to push aside the other, less important tasks in favor of the ones that will move you ahead.

Your *Inner Edge* Coaching Assignment: Your Focus Areas

Use the worksheet at the end of this chapter, "Your Focus Areas," to complete all of the final focus areas you want to guide your action now. You can find an electronic copy of this worksheet on the website (www.theinneredge.com).

FAQS

Q: What do I do with my focus areas once I have them?

A: Once you've established your focus areas, make them a part of the way you think. Vic Gregory, the president of a Midwestern power company, likes to put his focus areas into a single, logical sentence that rolls off his tongue:

As the president of the power company, I need to make sure the lights stay on, that every new customer gets hooked up, that the work is done safely, that prices for power are fair, and that we have the right infrastructure in place to provide exceptional customer service.

Kim, a real estate investor, put all of her focus areas into a motto: "Family, health, wealth, and the time to enjoy it." Other variations range from bullet points to sentences to paragraphs. Your focus areas might just be summarized in a short list that you keep in your calendar where you can see them every day. You might put them on your screensaver or post them on your desk. You can keep your focus areas in a file, on a sticky note, in a journal, on a notepad, or commit them to memory. Then use them as a guide for how you spend your time.

It's important for leaders to have goals for themselves. My goals are simple. First, I need to take care of myself. If I don't take care of myself, how can I take care of others? Second, it's about my family, my wife, because if I'm not taking care of myself and my family, again, how can I take care of my family at Cisco? If I do those two things, then I have the energy to think about the third goal—how to maintain that our services remain the best.
—Joe Pinto, Senior Vice President–Technical Services, Cisco Systems

---

Q: How often should I update my focus areas?

A: Be sure to revisit your focus areas often—at least every few months—to see if they're still current. If you're truly using them as a guide, they should change as your life changes and as you make progress on your goals. Know that this process will become easier and easier as you practice. If you discipline yourself to go through this process in its entirety at least once, preferably twice, you will establish the thinking pattern in your mind. After that, you'll move through the steps faster and faster until you can find your focus on the fly.

When you practice finding your focus, you break out of the "vicious circle of nonsense"[5] that characterizes the busy lives of many leaders. Your focus areas serve as a lifeline back to your vision. When you have a clear vision and focus areas to help you achieve it, you know your priorities, you can think about them all at once, you keep them from crowding each other out, and you find new opportunities for them to work together. Overall, when you find your focus, you show respect for yourself and your work as a leader. You're no longer just managing your workload. You're leading your life. Finally, when you set your focus areas, you tee them up for *action:* the next practice of personal leadership.

CHAPTER SUMMARY

Key Points

- Finding focus means choosing the select few areas that you must prioritize in order to achieve your vision.

- Finding your focus means highlighting, combining, minimizing, and even deleting priorities so your choices fit neatly in the greater context of your life. Then you know that the balls in the air are the most important. You can let the rest drop.
- The real trick isn't to figure out how to become a master juggler, but to realize that you can only gracefully manage so much before your life starts to feel like a circus.

YOUR FOCUS AREAS

Vision (What do you want?)_____

_____

_____

Focus Area 1._____

     1. *Now*_____

     2. *Then*_____

     3. *When*_____

     Commitment: *Time Frame:*_____

Focus Area 2._____

     1. *Now*_____

     2. *Then*_____

     3. *When*_____

     Commitment: *Time Frame:*_____

Focus Area 3._____

     1. *Now*_____

     2. *Then*_____

     3. *When*_____

     Commitment: *Time Frame:*_____

Focus Area 4._____

     1. *Now*_____

     2. *Then*_____

     3. *When*_____

     Commitment: *Time Frame:*_____

Focus Area 5._____

     1. *Now*_____

     2. *Then*_____

     3. *When*_____

     Commitment: *Time Frame:*_____

The Third Practice

Take Action: *What Do You Need to Do?*

Reaching goals is fine for a plan. Only reaching one's potential is fine for a life.

—*Max DePree, Leadership Jazz*

SUZANNE

It was January 3, two days after the New Year, and Suzanne was ready to start fresh. As the vice president of human resources at a Fortune 500 communications company, she felt her organization lacked resources for developing the next generation of young managers. She spent an hour brainstorming plans for a new leadership-development program. She organized the ideas into an action plan, e-mailed them to me, and put a copy on her desk where she would see it every day.

Once the year was underway, Suzanne's desk got cluttered. She put the action plan in a file so it wouldn't get lost. In the next few weeks, Suzanne's hopes for her plan kept getting squeezed out by "fire drills": sudden budget cuts, a hiring freeze, a systems crash, and other urgent workplace issues.

Suzanne and I had agreed to revisit her action plan every 30 days. When I asked her about it the next month, she blushed. "Oh, that. Well. First I have to find it!"

The number of times I've had conversations like these with leaders are too numerous to count. It's not that these are slackers. On the contrary, they're the most industrious people I know. The problem is that while they are taking care of the needs of the business, the needs of their employees, the other people in their lives, and their existing responsibilities, they're not taking action on the things that matter most to them.

Maybe you've fallen into the same pattern. It's easy to do. Fortunately, you can change the model to get better results. In this chapter, you will look at your actions in a new light. You will stop asking, "How can I do everything I need to do in a day?" and start asking, "What are the most effective actions I can take to move toward my vision, and how can I ensure that I take those actions now?" By investing just minutes in the planning process and then taking targeted action, you can shave hours, weeks, and even months off the time it takes to reach your goals.

You already have a long-term vision for your future and for yourself as a leader. You have divided that vision into a few prioritized focus areas. Now you need to move.

THE PRACTICE OF TAKING ACTION

It is not enough to be busy. The question is, what are we busy about?

—Henry David Thoreau

Taking action is the third practice of personal leadership. But it's not just any old action. This is not about time management. You don't need to learn more about how to put more tasks into those tiny boxes in your calendar. Taking effective action involves finding newer, fewer, more strategic ways of applying your energy and efforts to ensure success.

The Two-Step

Taking effective action is a two-part process:

1. Planning the action to align with your top priorities
2. Taking the action—and only the action—that gets results

These are two very different processes, requiring different time frames, different approaches, even different energy. But they're both essential. Action without planning is foolish, but planning without action is pointless. You need both.

Planning is using the clarity and focus you've gained by practicing personal leadership to decide how to get things done. That sounds easy enough, but as Wagner and Harter, the authors of *12: The Elements of Great Managing*, point out, "It's amazingly common to find individuals making large salaries who will confide, 'I really don't know what I'm supposed to be doing.'"[1] When you've planned well, you know *exactly* what you're supposed to be doing. The planning fuels the action.

Taking action is about motion. Your plan guides your steps. No more wondering and waiting, deliberating and deciding. You just go. When you take action, you move fast and get it done. Taking action is a practice. You practice getting better and better until you can stay on course for good.

Otherwise, you'll go back to business as usual. Good ideas will tumble around in your mind, and then tumble back out. You'll spin through the same thoughts over and over, and only random ones will stick. If you are lucky and have the time, you will get started on some of your goals. But if you get busy, stressed, distracted, bored, confused, sick, promoted, fired, arrogant, nervous, isolated, or forgetful, all of your plans will fade away. Later, if you even remember them, you'll be exactly where you started.

We're not going to let that happen. From now on, the action you take is going to make your vision a reality.

The Benefits of Action

When you plan and take effective action:

You Do Better Work. You become more valuable to your organization when you take effective action, because your actions are more purposeful and complete.

You Avoid Burnout. Taking effective action is the antidote to "the curse of the modern world: too much to do and too little time to do it."[2] Effective action is an escape to a saner, safer way of life. You honor your priorities and escape the bombardment of endless to dos.

You're in Control. Instead of being pulled away from the actions you want to take or waiting for the perfect moment to work on your vision, you take the offense. You no longer let circumstances dictate the way you spend your time. You make the decisions about what happens and when.

You Achieve Your Vision. Long term or short term, in personal life or and business, you'll find yourself charging toward your vision when you make sound decisions first and then act.

You Have Time for You. A happy benefit of taking more effective action is you need to take less action overall to achieve your goals. That leaves you time for rest and restoration, advancing other goals, or whatever it is you know you want. When you consistently plan your actions and then act on your plans, you put your energy where it will make the biggest difference.

How to Practice

Becoming more effective with your action is like speeding up a slow computer. You may have to tinker with your hardware—those entrenched thoughts and behaviors that determine how well you run. We'll take a look at some common action afflictions. Addressing them will automatically improve your ability to get things done.

Once you've managed the hardware (your thinking) you can move to the software (your behaviors). Your software systems—or as we'll call them, your action applications—are the specific tools you use to plan your action. Throughout this chapter, you'll find a number of action-planning techniques that can help you blow through your task list so you have more time to work on your goals. At first, you may find the shift to newer, faster action plans challenging. Eventually, effective planning becomes a way of thinking and a way of life— not something you have to discipline yourself to do but something that happens spontaneously, intuitively, and naturally. You'll start to feel less like you're learning a new program and more like you have a computer in your head.

Once you've rebuilt your thinking and behaviors, all that's left is to get into action. I'll offer you some suggestions for getting out the glitches as you go.

ACTION AFFLICTIONS

Why don't we take action on the things we say matter most? We all have our own reasons, but I've found that three common action afflictions seem particularly endemic to leaders. Like a virus, these faulty ways of thinking attack your ability to be as effective as you could be. See if any of these apply to you.

You Overbook Yourself

Taking on too many projects, saying yes too often, seizing every single opportunity—these are common habits of the overachiever. And while that may sound great for business, it really isn't. You're stretched too thin. You're constantly scrambling or letting things drop. You can't sustain that pattern and stay effective.

Suzanne provides a classic example of overbooking. She started every day with a full schedule then heaped onto it the demands of every person and project that crossed her desk. There was no way she could possibly do everything she committed to doing, and it was diluting her energy to try.

Overbooking isn't good for you, either. Taking on too much work is an abuse of your talent. Like an athlete who overtrains and injures himself, you can harm yourself and your company if you victimize yourself with relentless action. All those long days, the stress, the pressure—they weigh heavily on your shoulders and keep you from being your best.

You Mismanage Your Actions

As a leader investing in your own success, you plan and act all the time. Most leaders have everything from to-do lists to personal assistants to entire software programs all designed to help them take action. But just because your time is well organized doesn't mean it's well spent.

One of the activities I find most helpful for busy leaders is to do a calendar analysis to see how closely their actions align with their visions. When Suzanne and I looked at her calendar, it was clear that the activities filling her time were poorly picked. For instance, she spent all her time appeasing angry clients instead of coaching her employees to serve those clients better. She also planned every day by looking at her to-do lists and appointment schedule instead of starting with her vision and focus areas. As an organized person, Suzanne was managing her calendar—but she wasn't effectively choosing her actions to get closer to her vision.

None of the planning tools in the world will help you achieve your vision if all you do is shuffle around the same old tasks. That just deceives you into thinking you're managing your time well. In addition to managing your time, you also need to manage your actions.

You Underutilize Your Time

It's easy to get detoured from your vision and not take any action at all. You have so many other demands on your time.

- demands from clients
- demands from your boss
- demands from employees and peers
- demands of the market
- deadlines and disasters

What's scary is that while you feel like you're using every minute to meet all these demands, you could be wasting a tremendous amount of time.

Suzanne defended her lack of progress on her vision by pointing to these kinds of demands. She was indeed short on time, but she was also underutilizing the time she had. To give one example, Suzanne often spent two-thirds of a staff meeting covering administrative issues that could have been handled in a five-minute e-mail. She spent hours poring over reports that could be described in a 10-page memo. When we scrutinized her calendar for opportunities to work on the programs that added more value, she found hours and hours hiding in plain sight.

It's hard to find time to work on your vision. Plus, when you do sneak away, the work just piles up. So you exhaust yourself trying to be all things to all people. You respond to the demands, meet the needs, and put your vision on hold. But if you can learn to maximize the time you already have, you won't have to sneak away at all. You'll have all the time you need.

> *Flexibility and versatility is key. Certainly you have to have a game*
> *plan, but you have to be cognizant that things change. You have*
> *to be able to address whatever curves are thrown at you.*
> —John Futrell, President, Las Vegas Executive Speakers Bureau

All of the action afflictions that plague leaders make it difficult to take effective action. By raising your awareness about your habits, you make it possible to change and choose a more effective approach.

Exercise

What are your action afflictions? What keeps you from taking your most effective actions toward your long-term vision? Write down your answers.

ACTION APPLICATIONS

To take the most effective action, you need the most effective plan. You do not need to limit yourself to one kind of action plan. You can do so much more if you have a repertoire. To start, I'll introduce you to one of my favorite types of action plan: the CATA list. Then, I'll share some more surefire action plans—because the more you know, the more you can do.

The CATA List

What is the one thing you could do that would have the greatest impact on your vision? The answer is your *catalyst*. In the sciences, a catalyst is a substance that increases the rate of a chemical reaction without being consumed in the process. For you, a catalyst is an action that dramatically increases the rate at which you achieve your vision, without consuming *you*.

To take effective action, you can get the potency of a catalyst by using an action plan appropriately called the CATA list. The CATA list is a chart divided into four categories:

1. Catalysts
2. Achievements
3. Tasks
4. Avoidances

These categories help you sort interminable lists of to dos to find the ones that pack the biggest punch. Then you trim away the rest.

"C" Is for Catalysts

To find your catalysts, ask yourself, "What is the one thing I can do that will have the greatest impact on my vision?"

Any item you call a catalyst must be an action that drives all the rest, either because it causes the rest of the actions to happen, it frees you to put your time where you want it, or it unlocks a barrier to action. The main criterion for your catalyst is that you know this one piece will do more than any other to advance you in the direction of your vision. If you're writing a speech, a catalyst might be to stand up and practice. If you're leading a company, a catalyst might be to communicate the strategic direction. If you're trying to lose 50 pounds, a catalyst might be to go running or give up sugar. Looking at these examples, you can see how easily catalysts get crowded out by more pressing issues. Indeed, even though your catalysts have the most value, if you're not careful they can easily get pushed aside.

To find your catalysts, think about what action you would take if you could find uninterrupted quality time because you know it would make the biggest difference in your ability to attain your vision.

"A" Is for Achievements

The next category includes actions you classify as important. *Really* important. They may not have the transformational effect of your catalysts, but they are the kinds of achievements that matter on a day-to-day basis. These achievements typically take center stage in your life. They tend to include:

- daily actions
- key relationships
- priority projects
- deadlines

As a rule, working on achievements makes for a very productive day.

"T" Is for Tasks

You use the tasks category for the actions you'd like to take but can't justify as truly critical. Yes, they are things that may have to get done, but they don't have nearly the impact as your catalysts and achievements.

Tasks are big time consumers. Long meetings. Some networking. Obsessive perfecting of nonessential details. You might feel a little twinge when you admit these tasks are less-than-important, because you may want to do them. And you may get to. But only after the more valuable things are done.

"A" Is for Avoidances

Many leaders find the avoidances category the hardest to fill. The items in this category take more energy than they deserve. When you're trying to rid your action plan of excess, cut the fat by forcing yourself to put at least 25 percent of your to dos onto this list. To find actions to avoid, look for the ones that take a lot of time with little return. The avoidances list is a place to throw off extra baggage. Letting some actions go—undone—lets you to be lighter, more nimble, and available for the things that really matter.

As a whole, the CATA list takes the commitments that emerge from your focus areas and marries them in a single-page, concrete list of actions that ultimately lead to your vision for living and leading well.

When you create a CATA list, you have a quick categorization of everything you need to do, organized in order of value. As you think about all the actions on your to-do list now, can you see how categorizing your tasks in order of value might help you make room for working on your goals? Suddenly the most important thing you need to do isn't just the most pressing. It's the one that fits with your focus and leads to your vision.

To understand the effect of creating a CATA list, meet Salvador.

SALVADOR

Salvador was the COO of a construction company. A respected expert in his field and an accomplished business leader, he was a man of action. His department ran smoothly, he was a key leader in the company, and he was on several community service boards. In many ways, he was a role model for aspiring leaders. For Salvador, all of that was great, but something was missing. He wasn't sure what. I asked him to remind us both of his vision. "Salvador," I asked, "what do you really want?" His answer was clear: "I want to make a difference."

But Salvador felt like every day he was just "doing the work." He had a bigger vision for the company. He wanted it to be a model of service in the community.

I asked Salvador, "What is the single most important action you could be taking right now—the one thing that if you did it, would make the biggest impact?" He thought for a moment. "Truly, I think it's developing that vision." I knew Salvador valued service, leadership, and community, but when he identified a new vision for bringing those values together in a way that could transform the company, he not only found a catalyst, he found a new sense of purpose in his work. He started sorting out the tasks that would follow.

"If developing a vision is the catalyst, then some of the other things I've been doing—some of the day-to-day things like client relations—get bumped down to achievements. I still need to do them, but they don't change anything. Truth be told there are probably many things I'm doing now that I could delegate or phase out to fill out those tasks and avoidances categories. That would make more room for this new vision."

The thoughts he was speaking started to form Salvador's initial CATA list.

SALVADOR'S CATA LIST

Catalysts

- Develop vision for making the company a leader in client and community service

Achievements

- Client relations
- Project oversight

Tasks

- Weekly update meetings—change to a weekly memo

Avoidances

- Outdated processes

Recasting his vision for the company was a catalyst for Salvador. But that was just a start. The more he looked at his CATA list, the more it grew and grew. In the end, he generated a full-page action plan that covered everything from his long-term vision to his short-term goals to even his most trivial tasks. When he was done, though, it seemed to me we'd forgotten something important.

"Salvador, is there anything personal you want to add? Are there any catalysts that you want to name that are important to your quality of life?"

There was one.

"I need to make more time to see my father." He explained, "My dad is all alone now. His joy in life is to see me and my family, and he relies on us to take care of him. If it's really important to me to 'make a difference,' I need to honor that value in my personal life as well as my work."

Salvador added "See my father" to his CATA list. When his CATA list was done, he was ready for action. As coaches often do, I asked Salvador to give himself an assignment—a specific step to get the action plan off the page and into his life. "Okay. I'm going set up a meeting with the president and CEO to talk about this vision. I'll do that by the end of the day." One action.

"I'm also going to go see my dad. No excuses. I'll call him now and let him know we'll be there tonight." Two actions.

In two swift moves, Salvador had realigned with the actions that meant the most for his personal and professional success. Of course he still had to follow through with the action, but the decisions had now been made. When I left Salvador at the end of our meeting, he was standing at his desk adding to his CATA list, categorizing all of the many things on his plate into an order guided by his values and priorities.

Salvador's father died the year we made his CATA list, a poignant reminder to both of us that there's more to life than what's on our action plans. At 82, he had lived a full life and died peacefully at home. When Salvador shared the news with me, he was comforted by knowing he had spent special time with his dad in recent months. I'm sure that with all of Salvador's impressive accomplishments, his father was very proud of him, but I suspect that what heartened his father most in the last year of his life wasn't Salvador's success as a leader in his company or the reputation he developed as a service leader. It was having a son who made a difference.

Exercise

Try this process now using the "Your CATA List" worksheet, or go online (www.theinneredge.com) for an electronic copy.

The things you put on paper . . . they happen!
—Sam Barker, entrepreneur

More Action Applications

The CATA list is a surefire way to speed effective action. But there are others. In the Resource Section titled "More Action Plans," you will find several other approaches you can also choose to plan your actions your way.

Each of these action plans offers a different advantage. They can all help you take more targeted, effective action than those long, all-too-common, and not very strategic lists of "what I have to do today." But each one appeals for a different reason. You can choose the most powerful action plan based on a number of factors:

- your circumstance
- your style
- your personality
- your mood
- the benefits of a specific type of action plan
- the particular actions you're planning

The key to effective action planning is to familiarize yourself with all of your options and then choose the plan that matches the occasion, not just the

YOUR CATA LIST

Catalysts:

Achievements:

Tasks:

Avoidances:

one you use out of habit. As you read through the various action plans, look for the ones that naturally appeal to you. When you're ready to actually write an action plan, choose one. Just one. Keep it simple. Decide which one suits you now, and try the rest another time.

RESOURCE SECTION: MORE ACTION PLANS

THE 30-60-90 DAY PLAN

A 30-60-90 Day plan maps out your actions by *time*. You identify, for each of your focus areas (or goals or projects), what specifically you need to accomplish in 30, 60, and 90 days. You map those focus areas into a schedule, then return to the plan every month or so to keep it up to date. The basic plan looks like this:

	30 Days	60 Days	90 Days
Focus Area 1			
Focus Area 2			
Focus Area 3			

A 30-60-90 Day plan appeals to leaders who like to plan and who want to keep tabs on all of their focus areas at once. It gives you the opportunity to do all of your thinking up front, then move into doing—where you can stay until it's time to check back in with your plan and repeat the process. What the 30-60-90 Day plan does not do very well is capture those ongoing actions that don't have a deadline. For that, you might prefer a different plan, like the Walk the Talk plan.

WALK THE TALK

Ann Golden Eagle, my first coach, taught me this strategy. You use a Walk the Talk for enduring changes as opposed to finite goals you will someday meet. Examples:

• Skills	• Habits	• Repetitive actions	• Decisions
• Perspectives	• Daily practices	• Ways of being	• Commitments
• Questions	• Behaviors	• Ways of thinking	• Ideas

A Walk the Talk list is so called because looking at the list every day ensures you are walking your talk. For example, let's say one of your focus areas is to "have a commanding presence." On your Walk the Talk, you might write:

Commanding Presence

- Dress for success
- Speak loudly and clearly
- Walk purposefully

Notice you will need to repeat these things over and over—not "in 30 days" or "by April 10th." Notice, too, that you will never be able to check these items off a list. Presence is something you must constantly keep in mind. A Walk the Talk helps you do that.

FUTURE PACING

Future pacing is a concept from the field of neurolinguistic programming. You mentally rehearse yourself through a future situation in order to help ensure positive behavior. You can apply the process to your planning. You choose a goal, decide what you want to have accomplished in 120 days, then work backwards to decide what to do every day.

Imagine that in 120 days you want to hire a management consultant to improve your business results. That means that in 100 days, you will need to have presented the candidates with offers.

That means in 90 days, you need to have selected the candidates.
That means in 80 days, you need to have finished all of the interviews.
That means in 40 days, you need to have scheduled all of the appointments.
That means in 10 days, you need to start searching for viable candidates.
That means in 7 days, you need to have composed a job description.
That means in 4 days, you need to have input from your coworkers.
That means you need to set a meeting for . . . tomorrow.

Future pacing this way culminates in a list of dates and actions. When you're finished, you turn the whole thing upside down so your immediate first step is at the top, then you start at the beginning and work toward the end. Future pacing is best when you have a certain deadline and want to be sure you reach it, while giving yourself plenty of time to do it well.

MASTER TASK LISTS

The master task list, popularized by *Seven Habits* author Steven Covey, is similar to a 120-day plan but organized in the opposite fashion. You start at Point A and list in chronological order as best you can all the things you know you're going to have to do to get to Point B. Afterwards, you go back and plug in target dates. You revisit the list periodically, updating it as you go.

To give you a glimpse of how this might look, here are a few lines of a master task list made by Brant, an event planner for celebrity fundraisers.

Date	Task	Notes
11/1	Lock in play lists	Agent calls (Rakesh); tracking (Lydia)
11/15	Confirm guest list	Celebs (Vic); media (Jo); others (Rhiana)
11/30	Send final order to caterers	Check vegetarian and kosher options (Carolyn)
11/30	Send press release	Draft by 11/27 (Kyle); final by 11/29 (Kim)

Notice the "Notes" column to the right. That column provides space for notes like these:

- marking what you've done
- collecting reminders
- noting names and numbers
- recording steps and status

Of all of the action plans, master task lists are probably the closest to a traditional to-do list. But unlike a jumble of notes you have to constantly rehash, a master task list lets you see your neatly ordered actions at a glance.

FIVE FOR TODAY

For the chart-averse, a handy strategy is *The Success Principles's* author Jack Canfield's "Rule of Five."[3] This one makes planning easy. Every day, do five things to move toward your vision.

That's it.

The benefit of this strategy is it gets you moving. You don't spend a lot of time taking notes and organizing. You don't have to keep track of anything, and you don't have to know what's next. Five for Today is perfect if these apply to you:

- you prefer a less-structured approach
- you have an unpredictable schedule
- you tend to have complex, nonlinear projects

It's *not* so perfect if you use it to sneak out of the quality thinking that will allow you to get things done efficiently. It's also no good for procrastinators. If doing five things a day motivates you, and if you will commit to actually getting them done and not making excuses, you can shorten the planning process and start making things happen.

THE NEXT LOGICAL STEP

Even less demanding than the Five for Today strategy is the strategy of choosing the next logical step. This process is akin to finding your way in the dark.

1. Take one step at a time.
2. Complete it.
3. Ask yourself, "What's the *next* logical step?"

You know the next step so you do it. If you don't know, the next step is to find out.

JUST DO IT

Perhaps the most direct strategy, as Nike says, is to "just do it." No schedules, no lists, no delay. You just move. There are some things that you simply have to *do*; they won't happen any other way. If you want to slow down, you have to slow down. If you want to be more committed, you have to commit. No amount of planning in the world is going to help you if you don't, at some point, just do it.

This strategy works best when the following are true:

1. you know what to do
2. you're driven to do it
3. there's nothing to stop you

Without those three criteria in place, just do it becomes an excuse—a way to let yourself off the hook of quality planning. What you do not want is to say you'll just do it and then let time pass as you don't. What you do want to do is adopt a no excuses approach to taking action now.

CREATE A ROUTINE

A strategy that works well for leaders who don't like to plan but do like to achieve is to create a routine. Compared to strategies of taking the next logical step and making a commitment to just do it, this strategy is more structured. But unlike the master task list and future pacing, it doesn't require so much dating and itemization.

Creating a routine means developing new habits to create a new reality. Examples:

You read for an hour at three every afternoon to develop your expertise.

You follow the same five setup steps every morning to stay organized.

You review your finances the same way on the last Friday of every month.

The core of this strategy is the repetition. The sameness of the ritual becomes compelling. Once you establish the routine, you will feel drawn to follow through on the pattern. Each time moves you closer to your vision.

Exercise

Now that you have a more extensive collection of action planning strategies, choose one. Do a trial run and see how it works. What would this action plan look like if you created it just for this week? Do an action plan test run to mock it up. If you want to try more than one action plan, great. Experiment with the different options to see the benefits of each.

THE ACTION SUPERHIGHWAY

After you've implemented your planning strategy, it's time to act. As a coach, I can't actually help you take the action. You have to do that for yourself. But you're no longer going to just plow through those items on a to-do list like you used to. You're going to get on the action superhighway. This is where you start to link thoughts to behaviors, planning to action, and daily tasks to your big picture vision to navigate at cyber speed to your new ways of living and leading well.

Find Your Stopportunities. Stopportunities are those actions that you should stop doing because they don't help you achieve your vision. Take something off your plate for once. Free up some space. Refuse to do what doesn't make you a better leader or make for a better life.

Choose Your M-No. Change your M.O. to an M-No. If your modus operandi is, "Yes, I'll do it," try saying, "No, I'm sorry I can't." Think long and hard about why you need to say yes to some actions and no to others, then choose a new motto to match.

Do a Little Pruning. Trees and plants need pruning to stay healthy. So do you. Write down everything you're currently trying to do and hack off two-thirds. Even if you don't ultimately stop doing all of those things, the exercise alone will show you which of your current actions enhance your life and which impede your growth.

Only Do What Only You Can Do. Respect your talent by refusing to waste it doing what other people can do. Productivity expert and owner of the speaking and consulting firm Emphasis on Excellence, Dr. Meggin McIntosh (www.meggin.com) advises, "You should only do what *only you* can do." Someone else can do the rest.

Empower Others. Many leaders have excuses for why they do everything themselves.

"It's just easier if I do it myself."
"No one else knows how to do this."
"This needs to be taken care of right away."

While these statements may be true, they keep you from focusing on your most important priorities. Effective leaders don't do everything themselves. They empower others.

Take an Account. Keep track of your results. Research shows "people who regularly record specific daily and weekly results are nearly 50% more likely to make continued progress than those who don't."[4]

Notice the Impact. Taking action brings powerful results. To gain momentum, notice the impact of your actions. What results did you get? Was it harder than you thought or easier? Was it worth it? When you notice the effects of your productivity, you'll find it easier to do what you want to do, because you'll see that it works.

You will find more ideas for getting the best results from the actions you take on the website at www.theinneredge.com.

When something needs to get done, I do it. No pomp and circumstance. No drama. You put the blinders on and you go do it.
—Jennifer Kluge, President, National Association
for Business Resources

In preparing to write this chapter I asked myself what some of my clients had gained when they got serious about taking effective action on their visions. Here are a few:

- Adam increased his income 50 percent.
- Pankaj, Nicole, and Curtis got promoted.
- Jocelyn finally, *finally*, lost 30 pounds.
- Hope was able to stop saying, "I don't have enough time" and start saying, "I've got plenty of time."
- Tristan turned his small home-brewing hobby into a regional microbrew phenomenon.
- Eli ran a marathon.
- Caroline beat breast cancer.

What's possible for you when you finally take action? It's worth it. So get out your plan. Schedule the actions. Now go.

THE MIND-SET FOR TAKING ACTION

Decisive. Go with your gut to make decisions fast.

Entitled. You're entitled to take effective action in the direction you're leading. Without being selfish or irresponsible, a touch of irreverence will give you courage to claim the time you need.

Opportunistic. When the opportunity presents itself to take action, *do it.* Ten minutes? Half an hour? Take advantage of the time you've got. A quick glimpse at your action plan will tell you what to do. Do it now.

Patient. Changing patterns takes time. Be patient but don't make excuses.

Persistent. Results take time, too—maybe even longer than you thought. Just keep asking yourself, "Am I acting in line with my greater vision? Are these actions tied to my focus areas? Am I still headed in the right direction?" If you are, keep it up. You're going to reach your goals.

PERFECTING THE PRACTICE

For all sad words of tongue and pen, the saddest are these: it might have been.

—*John Greenleaf Whittier*

SUZANNE

At the beginning of the chapter, you met Suzanne, who had put her action plan, along with her good intentions to make a positive impact as a leader, into a file and forgot about it—something probably more of us have done than we'd like to admit.

But so much more was possible for Suzanne when she dug out that old action plan and started over. Over time, she used a variety of more powerful strategies for action to keep her focused and on track toward her goals.

In hindsight, the actions Suzanne took weren't so remarkable, but her transformation as a leader was. I attended one of Suzanne's staff meetings six months after she had re-created her action plan. What I saw was not the preoccupied, overcommitted woman I had first met. What I found instead was a confident, comfortable leader who kept her whole department—and herself—focused on what really mattered and taking the actions to make it happen.

A friend of mine once told me that a definition of "hell" is meeting the person you might have been. When you take action on your vision for your leadership and your life, you ensure that never happens. You stop procrastinating and refuse to be pulled off course. You don't forget what's important, and you stay true to your commitments. You bring your vision to life.

Your *Inner Edge* Coaching Assignment: Your Action Plan

Use the worksheet at the end of this chapter, "Your Action Plan," to overhaul whatever action plan you're using now. Then refer to the additional worksheets, planning guides, and templates available on the website (www. theinneredge.com) to become a true action expert.

FAQS

Q: Do I always have to have an action plan?

A: Yes and no.

Yes, you do need to be ever-conscious of what you're doing and why, how it fits with your focus areas, and how it contributes to your vision. You will always be more effective when you're guided by the kind of thinking behind the action planning process.

No, you do not always need a tangible action plan at hand. Whether in writing or in your head, the goal of effective action planning is not to obsess about the process but to be able to whip up a quick action plan whenever you need it.

With practice, you will get so good at the cycle of thinking and action that you don't need to put yourself through the paces of comprehensive action planning. You'll instinctively know what needs to be done, and you'll do it. And you'll know, because you've practiced this skill, that your actions do indeed synch up with your focus areas and the ultimate vision of what you want.

Q: Are there other ways to take effective action besides planning the work and working the plan?

A: Yes. As you've seen, several alternatives for getting into action hardly require any planning at all. You may decide to halt your action plan based on new information. You may leapfrog over half your list with one stroke of genius. You might act on intuition and take a totally different direction. The crux of action planning is just stopping for a second and saying, "Am I ready to begin? Do I know what to do? Is there anything I need to remember?" It's like a huddle in the middle of a game—a short break in the action before you go back out on the field. Sometimes that huddle is critical for winning the game. Sometimes, no huddle needed—the win just happens like magic.

When you have completed the exercises in this chapter alone, you will have given yourself a tremendous gift of time that you can now use for the actions you *want* to take. When you know your vision, your focus, and your actions, as you do now, you are ready to move to the next practices of personal leadership, which will power up those actions for truly phenomenal results.

But first, one more story. A friend of mine once told me a tale relayed to her by her pastor, Father Tom. Father Tom was given a jar of glass stones. The number of stones equaled the number of weeks, based on his age and demographic, that Father Tom could be expected to live. Every week he took one stone out of the jar. As he held the stone in his hand, he reflected on what it meant: one less week to live. Had he made that one week count? The way you spend your time is the way you spend your life. Enjoy it. Make it count.

CHAPTER SUMMARY

Key Points

- By investing just minutes in the planning process and then taking targeted action, you can shave hours, weeks, and even months off the time it takes to reach your goals.
- Effective action is an escape to a saner, safer way of life.
- None of the planning tools in the world will help you achieve your vision if all you do is shuffle around the same old tasks. By upgrading your ideas about time, you can find hours and hours hiding in plain sight.

YOUR ACTION PLAN

1. Review your vision and focus areas.

2. Choose an action plan.

_____ CATA List   _____ 30-60-90 Day Plan   _____ Walk the Talk

_____ Future Pacing   _____ Master Task List   _____ Five for Today

_____ Next Logical Step   _____ Just Do It   _____ Create a Routine

_____ _____   _____ _____   _____ _____
   (Other)   (Other)   (Other)

3. Use the space below to make notes, then use the templates online (www.theinneredge. com) to create your action plan.

4. What habits do you have to adopt or change to get into action on your vision?

_____

_____

_____

_____

_____

_____

The Fourth Practice

Tap into Your Brilliance: *What's Unique about You?*

Knowing others is intelligence.

Knowing yourself is true wisdom.

—*Tao Te Ching*

CHAD

Chad strode down the sidewalk in his dashing new suit, clutching his hot coffee on a brisk New England day. *Today,* he said to himself, *my new life begins.*

Chad had always been a star. At 16, he was the youngest captain of his high school basketball team. In college, he had been the student body president. He won awards for academics, for sports, and even for his Halloween costume the year he showed up to a party dressed like Marilyn Monroe.

But now, the stakes were higher. He'd graduated from law school, gotten a stellar clerkship, and landed a job in one of Boston's most prestigious law firms. If he was going to succeed at this job, he needed more than just a charming smile.

I hope I can do it.

As he crossed the street to the highrise that housed his new firm, a town car pulled up next to him. Out climbed one of the partners. Chad beamed at him with a day-brightening smile and held the door open for his new boss's boss. The partner disappeared into the lobby without a glance. Chad's heart sank.

Don't worry, rebounded Chad. *He'll know who I am soon enough.*

As Chad walked through door into the rest of his career, he had two options. He could do what most people do and start working *really, really hard*. He could mimic his role models, downplay his shortcomings, and spend the next several years striving to get ahead, believing all the stress would someday be worth it.

Or, he could skip the struggle and do it his way.

You have the same two options. Like Chad, you may also be striving to get ahead. You, too, might be working really hard, doing all you can to be like other successful people, and hoping to impress your boss. But did you know there's also another way? What if you could stop trying so hard and instead do things the way that is natural and fun for you? What if you could do things the easy way and still get where you want to be?

You have a choice. You can continue to do things the hard way, the usual way, the way you've always done them. Or, you can do things your way. The way you were made to do them.

In your efforts to be a better leader and lead a better life, you have been practicing clarity, focus, and action in order to achieve what you envision for your life and for yourself as a leader. Now, you're going to learn the one practice that amplifies all the rest.

You're about to learn how good you really are.

THE PRACTICE OF TAPPING INTO YOUR BRILLIANCE

Tension is who you think you should be. Relaxation is who you are.

—*Chinese proverb*

Tapping into your brilliance is the fourth practice of personal leadership. It means being able to identify, maximize, and leverage your unique attributes to be an effective, higher achieving leader.

When you tap into your brilliance, you get to do things your way based on where you naturally excel. If you could do that, how would it look?

- Would you surround yourself with a few key people who inspire and energize you, or would you be out and about, meeting and greeting people every day?
- Would you work in peaceful silence for hours at a time, or would you form teams to accomplish the work together?
- Would you be careful or take risks? Set goals or live in the moment? Learn or imagine?
- If you were able to manage your weaknesses, what activities or behaviors would you avoid?

What would life be like if you could truly do things your way? How good *then* could you be? You'll see what's really possible when you tap into your brilliance.

Leading with Your Strengths

To better understand the practice of tapping into your brilliance, it is helpful to understand the philosophy on which it is based: a strengths approach to leadership.

The idea is that in order to improve, we should build on our strengths and minimize our weaknesses. This idea was popularized by "the father of strengths psychology,"[1] Dr. Donald Clifton. Dr. Clifton, a scientist and the late chair of the Gallup Organization, sought to "start a global conversation about what's right with people."[2] His research touched off what is now known as the strengths movement—a groundbreaking way of thinking that capitalizes on strengths to help people grow.

A strengths approach brings your brilliance to life. In order to be your best, you maximize your strengths and manage your weaknesses. Then you are emphasizing the elements of you that are enduring and unique. You are growing in the areas of your inherent strength, where the possibilities for your potential are greatest.[3]

But even though a strengths approach to leadership primarily features our finer points, we also need to find our flaws. Your weaknesses are an influential part of your identity. As Claudia Shelton writes in her book *Blind Spots*, "The key is for you to be aware of your potential and your limitations."[4] Your brilliance is made up of both.

If you want to be your best, you need to build on what's brilliant about you. You can develop an approach to leadership that uses all of your attributes in the most advantageous way. You save time, energy, and effort. You get better results, because you are doing things in the way that works best for you. You discover what it truly means to achieve success with quality of life, because they become one and the same. Best of all, you do this not by changing who you are, but by becoming more of who you are. Because who you are . . . is brilliant.

The Benefits of Brilliance

When you take a strengths approach to work and life:

You Do Things Faster. What comes naturally tends to come easily, and when it's easy you tend to work faster.[5] You get more done in less time. With that kind of efficiency, you can accomplish more . . . or you can relax and enjoy the time you've saved.

You Make a Bigger Impact. No one else in the world has the same combination of strengths, expressed the same way, as you. When you bring your strengths to an activity, a process, or a group, you contribute something no one else can. That makes you valuable indeed.

You're Innovative and Resilient. When you are aligned with your strengths, you get better ideas and more of them. You are most creative when you are doing what you do well.[6]

You're Happier. It feels good to be yourself. That alone makes it worthwhile to discover your strengths; you get to be happy. When you are happier, you tend to build better relationships, see your work in a positive light, and become more solution oriented.[7] It's a lot more fun to succeed than fail, and you're much more likely to succeed with your strengths than your weaknesses.

You Gain an Advantage. One of the reasons a strengths approach to achievement is such a breakthrough is that so few people do it. If you can train yourself to capitalize on your strengths, you will be one of only 25 percent of people who work in their "sweet spot."[8] In the words of Dewitt Jones, distinguished photographer for National Geographic and creator of the inspirational film *Celebrate What's Right with the World,* you may not be able to be the best *in* the world, but you can be your best *for* the world.[9] If you want to be your best as a leader, you need to know what's best about you.

I was always interested in storytelling. Life as drama. While some people go into my line of work for the events or for the celebrities, the part I enjoy is telling the stories of companies to build and improve their reputation. Using my strengths this way brings me personal satisfaction and a feeling of accomplishment. I've been in this business 30 years, and I know my time has been worth it.
—Andy Tannen, SVP Strategy & Development, MS&L

How to Practice

I was explaining strengths-based leadership at a seminar one year when I met Chad, the attorney you met at the beginning of this chapter.

Chad listened intently to a discussion of strengths-based leadership in a corporate retreat. At the end of the presentation, he came up to ask a question.

"This is good," he said. "I get it. Right now I'm trying to work my hardest to impress my new boss, but what I really need to do is be more of myself."

You do get it, I thought.

"I have just one question. How do I know what's brilliant about me?"

It seems ironic that we would have to ask such a question. After all, we've lived with ourselves our whole lives. Why should it be so hard to know what makes us unique? The answer is complicated, touching on everything from psychology to confidence to self-awareness. But every one of us has the ability to discern our characteristics, and you don't need a Ph.D. in psychology to do it.

Your Leadership DNA

You are hardwired with certain characteristics that make you *you*—distinctly, irreplaceably, inimitably you. The way you live, the way you learn, the way you lead—all of these are guided by the gifts you were given at birth and the ones you have collected in the course of your life. Knowing these attributes gives you tremendous power.

To be able to tap into your brilliance, you must answer the question "What makes you unique?" You need to discover your distinct natural attributes— your DNA. Your distinct natural attributes include personal characteristics like these:

- strengths
- weaknesses
- personality
- preferences
- virtues
- vulnerabilities
- style

Like your genetic DNA, your distinct natural attributes define what's true about you. What's genuinely true about you—the good and the bad—is also what's great about you.

To tap into your brilliance, you need to understand your distinct natural attributes (your DNA) and be able to leverage them in the most powerful way.

Tapping into your brilliance involves three phases. First, you identify your distinct natural attributes. Second, you investigate those attributes so you see their full promise. Third, you learn to leverage your DNA to reach your vision and goals. Eventually, this process won't feel like a process at all. It will be the way you look at who you are and what you can do.

THE BEST OF YOU AND THE REST OF YOU

The first step in tapping into your brilliance is to identify and map your DNA. Your DNA map is a simple list of your strongest positive and negative attributes. Your strengths and weaknesses. The best of you and the rest of you.

To map your DNA—at first, anyway—you write down characteristics you've discovered in yourself so you can see them at a glance. When you do this, you'll want to include a mix of distinct natural attributes: your characteristics, behaviors, talents, learning styles, and so on. Other self-evaluation tools sometimes focus specifically on one aspect of your attributes—*either* your activities *or* your skills *or* your behaviors. For our purposes, that would be too narrow a view. We want to know it all. So we will take a very broad view of your attributes. Everything counts. Your talents, your activities, your character traits, the way you think, the way you behave—all of it is fair game at this stage for mapping your DNA.

You can get started identifying your DNA by using your own insight and self-awareness. When I asked Chad, the promising attorney, to guess at his DNA, here's what he wrote:

Chad's DNA Map	
The Best of You	**The Rest of You**
Confident	Superficial
Personable	Impatient
Analyzing Data	Dismissing New Ideas
Taking Charge	Neglecting Details
Making People Laugh	Thinking Too Narrowly

Eventually, we would get more specific about what we put on Chad's DNA map, but his initial ideas gave us a place to start.

Exercise

To get started mapping your DNA, try this short exercise. Off the top of your head, write down what you believe to be a few of your positive and negative traits on this short version of your DNA map.

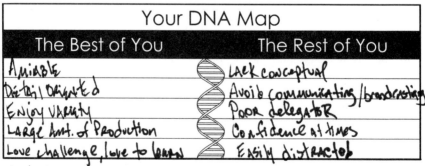

Your DNA Map	
The Best of You	**The Rest of You**
Amiable	Lack conceptual
Detail Oriented	Avoid communicating/broadcasting
Enjoy Variety	Poor delegator
Large Amt. of Production	Confidence at times
Love challenge, love to learn	Easily distracted

Adaptable
Relationship Builder
Analytical

This short, unscientific list will give you a glimpse of the attributes you can leverage in the service of your vision and goals. It gives you a place to start. But truth be told, this short DNA map is a fairly cursory list compared to the depths of greatness that make you the leader you are. If you really want to profit from your brilliance, you'll need a more extensive view.

A 360-Degree View of You

Getting a fuller picture of your brilliance is like checking your image in a mirror. You can get a sense of your appearance with a small hand mirror. You'll see more with a full-length mirror, and even more with a three-sided fitting room mirror. Even then, there are still some things a mirror can't tell you: the overall impression you make when you walk into a room, the way your presence makes people feel, and how you look when you walk around. For these, you need other sources of input.

Just so with your distinct natural attributes. You can get *some* information on your own, as you just did when you mapped a few of your DNA above. But the more strategies you use to find your distinct natural attributes, the more complete your view will be. A variety of strategies will help you flesh out your DNA map.

Reflective Questions

You can reveal some of your DNA by asking open-ended questions. To find out more about what's best about you, ask questions like these:

1. Where are you especially talented?
2. What do you love to do? *Improving process/things*
3. What do you do without even thinking? *Build relationships*
4. What do people count on you for? *Direction/guidance*
5. In your social life, what role do you play? *Humorous*
6. At work, what are you recognized for? *Availability?*
7. Given the freedom to do things your way, how do you do them? *Structurally*

To find out more about the rest of you, ask questions like these:

work that I dislike

1. What activities would you gladly never have to do again? *Mgr of Programs*
2. What do you wish you could pass on to someone else? *Communicate broadly*
3. When do you feel dragged down? *Problems outside of my control.*
4. What do you dread? *Broad communicating - Status updates*
5. When do you procrastinate? *When news is bad.*

As a coach, I deeply respect the insight leaders have into their own answers, and the knowledge you discover from these questions is invaluable. But it's not enough. In a report entitled "Why People Fail to Recognize Their Own Incompetence," researchers Dunning, Johnson, Ehrlinger, and Kruger wrote,

> People are unaware of their incompetence, innocent of their ignorance. Where they lack skill or knowledge, they greatly overestimate their expertise and talent, thinking they are doing just fine when, in fact, they are doing quite poorly.[10]

To find your DNA, in addition to asking yourself, you also need an outside opinion.

Outside Opinions

Sometimes what we do well is so much a part of who we are that we find it difficult to see. But it's easy for the people who know us well. In the words of emotional intelligence expert Daniel Goleman, "There are many ways in which other people know us better than we know ourselves."[11] Ask your friends, family, and co-workers what they notice about you. How would they describe you? Get the positive and negative take. You'll learn more about how you strike other people and discover more about what makes you brilliant.

Some people find asking for feedback to be a challenge. They feel shy about fishing for compliments, don't believe they'll get honest feedback, or fear bad news. If you'd like anonymity or a formalized, structured type of feedback, I recommend research-based profiles and assessments.

Profiles and Assessments

Profiles and assessments are research-based quizzes that reveal your attributes. Each assessment will yield different information. Some indicators assess personality traits, while others test leadership style or behaviors. Such assessments reveal information you might not come up with on your own, giving you fresh, new insight into your DNA. The drawback, however, is that profiles and assessments are necessarily based on a particular philosophy, theory, or body of research. The best assessment is the one that is based solely on *you*. For that, you need a 360-degree profile.

360-Degree Profiles

More customized and personal than most assessments, a 360-degree profile is a survey you conduct to get feedback on your effectiveness from the people all around you (hence the name). Traditionally, the survey is developed by a third party—say, a coach, consultant, or research group—then distributed to a group of people who know you well enough to give you input. They respond to the survey anonymously, and you receive a customized report of the results. The information you receive is filled with your DNA.

A 360-degree profile gives you some of the most up-to-date, relevant data you can get. Because the process is objective, you get more accurate data, but because it's personalized, you also get specific details. Unfortunately, a 360 can be somewhat unwieldy, especially if you're committed to ongoing improvement and want to get lots of feedback whenever you can. For an easy way to repeat the 360 process over and over, see the box entitled The 360-Degree Investment. Then visit the website, www.the360investment.com, which will show you how to do an efficient, high-quality 360 on yourself.

THE 360-DEGREE INVESTMENT

Management expert and author of *The One Minute Manager* Ken Blanchard once called feedback "the breakfast of champions." If you truly want to take leadership of your own excellence, you can't just take one 360 and expect to have all the answers you need for life. You need feedback *all the time.*

The best way I've found for doing this is to learn the process for doing a 360 on yourself. I call this *The 360° Investment*, because it brings in a fortune's worth of feedback.

The process is modeled on the formal, research-based 360s that have become a staple of leadership development. But unlike these extensive (and expensive) reports, the 360 you do on yourself is a fast, easy, flexible alternative —one you can engage in anytime you want for your own personal growth and development. It's based on the belief that, at its core, the 360-degree profile is really just a way of turning to the people around you and asking them, "How am I doing?" You can do that on your own with just a little bit of direction and advice.

To learn how to do your own 360, go to the website www.the360investment. com and download directions.

The 360° Investment isn't the only process you need to develop your DNA. But it is one you can use again and again to get the very best information about how you're succeeding in the areas that matter most to you. If you seek feedback as consistently and courageously as you can, you're likely to become the strongest leader you know.

Exercise

To get the most developed picture of your DNA, use the strategies above to build your DNA map over time.

To get started, choose one of the above strategies for learning more about your DNA. Over time, continue this process to learn more and more about what makes you unique. As you collect information about your attributes from various sources, keep track of them on the "Your DNA Map" worksheet at the end of this chapter. You can see an example of how complex and informative your DNA map will become by looking at the long version of Chad's DNA map, which we developed over time.

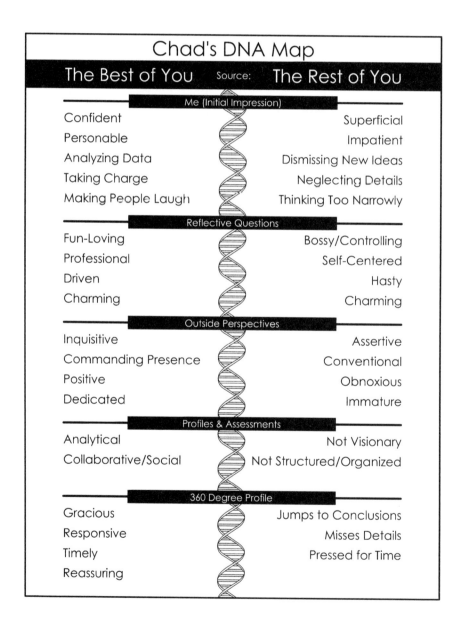

Your DNA map is an important stepping-stone on the path to seeing your brilliance, because when you know your strengths and weaknesses you can apply them more easily and creatively, with better results. Ultimately, though, the purpose of the complete process is not to make a list of your strengths and weaknesses but rather to get a sense of who you are and take the guesswork out of success.

To truly know yourself is a lifelong endeavor. As you learn more about your distinct natural attributes, you will spot themes. You will see nuances. You will know who you are. But no matter how much data you collect, it's all just information until you *do* something with it. The next step is to understand your attributes' characteristics and uncover their true potential.

POWER POINTS

It's important to investigate your strengths and weaknesses one by one to understand how they work for (and against) you. Doing so helps you find the salient elements of your attributes, or their power points. This is a necessary step, and one many people miss. As Clifton and Buckingham point out in *Now, Discover Your Strengths*, "the real tragedy of life is not that each of us doesn't have enough strengths, it's that we fail to use the ones we have."[12]

For each distinct natural attribute you find, do a little investigation. Describe it and ask questions to understand the nuances that make each attribute *you*. For each attribute you investigate, you will end up a one-page summary. You can see what this looks like in the box called Your DNA Report.

A DNA REPORT

What is this attribute?_____

Describe this attribute in a few words. _____
_____
_____

How does this attribute work *for* you?

How does this attribute work *against* you?

How can you use this attribute to meet your goals?

Describing Your Attributes

To start your investigation, every time you discover an important attribute, take a moment and describe what it means to you. The same attribute can vary from one person to the next. For instance, I have two clients who both say they are "good with numbers." But by "good with numbers," Frances means he can get a good sense of the overall financial picture of his organization by skimming reports. Tanya means she likes to crunch around in spreadsheets and play with figures. The same descriptor, good with numbers, means two different things to these two people. Defining your attributes keeps them personal.

Exercise

Try it now. Choose one of your positive attributes and describe it in your own words.

Examining Your Attributes

Once you have described your attribute, spend some time with it. For every attribute conduct a short, simple inquiry. Ask yourself the following questions:

- How does this attribute work *for* you?
- How does this attribute work *against* you?
- How do you use this attribute to meet your goals?

Examining your DNA using these three questions gives you a good, clear understanding of each attribute that you can later leverage for its distinct advantage. All three of these questions can be asked of both your positive and negative attributes. Although the questions themselves are straightforward, the thinking they inspire can be quite rich and complex. Let's look at these questions in more depth.

How Does This Attribute Work For You?

The first question to ask when trying to understand an attribute is, "How does this attribute work *for* you?" You can apply this question to both your strengths and your weaknesses.

Your Strengths Can Work For You. Choose a strength, or positive attribute, from your DNA map and ask, "How does this strength work for me?"

- What do you like about this strength?
- How does it feel to use this strength?
- What specifically does this strength do for you?

Examining your positive attributes this way helps you see the power points in your strengths. When you understand those power points, you know why you do things the way you do and how you can do more of what works to be even more effective.

Your Weaknesses Can Work For You. It may seem counterintuitive to think your weaknesses can work for you. Isn't the whole point to avoid them? Not necessarily. If you look, you can find value in your faults.

- Maybe you're not very flexible. That might work for you if it means you're consistent and dependable.
- Maybe you have a hard time selling yourself. That might work for you if it means you're humble and unassuming.
- Maybe you tend to be insensitive. That might work for you if it means you can be dispassionate in emotional situations.

To see the strength in your weaknesses, repeat the process you used above for a strength but substitute a weakness. Choose a weakness, or negative attribute, from your DNA map and ask, "How does this weakness work for me?"

Easily distracted

- Are there any ways this weakness could benefit you? *A variety of stuff gets done*
- Can you ever remember a time when this weakness worked in your favor?
- If you had to choose a weakness, would you choose this one, and why? *No, easy to procrastinate*

Questions like these help you understand the vulnerabilities posed by the weaker points on your DNA map. They also keep you from being too dismissive of the less flattering parts of your personality. Your weaknesses may not be your favorite traits, but they *are* a part of you.

How Does This Attribute Work Against You?

The second question to ask when investigating an attribute is, "How does this attribute work *against* you?" Again, you can ask this question for both your strengths and weaknesses.

Your Weaknesses Can Work Against You. Considering how much we dislike our negative attributes, it should be pretty obvious how they work against us. They make us look bad. They make us feel bad. They keep us from being our best.

To understand how a weakness can work against you, choose a weakness from your DNA map. Recall a time this weakness was present. Maybe you were acting in a way that didn't feel comfortable or doing something you didn't enjoy. Then ask yourself these questions:

- What don't you like about this weakness?
- How does this weakness slow you down, hold you back, or otherwise frustrate you?
- What is it about this weakness that makes it a challenge?

Considering the specifics of your weakness prevents you from throwing out the good with the bad.

Your Strengths Can Work Against You. Just as a weakness can sometimes be a strength, so can a strength become a weakness. You may be surprised to learn that your strengths can work against you. After all, aren't strengths supposed to be the best of you? Isn't that a *good* thing? Usually it is. But every strength can become a weakness if you take it too far.

To understand how your strengths can work against you, think about what happens when you take them to the extreme. In coaching, we call this over-expressing your strengths, and it happens when we are under stress, low on energy, or simply fed up. Consider a few examples. What happens when leaders overexpress their strengths in . . .

Q: . . . achieving?
A: They can become workaholics.

Q: . . . competing?
A: They can become cutthroat or vengeful.

Q: . . . building consensus?
A: They can neglect to make decisions.

What happens when you overexpress one of your strengths? When it comes to your strong suits, you *can* have too much of a good thing.

To reiterate, both your strengths and weaknesses make you who you are. Both can work for you and against you. If you don't fully appreciate the benefits of your strengths, you could be cheating yourself of their true potential. If you don't recognize the role of your weaknesses, you might view them as a necessary evil. If it's important to celebrate what's right with the world then we even need to celebrate what's *right* with what's *wrong*.

How Do You Use Your Attributes to Meet Your Goals?

The third question to ask about your distinct natural attributes is, "How do I use my attributes to meet my goals?" See what happens when you match your strengths and weaknesses to the goals you've set.

Chad used this question to think more strategically about how he could put himself on the path to partnership at his law firm. He became more conscious about the power of his strengths (like his charisma and charm); he became

A DNA REPORT

Attribute: _____

_____

How does this attribute work for you?

_____

_____

_____

_____

_____

How does this attribute work against you?

_____

_____

_____

_____

_____

How do you use this attribute to meet your goals?

_____

_____

_____

_____

_____

more cognizant of the damage done by his weaknesses (immaturity and the tendency to rush); and he learned to develop attributes that had previously popped up in unpredictable ways (like turning his assertiveness into a commanding presence instead of a bossy attitude). Knowing his distinct natural attributes, Chad was able to shape himself into the kind of lawyer and leader he wanted to be.

Before you consider your investigation of any attribute complete, be sure to connect it to your goals. You will get exponential results by going after your goals while you play up your most powerful traits. The more skillfully you apply your DNA, the brighter your brilliance will be.

Exercise

Now that you know how to develop an investigation into the power points of your DNA, develop a report using the worksheet called "A DNA Report." Try this with the positive attribute you described above. Go to the website (www.theinneredge.com) to get more copies for studying other attributes you find.

YOU, IN STEREO

You now know what's brilliant about you, and you understand how your attributes work for and against you. The last step in tapping into your brilliance is figuring out how to leverage all of your attributes—the entire set of your DNA, all at once—to achieve your vision, your goals, and your full potential as a leader.

At first blush, leveraging your attributes would seem to be a fairly simple proposition. Find your strengths and do more of that. Find your weaknesses and do less of that. That is, in fact, the point of a strengths approach to leadership. It makes sense to maximize your strengths and minimize your weaknesses. To do so will help you improve your efficiency, effectiveness, engagement, and results.

But there's more.

When you are committed to being a better leader and leading a better life (as you are), you don't *just* want to put your strengths to work—you want to attain your vision. You don't just want to be engaged—you want to achieve your goals. To do that, you can assess all your attributes for better or for worse, choosing which ones to put into play and which ones to bench. The more sophisticated you get about leveraging your DNA, the more you control your results.

Think of it like a stereo equalizer. You can turn the volume high, low, or anywhere in between to get your music how you want it. You can do the same for the treble, tone, and bass.

Off   **High**

|———————————————————————————X————————|

Treble

|————————————X——————————————————————|

Tone

|———————————————————————————————X————|

Bass

In the same way, you can adjust the controls of your DNA, bringing your strengths and weaknesses into play at different times and for different reasons to make the most of every opportunity. For instance, when you're having dinner with your mother-in-law, you might want to tone down your strengths in debating and assertiveness.

|——————————X————————————————————————|

Debating

|———X————————————————————————————————|

Assertiveness

But when you're in a union negotiation, you're going to want to turn those same strengths up.

|————————————————————————————————X——|

Debating

|————————————————————————————————X——|

Assertiveness

At the most basic level, you equalize your DNA by turning up the volume on your strengths and turning down the volume on your weaknesses. As you get creative with this strategy, you can turn any aspect of your self up or down, on or off, to create specific effects and get different results. Equalizing your attributes allows you to choose the right attributes at the right time to bring out your best and meet your goals. You, in stereo.

A Symphony of Success

When you get really good at equalizing your attributes, you'll find the perfect blend of attributes for succeeding your way, every time. You will be constantly changing and choosing which attributes to bring out and which to play down, conducting a creative approach to success using your DNA.

At this level, the lines between strengths and weaknesses blur. You move beyond "strengths = good" and "weaknesses = bad." You start to see *all* of your attributes as valuable, and you understand yourself to be the complex, multifaceted, integrated leader you are. You bring all of your attributes to bear on your goals, using your talent and gifts to make each moment a masterpiece.

Exercise

Try this now. Close your eyes. Think of an upcoming situation in which you really want to succeed—something representative of your vision and goals. Think about your goals for this event. How can you use your attributes to meet your goals?

Open your eyes and look at your DNA map in light of this upcoming event.

- Which strengths can you maximize?
- Which weaknesses could you minimize?
- Which other attributes can you intentionally turn up or down?

Use "The DNA Equalizer" worksheet to plot your DNA strategy with an important goal. Extra copies are available on the website (www.theinneredge.com).

THE MIND-SET FOR TAPPING INTO YOUR BRILLIANCE

Searching. Strong leaders look for opportunities to identify, investigate, and leverage their attributes.

Responsible. Your strengths are not excuses. I sometimes hear leaders saying they "have" to do something a certain way because "that's their strength." Just because you do something well doesn't mean it's the only way you can do it.

Fair. Your weaknesses are not excuses, either. Leaders sometimes claim they can't do something because it's a weakness. Just because something is distasteful to you, or because you don't excel at it, or you don't prefer it, doesn't mean you get to get out of it all the time.

THE DNA EQUALIZER

Attribute:_____

|—————————————————————————————|

Off   High

Attribute:_____

|—————————————————————————————|

Off   High

Attribute:_____

|—————————————————————————————|

Off   High

Attribute:_____

|—————————————————————————————|

Off   High

Attribute:_____

|—————————————————————————————|

Off   High

Attribute:_____

|—————————————————————————————|

Off   High

> *Balanced.* Beware of black-and-white thinking. Look for opportunities to leverage your strengths while remaining open to other ways of being. Be intentional, yes. Be a tyrant, no.
>
> *Respectful.* Your way is not the only way. The trap many leaders fall into is they impose their strengths on everyone else. They call their way the best way, or "the way we do it." Insisting everyone be like you will alienate you from other people, and possibly from exciting opportunities. Strengths-based leaders honor the attributes of others as well as their own.
>
> *Open-minded.* Even though we grow in the direction of our strengths, our minds are invigorated by change and novelty. In addition to maximizing your strengths, challenge yourself to do things differently once in awhile. Change for a change. You don't have to change forever. You don't have to adopt uncomfortable attributes for your own, and there's no "should" here about becoming well rounded. Give yourself permission to explore new possibilities and get outside your comfort zone. You might be surprised at what you find.

When you use this process to tap into your brilliance, you won't believe how much better you will be at leading the way to your vision and goals. If you don't, nothing will change. Sometimes your strengths will show up and sometimes they won't. Your weaknesses won't always take over but sometimes they will. Like a marionette on the stage of your life, you will be puppeteered by your implicit nature, which will sometimes work well for you and sometimes do you in.

You have another choice. You can truly see your brilliance. You can get to know your attributes. You can leverage your strengths and weaknesses so they consistently work in your favor. Maybe not all the time, but with practice, you can develop the skill to bring out your gifts for an extraordinary effect. Then watch for a brilliant performance.

PERFECTING THE PRACTICE

Be a first rate version of yourself, not a second rate version of someone else.

—*Judy Garland*

CHAD

Chad stands out in my mind as one of my most successful clients, mostly because he was so enthusiastically committed to his own improvement.

"'To whom much is given, much is expected,' Chad once quoted. "I want to make the most of the gifts I've been given."

One day I was taking my leave on the front steps of the building after a meeting with Chad. After we parted ways, a young man opened the door for Chad as he turned to walk back in. The gentleman looked inexperienced and innocent compared to confident Chad, but was well dressed and polite. I saw him look at Chad with admiration as he approached the door. Looking very much like the partner he would someday be, Chad nodded jovially and disappeared into the lobby.

By learning, understanding, and leveraging your distinct natural attributes, you have discovered a powerful message of personal leadership: You're brilliant. As you continue to learn about yourself, you will be able to apply the best of you and the rest of you to your goals, achieving them in the easiest, most natural, most enjoyable way. You know how your strengths and weaknesses work for or against you, and you can choose how to apply them for best possible payoff.

Your *Inner Edge* Coaching Assignment: Your DNA

Self-knowledge is a lifelong enterprise. As you continue discovering your strengths and weaknesses, you'll develop a robust understanding of your DNA. Keep adding to your DNA map at the end of the chapter and using the DNA equalizer to choose the right attributes at the right time. (Both worksheets are also available online at www.theinneredge.com). Your self-perception will expand, along with your confidence and appreciation for your gifts.

FAQS

Q: Do my strengths and values need to be reflected in my action plan?

A: Yes. When you first write an action plan, you're usually just concerned about getting the job done. Once you know your DNA, you can go back through your action plan and align it with your strengths. Some of the actions will change, and many of them will fall off the list altogether because you will have found a more powerful approach. Applying your strengths gives your action plan punch.

Q: Is it always possible to act on your strengths?

A: You would think with how effortlessly we apply our strengths that we would want to spend all of our time with them. So why isn't that always easy? Living through strengths, for many of us, means change. And change isn't always practical or painless. The realities of life (jobs, obligations, schedules, family life) sometimes make it easy to play to your strengths, and sometimes they don't. Little by little, if you keep integrating what you know about your strengths and applying them creatively, you will become more masterful at doing things differently. Better. You get to make the most of the gifts you've been given, but by all means, take into consideration the bigger picture of your life.

Does my job deepen and give me an opportunity to develop my core strengths? Does it allow me to use those things? Am I in an environment where those things are valued and rewarded? If you can say yes yes yes, you're in a great place, personally and professionally.
—Matt Modleski, Vice President, Stovall Grainger Modleski

Q: Is it really practical to minimize your weaknesses?

A: No matter how good you get at aligning your activities with your strengths, unfortunately sometimes it's just not practical. Whether your boss tells you to do something in your area of weakness, or the guy who usually does the task you hate is sick that day, or you can't figure out how to offload the activities that challenge you, or you haven't been able to approach a particular project using your strengths, you will end up working in your zone of weakness.

Don't sweat it. It happens. Just be aware of the emotions. Notice the difficulty, the struggle, the stress. Use the opportunity to pinpoint exactly what makes this activity so awful. Fantasize about how you could avoid doing it in the future, and then go one step further and make that fantasy a plan. With practice, you will avoid your weaknesses more often until they become less a part of your life. Get the task done as quickly as you can, and move on.

If there's one underlying message to this practice, it's this: If you want to be a better leader and lead a better life, you need to stop worrying about who you're not and start benefiting from who you are. You'll save time, struggle less, and succeed more. Best of all, you get to be yourself. In the words of Marcus Buckingham, "Capitalizing on your strengths is the best way to compete."[13] No one else in the world can be the incredible *you* that you are. See your brilliance. Give it life.

CHAPTER SUMMARY

Key Points

- You are hardwired with certain characteristics that make you *you*—distinctly, irreplaceably, inimitably you.

- To be able to tap into your brilliance, you must answer the question, "What makes you unique?" You need to discover your distinct natural attributes—your DNA.
- You can leverage your strengths and weaknesses so they consistently work in your favor.
- If you want to be a better leader and lead a better life, you need to stop worrying about who you're not and start benefiting from who you are.

Your DNA Map

The Best of You	Source:	The Rest of You

Me (Initial Impression)

Reflective Questions

Outside Perspectives

Profiles & Assessments

360 Degree Profile

The Fifth Practice

Feel Fulfillment: *What Motivates You and Makes You Happy?*

To love what you do and feel that it matters—how could anything be more fun?

—*Katharine Graham*

COLLEEN

Something was wrong with Colleen. As a corporate vice president in the banking industry, she had all the salary, stock options, and security she could want. But somehow she had lost her enthusiasm. Work had become drudgery, and she could barely drag herself in. She finally flopped onto the sofa in her boss's office and admitted, "I don't know what's wrong with me. I feel like I've lost my edge."

Even though nothing had changed in Colleen's life, she had somehow lost her spirit—a common challenge for leaders. Many talented people find themselves becoming restless in today's world—feeling vaguely dissatisfied, wondering if there's something better out there, looking around for that next move to make things right. Their experience starkly contrasts with leaders who are alive in their work and are driven by an invisible source of renewable energy from within.

You may have experienced the contrast yourself. Sometimes you lose your motivation, and sometimes you find it. Why? What makes the difference? And how can you stay motivated and inspired all the time? To be your best as a leader, it's vital you give some thought to what, specifically, makes you flourish and to understand the mysterious and sometimes elusive source of your success.

Otherwise, your achievements will feel empty. Your vision, your goals, your actions—they don't automatically lead to fulfillment. No matter how good you are or how successful you become, your accomplishments will feel meaningless if they're not congruent with the values in your heart.

The goal of this chapter is to create a foundation for fulfillment. You will clarify the values that guide your life, define the specific ways they enhance your experience, and learn to live in integrity with those values to find a renewed sense of purpose and joy. Your happiness is not an achievement, it's a choice.

THE PRACTICE OF FEELING FULFILLMENT

> A happy person is not a person in a certain set of circumstances, but rather a person with a certain set of attitudes.
>
> — *Hugh Downs*

The fifth practice of personal leadership is *feeling fulfillment*—the ability to connect to an internal source of vitality. As leaders, much of our energy goes into striving. We want to get ahead. We want to achieve. Finding fulfillment is understanding what you're striving *for*. The meaning. The purpose. The essence. Do you want to be happy? Are you trying to reach your full potential? Do you hope to make a difference? Do you want to feel at peace? These are some of the experiences leaders seek when they search after success. The key to finding fulfillment is to identify what success means to you—not the results but the spirit of a life well lived.

When you feel fulfilled, you feel full. Satisfied. Content. You are a wholehearted participant in your own life. You know what's important to you, and you use it as a guide. You feel confident. Energized. Engaged.

The Signs of Fulfillment	A Lack of Fulfillment
• Peace of mind	• Guilt
• Contentment	• Resentment
• Enthusiasm	• Boredom
• Energy	• Restlessness
• Satisfaction ("I have everything I need.")	• Discontent ("Is this all there is?")
• Contribution ("I make a difference.")	• Hopelessness ("What's it all for?")

When you *lack* fulfillment, like Colleen, you lose your edge. Your energy goes down. Your stress goes up. You may even feel guilty and resentful. You might be bored, either in an "I-can't-take-this-anymore" way or in a dull, channel-surfing kind of way. You might get short-tempered or edgy.

Losing touch with your values is like losing direction in the fog. You may have a vague, almost unconscious sense that you are off course, yet you convince yourself you know where you're going and head on. Then, in a moment of clarity, the fog lifts and you discover where you are is not where you wanted to be.

Leaders lose their sense of direction all the time; I see it often in my clients. Perhaps you've achieved what you set out to achieve, but it feels empty and meaningless, as it did for Keith, a CPA who felt like he "hadn't ever really done anything" with his life. Or maybe you've made some trade-offs in your life that no longer seem worthwhile, like Victoria, the stay-at-home mom who after 15 years started to wonder who she really was. We need guideposts to help us stay on course. We need to know our values.

To maintain a consistent sense of joy and satisfaction, you need to know what fulfills you and learn to make it a part of every day. When your days are fueled by fulfillment, *every* day feels like a success.

I've never been motivated by political clout or power or what someone can do for me down the road. Getting praise doesn't have much of an impact. I'm motivated by what I define as success.
—Dijuana Lewis, Executive Vice President and
CEO–Comprehensive Health Solutions, WellPoint

The Who That Leads

If clarity, focus, and action are the "what" of personal leadership and tapping into your brilliance is the "how," then fulfillment is the "why"—or perhaps more importantly, the "who."

In his work with educational leaders, author and educator Parker Palmer writes about the importance of the person behind the work. Although he often writes specifically about teachers, his ideas apply directly to leaders in any field. In this passage, paraphrased to apply to leadership instead of teaching, he talks about the importance of the self in our success.

The question we most commonly ask is the "what" question—what [efforts] shall we [lead]? When the conversation goes a bit deeper, we ask the "how" question—what methods and techniques are required to [lead] well? Occasionally, when it goes deeper still, we ask the "why" question—for what purpose and to what ends do we [lead]? But seldom, if ever, do we ask the "who" question—who is the self that [leads]?[1]

So often leadership is about results. The success of a company. The development of people, the perpetuation of good ideas. Those outcomes are critical. They are the work of the leader. But feeling fulfillment is about the well-being of the leaders themselves.

The Benefits of Fulfillment

Fulfillment may not sound like a top business priority. Critics will argue business is not about feeling good, but getting results. But although fulfillment may seem self-serving, it is actually smart business—not just for you but for your whole organization.

So many things happen when you find fulfillment.

You Make a Difference. So many leaders long to leave a legacy. In *The Eighth Habit: From Effectiveness to Greatness*, Stephen Covey writes, "Deep within each one of us is an inner longing to live a life of greatness and contribution— to really matter, to really make a difference."[2] Bolman and Deal, authors of *Leading with Soul*, agree: "Each of us has a special contribution to make if we can shoulder the personal and spiritual work needed to discover and take responsibility for our own gifts."[3] When you know what fulfills you, you are able to give of your gifts in a way that also gives back to you.

You Feel Rewarded. Many leaders are well rewarded for their work, but they also pay a price in long hours and extra stress—an unfortunate trade-off given the well-documented research that money simply doesn't equal happiness.[4] When you find fulfillment, you find gratification in both extrinsic and intrinsic rewards. You still get to keep the traditional benefits you earn for your work. Money is motivating. So are promotions and appreciation and power. But in order for your work to not just pay you back but actually drive you forward, you also need to experience the inner rewards of satisfaction and joy.

Your Quality of Life Improves. When you know what fulfills you, you can make a conscious effort to design your life around it. Then your work fits into your personal life, as well as the other way around. Your professional and personal lives can blend into one as you find contentment in both. You may still be busy. Fulfillment is not about whether your life meets someone else's preconceived idea of a balanced life. But when you look across your life, you feel not just successful, but also at ease with the choices you've made.

You Preserve Your Talent. Business journals in the last several years have been replete with stories about attracting and retaining employees. I often wonder how much time, effort, and expense would be saved if endeavors to develop strong leaders would focus on engaging the leaders they already have.

In an article entitled "Moments of Greatness," University of Michigan business professor Robert Quinn wonders, "As leaders, sometimes we're truly 'on' and sometimes we're not. Why is that? What separates the episodes of excellence from those of mere competence?"[5] Bill George proposes one answer in his book, *Authentic Leadership:* "Authentic leaders demonstrate a passion for their purpose, practice their values consistently, and lead with their hearts as well as their heads. They know who they are."[6] When you find fulfillment, you don't get burned out; you get fired up. You put your talent to work, but you're the one who feels rewarded. You experience those moments of greatness. You also get to lead a great life.

You Feel at Peace. When you live in accordance with your values, even when you have to make the occasional sacrifice, you do so with full awareness of what's important to you and make every effort to honor those values in your life. As authors Lee Bolman and Terrence Deal point out, "soul is not something one leaves at home."[7] You do not have to check yourself at the door.

Even if you generally feel happy and satisfied, it is still critical to maintain that sense of meaning. Fulfillment is not just a remedy for the disillusioned. It is the secret to a happy life. Even if you are already interested, enthusiastic, engaged, goal driven, and achieving, by all means, understand why! Then you'll never lose yourself on the way to success.

Before we talk about how to do that, let's first return to Colleen. Colleen was the banker you met at the beginning of this chapter. Her experience provides a good contrast between what happens when you do feel fulfillment versus when you don't.

How to Practice

COLLEEN

Colleen was a 45-year-old executive in private client services for a New York City bank. Having recently moved from a branch to the corporate offices, she was struggling with the change in pace and company culture.

Colleen had been promoted twice and was well regarded in the organization. That's why I was surprised when she sounded so clandestine. "I need to talk to you. You have to guarantee me this conversation is completely confidential," she insisted. After working with Colleen's organization for several years, I would have thought this could go unsaid.

"Okay." She let out a big breath. She paused. "I'm thinking of leaving."

In some ways, Colleen is a company's worst nightmare. The bank had invested years of time and resources in Colleen's career. They were counting on her to run the rollout of a new business stream. Instead, she was about to take her talent somewhere else.

"It sounds weird coming from someone who's been working 60 hour weeks for three months straight, but . . . I'm bored. I need a new challenge. I want to do something new. I want to feel like I'm actually helping people, not just making the company money. Life's really short. I want to be able to do things like go for a run in the mornings with my dogs and actually have time to stretch and read the paper before rushing off to work. I want to be able to make a real dinner in the evening, not just grab something when I get home at eight o'clock at night."

Were these unreasonable demands? A little stretching, a homemade meal? Not really. But were they possible at the bank? She doubted it. "This place controls me," she said. "It doesn't matter how hard I try to get in some flexibility or take a little time off. Something always comes along and gets in the way. I'm thinking of leaving next summer." Next summer. Eight months. The bank had eight months to replace 15 years of experience and a top-flight leader.

She sighed. "The scariest thing is not knowing whether it's the right decision. I don't really know what I want. I just know I don't want this."

For many people, this is as far as they get. Then one of two things happens. Either they abandon ship—quitting their job in a moment of frustration—or they paper over the emotions and pretend to be fine. They remain disengaged but collect a generous enough salary to placate themselves until the feeling goes away.

Colleen's situation is not uncommon. Her bosses had given her opportunity, responsibility, a title, the promise of advancement, freedom, and money. But they couldn't give her fulfillment. She had to find that on her own. If she didn't, she would leave. For Colleen, moving on might be the right decision. Compared to trudging through a job that had lost its meaning, her leaving could be best for both Colleen and the company. But if it wasn't the right decision, she could be giving up a very successful career, and her company could be losing treasured talent. How would she know? She wouldn't, unless she gave some serious thought to what was important to her and what it would mean for her to feel fulfilled. In this chapter, we will use your values as a way of finding out what fulfills you.

The Value of Values

Values are the cornerstone of fulfillment. When you live in alignment with your values, you experience harmony. When you live out of synch with your values, you experience dissonance and stress.

To understand the concept of values, it's helpful to know what a value is and is not. Values include principles, standards, and qualities. If you can see it, feel it, or touch it, it's not a value but the expression of a value. A value is the experience behind those things that gives them worth. Here are a few key distinctions.

Material Goods Are Not Values. Money may be important to you, but money is not a value. What is it about money you value? Security? Freedom? Prosperity? Now, those are potential values.

People Are Not Values. Your spouse is not a value, but *love* is. Your best friend is not a value, but *friendship* is. Even deeper are the words you would use to describe the importance of love and friendship. What matters in love and friendship? Belonging? Laughter? Support? Again, these are possible values.

Goals and Activities Are Not Values. Even though you might want to ski the Alps or take your company public, those are not values. What's behind those goals or activities that make them so compelling? Vibrant health? Adventure? Success? All of these are values.

Expectations, aspirations, things, places, and even fears can masquerade as values. But values are intangible, not concrete. Expansive, not limiting. Universal, not particular. Take a look at the following list of values to get a feel for what counts as a value.

Abundance	Consistency	Frugality	Justice	Relationship
Acceptance	Control	Fun	Learning	Respect
Achievement	Courage	Generosity	Love	Safety
Adventure	Courtesy	Gratitude	Loyalty	Security
Authenticity	Creativity	Health	Openness	Service
Balance	Discovery	Honesty	Order	Simplicity
Beauty	Excellence	Humor	Peace	Spirituality
Choice	Faith	Imagination	Pleasure	Trust
Clairty	Family	Impact	Power	Truth
Compassion	Freedom	Independence	Prosperity	Wellness
Confidence	Friendship	Integrity	Quality of life	Wisdom

You search for your values in three stages:

- mining
- defining
- refining

Think of it like you're panning for gold. You sift through the rubble to find the precious nuggets. Then you can dust them off, hold them up, and polish them so you can see their true worth. The reward is a priceless collection of values that add up to one golden life.

STAGE 1: MINING FOR VALUES

The first step is to mine your experiences to find values. Your values hide in peak experiences—real or imagined. To reveal them, you can revisit good memories, dream up ideal scenarios, or recreate the imagery you saw when you envisioned a you-and-improved future. Those experiences are infused with your values. After you've spent some time remembering what makes you feel fulfilled, you will be able to sort through the memories and pick out the values.

To mine for your values, you'll start by visualizing an ideal experience.

Recall a time in your life when everything was just right. You could choose a time when you were a child, a teenager, or an adult. You can remember a time from your personal life or your work. You might revisit a moment, a particular event, or a whole phase of your life. It could be anything from backpacking through Europe to a day at the California coast to the first moment you stepped into your new office. The trick is to clear your mind of everything, release all expectations, and just ask yourself, "When in my life did it feel like everything was just right?" See what comes to mind. If you like, do more than one.

Once you've allowed yourself some time to explore the memory, ask yourself what it was about that memory that made it so memorable, so significant, so right. What made it a peak experience? Write down any ideas that come to mind—words, phrases, images, and symbols. Don't worry about whether your words are values yet. Just brainstorm.

When you've finished with your notes, circle the words that meet our definition of values as principles, standards, and qualities. If you come across a word that doesn't quite seem like a value—perhaps a specific person, object, or goal—ask yourself, "What is it about this thing that matters to me?" Look for the value underneath the words to get at the essence. For instance, let's say your peak experience was set in the mountains—hiking with family, maybe, or rock climbing with friends. You love the mountains, so you write "the mountains" in your notes. Fine. But now as you think about the mountains in terms of actual values, you can see that "mountain" is not a value after all. What is it about the mountains that you value? Nature? Peace and quiet? Those are values. As you find your values, avoid judging. There is no right or wrong about what makes a good value. Use your own words and your gut to tell you what your values are.

Some people prefer to have a coach walk them through this process to help them visualize or find their values. You can find audio and links to coaches on the website to help you mine for values at www.theinneredge.com.

THE MIND-SET FOR FEELING FULFILLMENT

Genuine. Your values come from the deepest place of authenticity. Be honest.

Heartfelt. You'll find your values more readily if you start with the right sentiment. Don't try to crank this out sitting in the dentist's office. Wait until you're feeling grateful and connected, or create the opportunity by taking some special time to give the process your fullest attention.

Vulnerable. As a culture, we don't talk much about our values. We definitely don't talk much about them in our places of business. It may feel vulnerable and strange to be so open about your feelings if you're not used to it. On the other hand, those emotions are an important (if hidden) part of who you are. It's not soft or touchy-feely to acknowledge what matters most to you. It's human.

Colleen and I used this process of mining for values to help her understand what was bothering her, in hopes that she could make a decision about whether to stay or leave the bank.

COLLEEN

When I asked Colleen to recall a time when everything was just right, she described a recent memory—a surprise party her kids had thrown for her and her husband's 25th anniversary. As she described the details of the event, potential values emerged between the words.

"We could just laugh and be ourselves," she said (value: acceptance/being myself).

"There was nothing to do but just kick back. I was totally unplugged from work," she said (value: relaxation/being unplugged).

After a little more conversation about her anniversary, I asked Colleen to remember something different: a time when everything was just right at work. What came to mind was her previous job.

"Everything at the bank just hummed. It was challenging, but it was exciting. It was never too much. It was demanding without being over the top" (values: trust, challenges, and reasonable demands).

When I dug a little deeper into this memory, we found a value that I suggested might be empowerment. "That idea of empowerment is important to you, isn't it?" I asked.

"Yes!" Suddenly the dam broke. Colleen leaned forward, instantly animated. "Empowerment is what it's all about! That's exactly it. When I was at the branch, I felt empowered. We were all empowered to do our jobs. My parents raised me to be empowered. Everything I am today came from their insistence that I do things for myself and understand that I can do anything. It's crucial that we empower people, especially in this economy where so many people are just struggling to get by. We need to give them tools and the opportunities to improve their lives."

When Colleen hit on the value she held most deeply, she suddenly became herself. Empowerment wasn't just a value to Colleen. It was a purpose.

Throughout this exercise, Colleen wasn't thinking about her values at all. She was just reliving the moments. Her memories allowed her to get away from the things she felt she should care about to the ones that genuinely and instinctively mattered. My job was to listen and take notes. Every time I thought I spotted a value, I wrote it down. After Colleen had described a few ideal scenarios, we mined the memories together for the rest of her values.

By the time Colleen and I had finished, we had mined 13 values from the experiences she described. You can see these in the Colleen's Mined Values box.

COLLEEN'S MINED VALUES			
Family/Friends	Relaxation/Being unplugged	In control	Service
Comfort	Trust	Responsibility	
Security	Challenge	Empowerment	
Acceptance/ Being myself	Reasonable demands	Diversity	

Our next step would be to narrow down the values to a shorter, more memorable list. You can use the same process I used with Colleen to mine your memories for your values.

Exercise

1. Recall a memory of a time when life was just right. If you choose, do more than one.
2. Use the memory to identify values that are important to you.
3. Write down the values you find in the space below (see Figure 4).

Peak Experience(s):	Potential Values:
Memory #1	
Memory #2	

FIGURE 4 Mining for values

STAGE 2: DEFINING YOUR VALUES

The next step after you collect a list of potential values is to define them. You're choosing your top 5 to 10 values and describing what each one means— the significance it has for you and how it looks and sounds in your life.

Take, for instance, integrity. When I ask leaders to list their values offhand, 9 times out of 10 they start with honesty and integrity.

"And what does that *mean?*" I ask. "What does it mean to you?" Their responses vary widely.

Navarro: "Integrity means doing what you say you're going to do."
Pat: "Integrity to me is having the courage to stand up for my beliefs."

Mark: "Integrity is being honest with myself to see if I'm being the person I claim to be."

Bobbie: "Integrity: reliability. Being able to count on someone. Having them be able to count on me."

Four leaders, four definitions of integrity. Defining your values moves them from platitudes to personal priorities.

You get to define your values to capture the meaning they have for you. To do this, first whittle down the list so it contains only your most significant values.

- Which values seem most important? Circle them.
- Are any important values missing? Add them.
- Can you combine any words? Do so.
- Can you delete any words? Cross them out.

As you mark up your list, reduce the number of values to keep it under 10—enough to capture the important ideals but not too many to remember. Then, describe each remaining value in your own words so it accurately reflects your highest ideals. Write a sentence or two about what each value means to you. Defining your values gives them specificity and clarity.

Notice how much more cohesive Colleen's values became when she took this step.

COLLEEN

When Colleen and I defined her values, her list shrank from 13 to 7, which you can see in the box titled Colleen's Defined Values.

COLLEEN'S DEFINED VALUES

Family/Friends—Spending time with people with whom I have history and who know me as a person

Acceptance/Being Myself—Not worrying about expectations; knowing that others accept me as I am

Relaxation/Being Unplugged—Getting away from it all; complete detachment

> *Trust*—The opposite of micromanaging; being trusted to do what I need to and extending trust to others
>
> *Challenge*—Rising to the occasion; setting high expectations and meeting big goals
>
> *Responsibility*—Taking ownership for one's own part, whether it's in a project or the world we create
>
> *Empowerment/Diversity*—Giving people opportunities and access that they might not otherwise have

Exercise

Choose one value now and write a definition. Later, take the time to identify the 5 to 10 values that matter most and define each one.

STEP 3: REFINING YOUR VALUES

After you've defined your values, refine them with a process of prioritization. It can be tough to prioritize the most important aspects of your life. Chances are you'll want to keep them all. And you can, but it's revealing to understand which values truly matter most.

To refine your values, imagine you are starting over in a brand-new world. Looking at your draft list of values, ask yourself: If you could only be certain of having one value honored, which one would it be? Test it. If you had to live a life where you could count only on this one value, could you survive? Would you want to? And if you could have two values? How about three? Continue ranking your values in this manner until you're satisfied you have them in priority order.

COLLEEN

When Colleen did this exercise, she was able to reorder her values using the prompt, "If I could only have one. . . ." It sounded like this:

Joelle: You have seven values on this list. If you could only have one, which would it be?

Colleen: That's tough. Let me see. The value I called "Empowerment and Diversity" really is my purpose for living. If I had no friends or family, if I lost my job, if there was some kind of crisis that left me lost and alone, I would be okay if I could still empower other people. I felt that way when Hurricane Katrina hit New Orleans. My first instinct was to get in there and get those families the support they needed. I became an instant advocate for our Louisiana employees so they wouldn't be left helpless. I'll put empowerment and diversity first on the list.

Joelle: What would be second? If you could only have one more, what would it be?

Colleen: Hmm. That's also tough. That value of "Responsibility" is hugely important to me. I need to take responsibility for myself. We all do. No matter what happens in life, I will be okay if I remember that I have a responsibility for making things happen. I'll put responsibility as number two.

Continuing this process, Colleen and I eventually formed her final list, which you can see in the box of Colleen's refined values.

COLLEEN'S REFINED VALUES

EMPOWERMENT/DIVERSITY

Giving people opportunities and access they might not otherwise have.

RESPONSIBILITY

Taking ownership for one's own part, whether it's in a project or in the world we create.

ACCEPTANCE/BEING MYSELF

Not worrying about expectations; knowing that others accept me as I am.

FAMILY/FRIENDS

Spending time with people with whom I have history and who know me as a person.

CHALLENGE

Rising to the occasion; setting high expectations and meeting big goals.

RELAXATION/BEING UNPLUGGED

Getting away from it all; complete detachment.

TRUST

The opposite of micromanaging; being trusted to do what I need to and extending trust to others.

Throughout this conversation, you can see Colleen is using worst-case scenarios to help her isolate her values. While imagining tragedy may seem like a grim passageway to fulfillment, it can connect us suddenly and deeply to who we really are. In times of tragedy and sorrow, we *know* what's important to us. Our values show themselves in sharp relief against a world that suddenly seems harsh and uncertain. Getting honest about what matters to you above all else will help you refine your list to the values you hold most dear.

Exercise

Rank your values in priority order. Many leaders find it helpful at this point to create a final version of their values in their own style by typing them up, writing them in calligraphy, and so on. As a final step, post your values where you can see them. What a shame it would be to find what makes your eyes sparkle and then forget all about it. Don't let that happen. Take the time to write down your values and put them where they will call you forth to be who you are at heart.

TIPS FOR CLARIFYING YOUR VALUES

- Dig to find the values that are most important to you.
- Remember, a value is not a thing but a principle, standard, or quality.
- Spend the time to personalize your values.
- Go easy—let your values be a work in progress.
- Make your values a part of your life. Keep them in view.

THE GOLDEN LIFE

After mining, defining, and refining your values, you have collected the raw materials of a golden life. Now you get to decide how to use them. You do that by looking at the role your values play—or could play—in helping you achieve fulfillment. In coaching, we call this *living your values*. You are living your values when you're not only clear about what you value but use it a basis for action. So says Jeffrey McCollum in his essay "The Inside-Out Proposition: Keeping (and Finding) Our Balance in Contemporary Organizations."[8] He concludes that when you're able to live your values, you will "recover enchantment."

To What Degree Are You Living Your Values Now?

When you live your values, they define who you are, not just who you want to be. If family is one of your top values, to what degree are you prioritizing your family? Are you spending time with them? Are you enjoying them, helping them, involved with them? If trust is one of your top values, are you being trustworthy? Are you trusting others? Are there any ways in which you might not be, or are there ways trust is being violated in your life? Questions like these aren't meant to grill you or shame you, just to compare. Asking this question helps you hold up your life against your values to see how well they match. Then you know where to make adjustments to feel more fulfilled.

How Would Life Be Different If You Were Living Your Values?

When you live your values, they become an integral part of your life. How would it look for you to live your values? How would your personal life be different? How would your professional life be different? How would you act and be different as a leader? Knowing the answers to questions like these helps you make positive changes in keeping with your values.

- Tyler valued spirituality. His work as a judge took on new meaning when he chose to see it as an act of faith.
- Johanna valued beauty. She was able to express that value by having a gray floor of cubicles redecorated to create a warm and colorful environment.
- Paulo valued nature and the environment. He found fulfillment in enacting environmentally friendly changes and green policies at work.

When you practice this kind of thinking, you can give up complaining about the parts of life that seem meaningless and actually infuse them with meaning.

How Can You Live Your Values Now for a More Fulfilling Experience Every Day?

When you live your values, you use them to make decisions. Your values are like the gas in a car. When you apply your values to your life, you drive positive energy into everything you do. Otherwise you are just idling and wasting power. Your values are especially helpful in making decisions, choosing perspectives, and resolving conflicts.

Using Your Values to Make Decisions. Your values can help you make the big and small decisions that define your life. When you have to make a decision, big or small, ask yourself, How do your values influence this decision? Being explicit about your values gives you a basis for comparison when considering the opportunities that come along.

Using Your Values to Choose Your Perspective. Fulfillment doesn't just come from using your values to decide what to do. It also comes from using your values to decide how to think. When you're feeling challenged or struggling with a difficult situation, the question to ask is, How could your values enhance this moment? Even a chore like raking leaves takes on meaning when you connect it to a value of having a pleasant, comfortable home, and working for hours on the copy for a web page seems more palatable when you realize it fulfills your value of having a professional presence in the market. The right perspective can be the difference between a mundane and a fulfilling experience.

Using Your Values to Resolve Conflicts. Values serve a practical purpose in relationships. They help you resolve difficult issues. Many conflicts stem from a values clash. One person values speed, the other values meticulous correctness. One person values serenity, the other values excitement. One value crashes into another, creating tension and slowing progress. Simply by naming the values ("It seems like we have a values clash. I value loyalty, and you value freedom."), you can move quickly into more productive questions, like "Is there a way we can meet both of our needs?" and "How can we get around this issue?" Often these questions will lead to answers. If not, you'll need to consider which values are worth your taking a stand and which must be subjugated for the sake of a solution.

It's not always possible to honor your values. That's why feeling fulfillment is a *practice*. You practice aligning your choices with your values. The more you practice, the better you'll become at creating a life of fulfillment every day.

Colleen applied her values in these ways when she was trying to recover her commitment to her job at the bank.

COLLEEN

Colleen decided to use her values to figure out what to do about her job. When she held up her value of empowerment against her daily activities (meeting with clients, sitting in conference rooms, and busying herself at her desk), she didn't see much of a connection.

Then she asked herself, "How can I connect my work at the bank to my value of empowerment?" She suddenly realized: Money empowers people. Following that line of thought led her to start asking how the bank could do more to empower customers. This generated several ideas, like developing a financial management workshop series for the community and offering new low-interest loans. Colleen's values helped her see banking in a whole new light—as a way of empowering families and businesses through financial management—that became a new purpose for her work.

Exercise

Take some time now to reflect on your values. Write down answers to these questions.

1. To what degree are you living your values now?
2. How would life be different if you were living your values?
3. How can you live your values *now* for a more fulfilling experience every day?

There's an ancient Hindu story about the gods arguing over where they should keep the secret of happiness. Afraid that humans didn't deserve or couldn't handle this secret, they debated where to hide it. At first they considered putting it at the top of a high, high mountain, but reasoned that humans would eventually be able to find it. Likewise, they might find it in the darkest forests or at the bottom of the ocean. Finally, an idea struck one of the gods:

"I know the perfect place. We will hide the secret of happiness in the deepest depths of their own hearts. They will never bother to look there."

It's not easy to find the secret of happiness and fulfillment. But you have the ability to do it. The answer lies within you.

PERFECTING THE PRACTICE

Becoming a leader is synonymous with becoming yourself.

—*Warren Bennis*

COLLEEN

One day in our work together at the bank, I noticed that Colleen seemed particularly enthusiastic and engaged. Clearly Colleen had overcome her discontentment, and she was as vibrant as ever. I asked her about the change. "What do you think made the difference?"

As we walked down the hall, Colleen reflected on her coaching. She talked about her values and new sense of fulfillment. Then she stopped at the elevator and faced me.

"You know, I've been given a lot of opportunities. But I will never forget the moment I realized I needed to create my own opportunities for inspiration. It's great to be successful, but I'd already done that. Now I've moved from success to significance."

What made it possible for someone who was so obviously disillusioned to bounce back with such resilience and verve? What helped Colleen feel fulfillment? The answer is a solution that can benefit every leader, including you. Colleen was finally living her values.

You may not know it yet, but like Colleen, when you fully grasp the potential of your values to bring you fulfillment, you will feel as if you've reached your vision. The stress and striving will stop. The world will slow down. You will feel at peace. You can have all of that now. You don't have to wait. You can still set high goals, go after long-term visions, challenge yourself, and be an amazing leader, but you can do it in a way that gives back to you. You are going to feel as if you've made it when you find fulfillment.

That's because fulfillment is almost always what we're searching for. So the entrepreneur who still works a 50-hour week feels like she doesn't work a day. The executive who decides to be a stay-at-home dad still feels powerful and accomplished, and the president of a multibillion-dollar company feels as relaxed as if he'd already retired. They feel this way not because they're no longer chasing their dreams, but because they've already reached the most important part. They feel fulfilled.

Your *Inner Edge* Coaching Assignment: Your Values

Develop your list of values using the "Your Values" worksheet at the end of this chapter, and keep it current. Let it evolve. Remember you can always find fresh copies of the worksheet on the website at www.theinneredge.com.

FAQS

Q: Will my values change?

A: Most likely, yes. I often read in business journals that core values—particularly corporate values—should not change. For organizations, perhaps that's true. But leaders are people. We change. As we are shaped by the events of our lives, the values that have the most meaning for us change, too.

To me, the question "Do our values change?" isn't nearly as important as the question, "What are your values today?" Whether they change or not, the important thing is that you know, understand, and protect the core values that are important to you *now*. The point of identifying your values isn't that you will nail your values down once and for all. It's to learn a practice you can use time and again to find fresh motivation.

Fulfillment is something that keeps shifting. It's a personal responsibility to keep using those values as your guideposts and to say, now what do I need to adjust? And now? And now? What was fulfilling a year ago, for me, has shifted, because now I want a different balance. Two years from now that might not be the case. What is fulfilling to me now, and what do I need to do to get it?
—Amy Kovarick, executive coach and author of *Baby on Board: Becoming a Mother without Losing Yourself*

Q: How do my values relate to my strengths?

A: Both your values and your strengths describe who you are and what's important to you. But they are not the same. You can be working in your areas of strength and still be out of step with your values. Just look at the subprime mortgage scandals or other high-profile catastrophes where clearly bright people who were leveraging their strengths made disastrous errors in judgment. Leaders lose their connection to their values all the time. You can easily be maximizing your strengths and still abandon your faith, neglect your health, compromise your integrity, or neglect your values in a hundred other ways.

When it comes to finding fulfillment, your strengths contribute efficiency, accomplishment, and fun. Your values give it all meaning. Even though your strengths help you excel, if you're not living up to your values the effort might not be worth it. On the other hand, if you can align your values with your strengths, then you'll really be on fire. Colleen found a renewed sense of purpose when she married her job responsibilities with her value of empowerment. What could you do if you unleashed your values on your strengths?

Q: What do you do if you find yourself in a situation where you don't feel fulfillment?

A: Leaders ask this question all the time. Especially in a post-9/11 world, fewer and fewer leaders, especially those who are committed to being better leaders and leading a better life, are willing to sacrifice a personal sense of fulfillment for superficial versions of success.

As I see it, if you find yourself in a situation where you don't feel fulfillment—a job, a career, a relationship, a particular way you've configured your life—you have three options.

1. You can stay.
2. You can change.
3. You can leave.

Any one of these can be right. It all depends on your values.

1. *You can stay.*

You can often stay where you are in your work and life and find new ways of honoring your values. Colleen, the banker, provides a stellar example of how you can feel fulfillment in the exact same situation in which it was lacking. Colleen went through the whole process to get there:

a) She acknowledged her loss of motivation.
b) She mined, defined, and refined her values.
c) She assessed her current life in terms of her values.
d) She saw a vision for a more fulfilling life.
e) She asked herself how she could feel more fulfilled.

This process helped her find her way back to herself. She did this all on her own, with very little change in her life except a new perspective and a renewed sense of purpose. But that's not always possible. When it's not, you will need to take more drastic measures. You may need to make a change.

2. *You can change.*

You may not be able to find your values in your current circumstances, in which case you'll need to look for ways to alter the situation. One leader I coached, Mindy, discovered that by exploring new ways of working (telecommuting, using flex time, starting a job share, and delegating more creatively) she was able to keep her job as a high-powered corporate attorney while spending time with her newborn son. If your values don't seem to be honored by your circumstances, you may be able to change your circumstances to suit your values.

3. *You can leave.*

In the scenarios above, Colleen and Mindy were able to either flex their perspective or their situation to fit their values. Sometimes, that's a compromise neither you nor your organization are willing to make. The sooner you can realize that, the sooner you can move on. Here are some leaders who had to make that decision.

- Larson valued service. He resigned from his job as the CFO of a health benefits company when it was clear the dominant value of the president was profit—or as Larson put it, "the margin above the mission."
- Noah valued rest and restoration. He gave up his stressful two-hour commute to the city for a less flashy but equally rewarding job close to home.
- Marcus valued compassion. When the partners in his radiology practice doubled their caseload and became, as he put it, "a patient mill," he switched practices and joined a group that allowed for more patient consultation and long-term relationships.

When you can identify your values, you can hold them up against the circumstances you face and decide how to renegotiate the situation to make it work—or else, to realize more quickly that it can't.

Q: Why should my company care about my fulfillment?

A: Although it's been mentioned before in this chapter, it bears repeating that fulfillment is not just a personal matter. In a competitive market—especially one that's short on qualified leadership—organizations and cultures need to be protective of their human assets. Business leaders and their organizations need to be concerned about the degree to which their people feel fulfilled, committed, and engaged.

What businesses do now is expect more and more from fewer people in less time. When change happens fast and budgets are tight, it may seem like getting more out of proven high achievers is the only way to compete. Slowing down could mean risking competitive edge, market share, or both.

"So what?" you may ask. "Can't they just replace the people that leave?" Statistics say no. With the number of workers age 35 to 44 declining,[9] millions of Baby Boomers retiring, and a "strong to severe talent crunch for leadership skills,"[10] it's getting harder and harder to replace the leaders that leave. And even if they could be replaced, they take with them valuable institutional knowledge that simply cannot be replaced.

Business leaders do need to worry about fulfillment and the degree to which people in an organization can act, think, contribute, and be rewarded in line with their values. When businesses do this, they re-establish some of the loyalty that has eroded between companies and their people in recent years. Viewed in this light, the process of choosing fulfillment redefines the term "competitive edge."

Recently a friend of mine overheard a conversation between his mother and his son. They were at a soccer game, and six-year-old Garrett had gotten trampled by another player. Blotting his grass-stained scrapes with a wet cloth, his grandmother proclaimed the old adage, "No pain, no gain."

"But Grandma," Garrett replied, "I scored a goal off my knee, and *that* didn't hurt."

Garrett understood at six what many adults never realize all their lives. It doesn't have to hurt to succeed.

CHAPTER SUMMARY

Key Points

- To be your best as a leader, it's vital you give some thought to what, specifically, makes you flourish and to understand the mysterious and sometimes elusive source of your success.
- Your accomplishments will feel meaningless if they're not congruent with the values in your heart.
- Values are the cornerstone of fulfillment. When you live in alignment with your values, you experience harmony. When you live out of synch with your values, you experience dissonance and stress.
- Your happiness is not an achievement, it's a choice.

YOUR VALUES

Value: _____
Definition: _____
_____
_____

Value: _____
Definition: _____
_____
_____

Value: _____
Definition: _____
_____
_____

Value: _____
Definition: _____
_____
_____

Value: _____
Definition: _____
_____
_____

Value: _____
Definition: _____
_____
_____

Value: _____
Definition: _____
_____
_____

The Sixth Practice

Maximize Your Time: *How Can You Achieve More with Less?*

The greatest geniuses sometimes accomplish more when they work less.

—*Leonardo da Vinci*

YOU

What would you do if you had more time?

_____ Take a nap	_____ Get outside	_____ Catch up on work
_____ Do some visioning	_____ Take action on my focus areas	_____ Spend time with friends
_____ Take a class	_____ Call my family	_____ Take a vacation
_____ Plan my future	_____ Get organized	_____ Identify my values
_____ Do my 360	_____ Throw a party	_____ Read
_____ Work on a big project	_____ Join a business networking group	_____ Go to a museum or ballgame
_____ Get involved in charity	_____ Develop my action plan	_____ Do some financial planning
_____ Run errands	_____ Slow down	_____ Strategize

_____ Start a business	_____ Brainstorm	_____ Create
_____ Get a massage	_____ Travel	_____ Be more present
_____ Work out	_____ Work on a hobby	_____ Build my clientele
_____ Write or journal	_____ Meditate	_____ Hang out at home
_____ Empty my inbox	_____ Play music	_____ Develop my team
_____ Be a better friend	_____ Clean my house	_____ Go fishing
_____ Have an important conversation	_____ Meet with my mentors and coach	_____ Have a long, leisurely day
_____ (Fill in the blank)	_____ (Fill in the blank)	_____ (Fill in the blank)

In this chapter, we're going to make that happen.

The list above was created by asking leaders in my workshops the same question I asked you: "What would you do if you had more time?" Your answers may not have equal value. In the grand scheme of things, emptying your inbox probably doesn't mean as much as, say, strategizing or meeting with your coach. Unless, of course, emptying your inbox contributes in some way to your quality of life, frees you to do more important things, helps you feel less stressed and more settled, revives your energy, makes room for more important actions, or in any other way makes room for what you really want to do.

In this chapter, you will learn how to get more time as well as how to maximize that time so you can do the things you want to do, whatever they may be. In the previous chapters, we've been discussing how you can think and plan to achieve your vision for your life and leadership. Now you're going to get the time to carry out those plans.

THE PRACTICE OF MAXIMIZING TIME

If you obey all the rules, you miss all the fun.

—*Katherine Hepburn*

Maximizing time is the sixth practice of personal leadership. You will learn how to maximize time in several ways:

- save time
- spend time

- find time
- create time
- free time

You will have more time for the activities that help you lead and live well.

Imagine you had three extra hours this week to devote to your own im-provement as a leader—perhaps to do some of the exercises in this book or to complete specific actions that lead toward your vision. What kind of difference do you think this would have on your effectiveness? Your accomplishments? Your long-term success? Or imagine you had half a day this week to catch up on some of the backlogged work that never seems to get done. How would that help you clear the way to your bigger goals? Or imagine you actually had a whole day off this week to use for rest and renewal. What would you do? Do you suppose that would make you feel more refreshed? More relaxed? How would a dose of restoration affect your mood, your thinking, your relation-ships, and your decisions?

All of us can think of valuable ways to spend our time, and chances are some of those ideas are more valuable than the ways you're spending your time right now. When you maximize your time, you actually do have more hours in the day. If you've ever wondered when things would slow down, now you know: it's time.

Time for a Change

We need to learn to think differently about time. It's not as if we haven't been trying. Time-management courses have been around for decades, and work/life balance has become a cliché. Some question whether work/life bal-ance is even possible. Others argue we shouldn't be talking about balance at all, but time/life choices.[1] Many people feel they don't even *have* a choice about their time in a fast-paced, high-pressure world, which makes the whole discus-sion about which vocabulary to use entirely moot. We talk and talk about new ways to manage time, do things faster, tinker with our calendars, and apply technology to squeeze more into a 24-hour day.

But it's not working. We're busier than ever, and it seems to be getting worse. High standards, coupled with an uncompromising work ethic, de-manding bosses, business growth, job promotions, new technology, day-to-day operations, future planning, business travel, innovation, competition, family obligations, and the details of daily life all combine to create the kind of pressure that, as one leader put it, makes it hard to breathe. All of us who suffer a scarcity of time must learn to be more effective in our use of time or risk becoming victims of our own success.

The fact is, you will never have control of your time unless you take control of your time. That means stopping long enough to get a handle on what's happening, reflecting on whether it's working, and learning new ways to maximize the time you've got. Rethinking your relationship to time takes an open mind, it takes commitment, and (ironically) it takes time. But the investment you make in maximizing your time will pay you back hour after precious hour.

The Benefits of Time

There is one primary benefit to this practice.

You get more time. When you practice personal leadership, you think of time differently. Time isn't just a supply you use up to get things done. Time is a gift you can use as you choose. By thinking creatively about how to use your time, you give yourself the opportunity to gain on your goals and live in line with your vision and values.

The whole work/life balance thing has changed. It's not like
you have a work life and a play life. It's your life.
—Paul Melchiorre, VP Global Strategy, Ariba

How to Practice

In this chapter, I will give you some of the concepts and strategies I have found most helpful in turning around leaders' perspectives on time to get them much more of it. First, you will learn to challenge unhelpful myths about time and replace them with more beneficial thinking. Then, you will learn seven shortcuts that allow you to do everything you need to do and still have time left over. Before we close this chapter, you will make some commitments about your time so you're not just changing your thinking, but actually changing your life. The strategies you learn in this chapter aren't rocket science, but they have a meteoric effect. You go further, faster. You work smarter and better. You get more, with less.

We'll start with a discussion about time, challenging unhelpful myths to move you out of the old fast track so you can find the shortcuts.

THE MIND-SET FOR MAXIMIZING TIME

Creative. See the possibility. What's possible if you think about time differently?

Proactive. Treat time like a game. How much more can you get?

Rewarding. Use the time you save for yourself. You've earned it.

THE FAST TRACK VERSUS THE SHORTCUT

As a culture, we once had a reasonable relationship with time. Think about your parents and grandparents reflecting on their childhood. So often they reminisce that "life was slower then."

Then we got on the fast track. The implication was that those who were going to win were the ones who were moving fast. Faster equaled more efficient, more productive, and therefore more successful. We practiced new techniques with our planners and PDAs to get more done in a day. *Fast* became synonymous with *better*—an association we have been paying for ever since.[2]

Now we've moved from the fast track to warp speed. We keep trying to somehow fast-forward ourselves to do more and more, faster and faster, all at once and all the time. In some cases the pace becomes absurd as we try to do more of what we've always done faster than is humanly possible. But there's a limit to our capacity. Even if you see yourself as a Porsche in the fast lane of life, Porsches can only go so fast. At some point you're going to crash. In order to avoid breaking down, we need to stop trying to go faster and faster and cross into a new way of thinking altogether. We don't need to go faster from Point A to Point B. What we need is a portal. A trapdoor. A shortcut.

Physicists call it a wormhole—a way to link distant points in space that would otherwise take years, decades, or centuries to travel even at the speed of light. To get the image of a wormhole, imagine a worm traveling over the skin of an apple. To get to the opposite side, the worm can travel the entire distance around (the long way), or he could take a shortcut by burrowing through its center (the short way) (See Figure 5). To date, wormholes are more science fiction than science, but the concept can help us rethink what's possible with time.

You, too, can become a time traveler, slipping through time using shortcuts that lead almost instantly to a new way of life. To do that, you've got to shift your thinking. Let's look at a few examples of how we're used to thinking on the fast track and how you need to think differently to find the shortcuts.

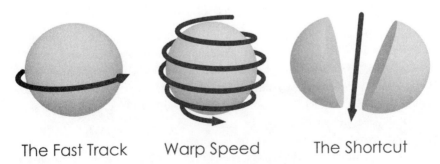

The Fast Track   Warp Speed   The Shortcut

FIGURE 5 From the fast track to warp speed to the shortcut

The Fast Track: You Have to Be Stressed to Be Successful

This way of thinking is a trap. If you fall into it, you will forever be caught in the black hole of busyness, trading your life for your success.

Research shows what we get in return for our stress is no American Dream. Health care costs for people who are stressed are 147 percent higher than other workers,[3] and 60 percent of doctor visits involve stress-related complaints.[4] Other problems occur when you're stressed:

- your performance slides
- your productivity decreases
- your relationships get damaged
- your decision-making ability declines
- your health suffers.[5]

The stress isn't just bad for leaders. It wreaks havoc on business in the form of lowered productivity, absenteeism, turnover, disability, insurance costs, workplace accidents, violence, workers' compensation, and lawsuits.[6] Does that sound like success to you?

Some stress is unavoidable, and the right amount of stress can even be good for you. But too much stress eats away at your quality of life, and the extent to which you enjoy your life is part of your success. Ironically, by trading your achievement today for happiness tomorrow, you give away some of the results you're trying to gain. There's no way to win at that game. Try thinking this way instead:

The Shortcut: You Can Succeed without the Stress

Stress and busyness do not equal success. Goal clarity and commitment do. Two leaders I coached provide examples of this distinction. Meet Vinh and Lucas.

VINH AND LUCAS

Vinh, an executive vice president of sales for a leading medical equipment company, was always behind. When he talked about time, he always seemed to me rather glib. He was always on the run, he was constantly behind, and I could see from his expression it wrung him out. But as soon as he saw me, he would paint on a smile. Grinning, he'd cry, "Ah, too much to do, too little time! But I guess that's true for everyone, right?"

But it's not. Right next door sat proof.

Lucas, Vinh's counterpart, had almost the same job but in another territory. Same responsibilities. Same boss. Same number of hours in the day. Lucas had just gotten back from a two-week scuba diving vacation. As a general rule, he was rested, relaxed, and on top of things.

The difference was more than their personalities. As I worked with these two executives, I looked at their views on time. Vinh was constantly stressed but covered it up with solace ("That's just the way life is.") and a happy face ("It's all good!"). He worked a long day every day, stressed himself out, and fell further and further behind. Lucas stayed focused on his priorities and insisted on a high quality of life ("Otherwise, what's it all for?") He made the way he spent his time a constant focus, a conscious and ongoing decision.

Six months later, Lucas was promoted and Vinh was fired.

I'm not suggesting Vinh was fired because he didn't use his time well, but all that rushing around certainly didn't pay off. Lucas was rewarded for his contribution even though he had sustained a comfortable pace and a joyful quality of life.

You've already seen several shortcuts to a life with less stress in the first five practices of personal leadership. When you take effective action, you stop rushing aimlessly about: less stress. When you leverage your strengths, achievement is easier: less stress. When you live your values, your life has meaning: less stress. One of the most beneficial rewards of personal leadership is *less stress*.

It's not that there aren't any costs to reducing your stress. There are. In a 1998 essay titled "Lives in the Balance," Diane Fassel (author of *Working Ourselves to Death*) described a disturbing trend:

> In corporations the tendency [is] to judge those employees who work at a human pace—say forty hours a week—as the deviants, while those whose loyalty knows no bounds, who work without to regard to limits are considered 'normal.'[7]

In this way, she suggests, stress acts like an addiction—the "drug of choice in corporate America." Even if you wanted to get out from under the stress, you'd still have to manage the consequences (like backed-up work or postponed goals), which may be why Americans neglect to take all of the vacation time they have coming to them.[8]

But you now know. The idea that the stress is somehow worth it is a lie. Fassel sums it up like this:

> Many myths underlie our fascination with workaholism. . . . The first myth is that workaholics are more productive and therefore profitable to organizations. Repeatedly, this myth has proven to be wrong. . . . The second myth states that no one ever died of hard work.[9]

The Japanese even have a name for it: *karoshi,* or sudden death by overwork. Workaholism kills in stages, starting with such symptoms as headaches and high blood pressure, and too often culminating in substance abuse, heart attacks, even strokes. If you're not careful, you can literally work yourself to death.

Some people see busyness as a badge of honor, brandishing Bluetooth devices and BlackBerries to prove their importance. Real worth comes from proper focus and perspective. No matter how universal stress is, it will never bring you complete and fulfilling success. You don't have to be stressed to be successful.

The Fast Track: Life is Busy

A common way people placate their busy selves is by believing busyness is just a matter of fact. "That's life," they shrug, as if time were completely out of their control. The truth is, busyness is a choice. Your life will be more in control when you take control. Your time is your own, and your time is your life. Relaxed, successful leaders see a different reality:

The Shortcut: Time is Life

Every moment you spend is a tiny chunk of your life. Every moment you give to inefficiency, overwork, or stress is one less you have for your happiness, well-being, and the ones you love.

It's too easy to abdicate responsibility for your life choices when you believe life is just busy. You become a victim.

"But it's not my fault!" you object.
"My boss is relentless!"
"I need to be there for my clients!"
"My kids need me!"
"There's just too much to do!"

Every time I hear these excuses, I have to nod in understanding. I have the same problems, and I feel the tension just like you. No one's saying you have an *easy* choice. No one's saying there aren't consequences for each choice you make. What *is* true is you choose those priorities and you choose the result.

Fortunately, says stress expert and physician Dr. David Posen, "you have more control than you think."[10] For some reason very few people seem to believe that. I'm especially amazed at how many empowered, decisive, capable leaders throw up their hands at a full schedule and declare themselves defeated. "You win!" they seem to be saying. "I give!" No matter what they would rather be doing with their time, they give into the pressure and do what they think needs to be done. The result is a very busy life. In *The Overworked American,* Juliet Schorr reported Americans work up to the equivalent of a month longer per year than they did 20 years ago, cutting into sleep, family, and personal time.[11]

I want to be clear that I'm not judging long hours and dedicated work. You don't have to stop giving it your all to get ahead. But you should know that the research is clear. Working more hours does not mean you're going to succeed. In his 2001 *Harvard Business Review* article, author Seth Godin summarized the research:

> People who run huge corporations, superpower governments, and insanely profitable, tiny proprietorships are all working fewer hours than you are. It's time to stop the madness and reset your internal clock.[12]

So put in that extra-long day when you need to, finish that project, go on that business trip. But recognize you *do* have a choice. Those choices add up to your life.

The Fast Track: There Are Only 24 Hours in a Day

This is a hard one to dispute if you think traditionally about time. But remember, there's a shortcut. When you get creative and conscious about the way you use time, one hour can feel like several, and a shortage of time becomes more than enough.

The Shortcut: You Have More Time Than You Think

The primary shift to believing you have plenty of time for everything you want to do (and more) is from quantity to quality of time. If you improve the quality of your time, you will save an unbelievable quantity in exchange.

You may have noticed that your work expands and contracts to the time it's allotted. If you have 15 hours to prepare a brief, it will take you 15 hours. If you have 15 minutes, that's all it takes. How do you do it? You gather up all of your mental resources and unleash them all at once to blast through one very specific target. Why not do that all the time? Instead of giving yourself 15 hours in the first place, give yourself 15 quality minutes, stay focused, and get it done. Then you will have saved 14 hours and 45 minutes to do other things.

This is just one example of how your experience with time will change when you start to focus on quality rather than quantity. Here are some more.

> Alex used to have weekly two-hour staff meetings to get face time with his direct reports and stay up-to-date. Now he receives updates in a bulleted summary and gets his face time in a monthly catered lunch with his staff.
>
> • Time saved: six hours per month

Geneva used to steal every second she could with her e-mail in an attempt to keep the deluge at bay. Now she zeros in on it for 20 minutes three times a day and has developed new rules to prioritize her messages.

- Old inbox: 677 messages
- Today's inbox: 33

Hunter used to work evenings and weekends to stay in step with his high-speed global company. Now he has redefined his time so he can focus on specific types of work for set amounts of time with better quality of thought and action. Every week he has the equivalent of at least two days of concentrated office time, one day of dedicated customer service time, and two days of meetings and miscellany.

- Time elapsed between vacations last year: nine months
- Time elapsed between vacations this year: every weekend feels like a vacation

There's only so much time in a day, but some minutes are worth more than others. Two days before a deadline can race by, but two days on a tropical beach can stretch out lazy and slow. When you realize it's the quality of time that counts, not just the quantity, you will no longer feel pressed by the fact that there are only 24 hours in a day. You will have plenty of time for everything you want to do and more.

When you accept that you don't have to be stressed to be successful, when you realize time is life, and when you believe you have more time than you think, you will start thinking differently about time. You can then use that time in these ways:

- to be strategic
- to be reflective
- to be intentional
- to be creative
- to prioritize what's most important
- to take action
- to enjoy yourself

Changing your ways won't always be easy. It won't even always be possible. It is a challenge to make all of your time quality time, and even then, you may still have more to do than you can fit in a day. I practice thinking productively about time every day, and I still occasionally find myself working extra hours—sometimes for a few weeks in a row. The point is not that you'll never be busy again. But you will be in control. To find the shortcut through time, you don't just have to change your scheduling habits. You actually have to *change* your *mind*.

If I have mental space, I'm so much more creative.
—Bradley Charbonneau, branding expert

THE SEVEN SHORTCUTS

Now that you're getting accustomed to shortcut thinking, you can also take advantage of shortcut strategies for maximizing your time. Below are seven shortcuts that will dramatically reduce the time you spend racing around the fast track so you can exit into a life of leading and living well. You will find that these strategies are very simple—the kinds of strategies you can do in your head or on a piece of scratch paper. The goal isn't to stock you up on more complicated notions of how to manage time. Instead, these strategies are meant to take what you already know about time and twist it—just a little bit—so you see powerful new possibilities. Because they are simple and designed to help you achieve what you want to achieve, it is not overstating the case that these easy strategies can change your life.

Before you begin, take just a moment to refresh your reasons for maximizing time in the first place. Why do you want more time? Do you just want to do more faster? Or could you use this time in a more strategic way to stay on track with your vision? How much more time would you like to have, and how would that feel? Thinking about how you want to use the time you find will motivate you to use it well.

Exercise

Be specific. If you had all the time you needed, how would your life be different? Write down your answer.

Just that little bit of clarity will help you get better results as we turn now to seven strategies that will get you that time.

SHORTCUT 1: MODELING

In many industries (construction and fashion come to mind), modeling is a strategy used to mock up an end product before investing the time, effort, and expense required to complete it. Your time may be the most precious resource you have. Make a model before you go out and spend it.

Modeling your time means figuring out what the ideal schedule would look like. You sit down with a pencil and a sheet of paper and sketch the way you'd like the next stretch of time to look. In just a few minutes, you can design your ideal week—or for that matter, your ideal day, month, or year. I even have one client who has mapped out the rest of her career all the way to retirement, and she's only 43. It will take time to turn the model into reality, but now you know what's possible. You may actually find creating the real thing to be easier than you think.

Exercise

To make a model of your time, sketch your ideal schedule into the blanks of an empty calendar until you're satisfied with the way it looks on paper. Use these three guiding questions:

1. In a given time frame (a day, a week, a month, a year, or longer), what are all of the different ways you want to spend your time?
2. Ideally, when would you like to be able to do them?
3. Mock up an ideal schedule so you can see on paper how it would look.

You can use the following worksheet to create "Ideal Schedules" (the Ideal Day, the Ideal Week, the Ideal Month) with more worksheets available at www. theinneredge.com.

SHORTCUT 2: DEFINE YOUR TIME

A complementary strategy to modeling, defining your time means figuring out what *types* of days you need. Just as you have different kinds of clothing (work clothes, formal clothes, weekend clothes) and different kinds of friends (professional acquaintances, neighbors, college buddies), you can also have different kinds of days. Which kind you choose depends on your needs.

You can define your time by thinking about the various activities that take your time and grouping them together. Start with the basics:

Meeting days when you are available to meet with other people
Work days that you keep to yourself to do your own work.
Flex days that are flexible to provide a cushion for spillover activities.
Admin days for catching up on paperwork and other administrative tasks.
Days off for rest and renewal.

If a whole day seems too long to devote to a single kind of work, then go by half days or even two-hour blocks. You can make your days as specific as you want, as these leaders did:

- Porter, a sports agent, has meeting days, client days, and office days.
- Jeannette, a public relations executive, has writing days, interview days, and administrative days.

IDEAL SCHEDULES

The Ideal Day

Time: Task:

_____:_____   _____

_____:_____   _____

_____:_____   _____

_____:_____   _____

_____:_____   _____

_____:_____   _____

_____:_____   _____

_____:_____   _____

The Ideal Week

Sun	Mon	Tues	Wed	Thurs	Fri	Sat

The Ideal Month

Sun	Mon	Tues	Wed	Thurs	Fri	Sat

Week 1

Week 2

Week 3

Week 4

- Clarissa, a bank president, has public days, professional days, and private days.
- Jonathan, a stockbroker, has only two kinds of days: on and off.
- Sanchez, the owner of a marketing company, has semi days, half days, full days, and long hauls.

Defining your time allows you to get into one mind-set for a particular type of activity and stay there. You can find your rhythm. You can get into a groove.

If you don't define your days, then every day you bounce around from one activity to another to another, all day long. Time is lost as you try to transition from a high-energy activity to one that requires you to be calm and quiet. You have a harder time *getting* focused, because you're constantly *changing* the focus.

At this point, you might be thinking, "This strategy won't work for me. Every one of my days is the same: busy, totally unpredictable, and driven by everyone else's needs." That's fast-track thinking. You can take the shortcut. Time is life. Whose life is it, anyway? If it's yours, then take some control. The people who want a piece of your time don't just want any time. They want quality time. You, at your best—not you flying in from one meeting with half of your mind on the next.

Exercise

What decisions can you make now about how to define your time? Write down your answer.

SHORTCUT 3: MAKE APPOINTMENTS WITH YOURSELF

This strategy is so simple, I'm amazed people don't use it more often. Make appointments with yourself. Think about it. You make appointments with clients, and you keep them. You schedule time with your boss, and you show up. You commit to meetings, and you attend. Now apply the same concept to yourself. Set a meeting with a specific purpose and be there to get the job done.

Here are some of the appointments I've seen leaders make (and keep) for themselves.

4:00	every day	e-mail catch up
10:00	Tuesdays	coaching appointment
2:00–4:00	Fridays	office time for loose ends
7:00–9:00	Wednesdays	read up on industry news
8:00–10:00	every other Friday	review financials
All day	first Monday of every month	strategic planning

All of these activities are the kinds of important-but-not-urgent events that can easily be pushed off the calendar, making you feel like you never have enough time because you don't have time for the things that are important to you.

What kinds of appointments do you need to make? Don't feel you have to set a recurring meeting that happens every week. You might just need to make one appointment to do some quality thinking or make some important phone calls that keep getting brushed aside. The important part of this strategy isn't the "what" or the "when" or the "how many" of the appointments. The important part of this strategy is the fact that you do the following:

1. Recognize there's something specific you want to do.
2. Decide when you're going to do it.
3. Schedule the time.

Keep that appointment, and you'll have the time you need, guaranteed.

Exercise

Make an appointment with yourself for the following week. What will you do and when? Write down your answer.

SHORTCUT 4: BREAKING TIME RULES

Whether we know it or not, we are all operating on unspoken time rules. This strategy is about breaking those rules. Here are some of the unstated time rules that tend to guide us:

- You must work 8 to 10 hours per day.
- You must take time off on Saturdays and Sundays.
- You must be available by phone and e-mail at all times.
- You must take vacations in full-day or full-week increments.
- You must be available to other people before you can make time for yourself.

But you can escape the rules of time. How you spend your time is a choice.

For instance, maybe you'd rather leave work every day at 3:00 P.M. but work six days a week. Maybe you'd rather get a long massage once a month instead of a full-week vacation. You might start defining the length of your workday by the results you achieve instead of the hours you've worked. Time rules don't necessarily mean working less, but they do mean working with more freedom and choice.

You may be objecting that your boss or your work environment will keep you from breaking time rules. To this I say, "Have you checked?" A host of creative work options from video conferencing to traveling offices to job shares have become available as people and their companies look for ways to use time that works for them. And if not, there are plenty of creative ways for you to break time rules within your existing agreements. See if you can break the rules while still meeting important expectations. Ask for what you want. Make a proposal. See if you can make it work. If you're willing to be fair, negotiate, and persist, you will be surprised at how accommodating others will be to help you break the rules to make better use of your time.

Exercise

Which time rules do you live by? Put an X by the ones you need to break.

_____   _____

_____   _____

_____   _____

_____   _____

_____   _____

_____   _____

Choose one of the rules above to break. What would it take to break it? What ideas do you have for a new way of working around this old rule that will be better for you?

SHORTCUT 5: MAKING TIME RULES

One strategy many leaders love in addition to *breaking* the rules is *making* their own.

Financial advisors often advise people to set money rules, like "pay yourself first" or "save 10% of every paycheck." Money rules help you be decisive and stay true to your financial goals. For efficiency and quality of life, you can apply the same concept to your time by setting new time rules.

Here are some of the time rules other leaders have set.

- Never open my e-mail before planning the day.
- Never schedule a meeting before 9:00 or after 4:00.
- Turn off my computer after 7 P.M.
- Keep my PDA off during family time.

- Always eat dinner at home even it means working in the evening.
- Spend no more than one evening away from home per week for a work event.
- Work on my personal goals during "my time" and work at work.
- Be home in time to tuck in the kids every night, or at least call them to say good night.

Would any of these rules work for you?

To set time rules, follow this simple formula:

- − Notice what's not working about the way you spend your time.
- + Write down what would work—the way you wish you could spend your time.
- * Make a time rule that makes your time work well for you.

Example:

- − It's not working for me to have people walking into my office all day.
- + I would prefer to have at least two consecutive hours a day with the door closed.
- * Rule: I close my door for two hours a day.

Time rules, even small ones, have the advantage of being concrete and explicit, making it easier to hold yourself accountable. Once you set a rule, you'll want to communicate it so you can accommodate the people in your life. They can only respect your boundaries if your boundaries are clear. Said another way, they can only follow the rules if you set them.

Exercise

What rules would you like to set? Use the following format to make the rules:

- − What's not working about the way you spend your time?
- + What would work better? How do you wish you could spend your time?
- * Set a time rule.

− _____

+ _____

* _____

− _____

+ _____

* _____

− _____

+ _____

* _____

SHORTCUT 6: REPLACE MULTITASKING WITH "UNITASKING"

Research has shown multitasking to be "an enormous waste of time, cutting productivity by 25–30%, destroying focus and undermining spirit."[13] Face it. As a strategy for using your time well, multitasking doesn't work.

Of course, you'd never know this by watching the action in the business world. Rare is the commuter who's not hooked up to a cell phone or a laptop or both. Commonplace are the meeting attendees with eyes at half-mast, fiddling with their PDAs just under the table. At one organization where I've consulted, every single person is triple booked almost every day as meetings are heaped one on top of another: multitasking applied to an organization. It's ridiculous. The message seems to be, it's not going to be possible to do all of this anyway, so let's just pretend. You end up working twice as hard but very badly.

Need proof? One market-research firm discovered on average companies lose 2.1 hours per day of employee productivity because of multitasking and related interruptions. Do you have 2.1 hours a day to spare? I know I don't, and unless they want to throw away profits, neither do U.S. businesses. This "distraction disaster" costs them up to $588 billion per year.[14]

Defenders of multitasking will say it befits today's just-in-time, networked work style, and I can see that. In an *Inc. Magazine* article David Freeman argues, "We need to appreciate the ways in which multitasking and interruption have become essential to meeting the increasingly nonlinear demands of our jobs."[15]

Conceded. Multitasking is a fact of life in a high-speed world. And it does work to help you manage complex, nonlinear tasks, like being available to people whenever they need you; responding on a moment-to-moment basis; staying on top of moving targets, like projects that move ahead in fits and starts; and handling phone calls and requests that come in at random. Naturally you're not going to shirk your responsibilities to focus on a single project for weeks on end without addressing any other needs. That's just not realistic.

But recognize the impact multitasking has on you. Your actions become fragmented, your thinking is interrupted, you make hasty decisions, and you do things poorly. To get the focus you need to be effective in achieving your vision, try replacing it with "unitasking." The whole strategy is this: Do one thing at a time.

Doing one thing at a time—even for a short time—improves concentration, calms you down, and allows you to get more done in less time. Considering that on average only about three minutes out of every hour are used with maximum focus,[16] you can improve your "concentration rate" with just five minutes at a time. Then fifteen. Then twenty.

You don't have to unitask all the time, just when it counts. Some tasks lend themselves especially well to unitasking, because they require your undivided attention:

- strategizing
- visioning
- goal-setting
- brainstorming
- working on projects
- thinking
- planning
- conversing one-on-one
- spending time with the people you love

These are the kinds of activities that benefit from unitasking. Unitasking communicates a respect for the people and processes that deserve your full attention. As much as you possibly can, practice dong one thing at a time. Set the time aside, focus, concentrate, and you'll get your tasks done both fast and well.

Exercise

For the rest of the day, consciously do one thing at a time. Unitask. Feel the difference? What do you notice? Write down your answers.

SHORTCUT 7: POWER DOWN

Power down means turn off the technology.

The wonders of technology are just short of miraculous, and I'm always cautious about making technology the enemy. So much of technology can help us maximize our time. We can use it to transform not just the way our world works but the way we work. It can buy us time, save us time, leverage time, and organize our time.

But if we're not careful, technology can also use up all of our time. Just because you can be available 24/7 doesn't mean you should. Just because you can instant message at the same time as you're trying to write a report doesn't mean you should. Just because you can perch your laptop on the passenger seat of your car to tap out ideas during traffic doesn't mean you should.

Freedman speaks bluntly about the futility of multitasking:

> You might think that your email, BlackBerry, smart phone, always-on Web connection, and ever-growing array of computer applications make you smarter and more efficient. But you're wrong. Instead, all those shiny new tools make it impossible to concentrate on any one thing for more than a few minutes. And that is why you have become dumber and less effective.[17]

Not only does misuse of technology undermine the quality of your work, it also can also strip away your gains.

- Example: You've decided to honor your values by spending more time with your teenagers, but you interrupt their stories every ten minutes to answer your phone.
- Example: You've decided to use an electronic planning system to organize your master task lists but you spend all your time playing with the software instead of taking action.
- Example: You're already living part of your vision by taking a vacation, but the PDA in your pocket is a constant reminder that somewhere, work is waiting.

The trouble is not with the technology itself; it's the abuse of the technology that's the issue. Did you know . . .

- . . . our brains get a stress signal every time an e-mail comes in?
- . . . people are yanked off their tasks an average of every eleven minutes?
- . . . it takes twenty-five minutes to get back into a task you've left?[18]

To combat the downsides to technology, a CBS News report offered this common sense advice: "Give the brain time without stress, relaxing with family, exercising, eating well and sometimes, just sometimes, ignoring those emails."[19]

Take the step occasionally to power down. Turn off the technology, and do what will bring you progress and fulfillment.

Exercise

Spend a few minutes reflecting on your use of technology.

1. How does technology help you maximize your time?
2. How does it hurt?
3. When, where, why, and how could you power down to make even better use of your time?

PERFECTING THE PRACTICE

Beware the barrenness of a busy life.

—Socrates

You started this chapter by thinking about what you would do with your time if you had more of it. Maybe you want more time for yourself for rest and renewal. Maybe you want to be scuba diving in Australia, or riding your bike, or hiking in the mountains, or traveling somewhere new. You might need a nap, a vacation, or a whole year off. Maybe you don't need any time to rest; what you really want is to apply all of your creative energies to your work—both your current responsibilities and the new ones that challenge you as you move up in your career. That's why it's so important to you to determine how you want to use your time. Once you apply the strategies for maximizing your time, you will discover you have plenty of time for both the responsibilities and the rest, for the work and for you, for the success and the quality of life.

The shortcuts for maximizing time are your exit off the fast track. You can do things so much more quickly, easily, and enjoyably than the rest of the world by taking a different route.

Your *Inner Edge* Coaching Assignment: Your Shortcuts

Any one of the seven strategies above for maximizing time can help you find a shortcut through all of the things you need to do so you can get to what you want to do. But they only work if you try them. Use the worksheet at the end of this chapter, "Your Shortcuts," or go to the website (www.theinneredge.com) for a downloadable copy to figure out where to start. Directions and templates for all seven shortcuts plus several more are also available online.

FAQS

Q: I've taken a lot of time management classes, and they never seem to work. How is this any different?

A: You're not alone. Leaders everywhere have tired of time management, concluding that it doesn't work. Either they feel as if they've heard it all already, or they bristle at the idea of "managing" time when what they really want to do is live their lives. Valid points. In his book *First Things First,* Stephen Covey agrees: "More than an evolution, we need a revolution. We need to move beyond time management to life leadership—to a fourth generation based on paradigms that will create quality of life results."[20]

Personal leadership is part of that paradigm.

The strategies you choose for maximizing time aren't a program. They don't force you to do things a certain way because some expert says it works best. They're not complicated, they don't cost anything, and you don't have to upgrade them every year. These strategies offer choices and concepts you can use anytime and any way in order to use your time the way you want to, and to get time for the way you want to live. Maximizing time is not about a process. It's about the possibility.

Another reason I think people find these changes hard is because they see them as one big obligation. "I know I *should* manage my time better," they say, as if they were talking about eating flaxseed or flossing their teeth. Maximizing your time is not about what you should do, it's what you choose to do. Do you *want* to work more and achieve your goals? Then use these strategies to do it. Do you want to have more time to yourself and find ways to be rested and renewed? Again, these strategies can help. There's no pressure here, only potential.

Q: This all seems a little indulgent. Am I going to jeopardize my job if I take extra time for myself?

A: This is a good question and a very real fear. I wish I could answer it for you, but the only answer I can give is, "It depends." Your ability to maximize your time depends largely on you, but at work, your boss, your colleagues, and your organization also get a say. You need to work with them to communicate openly about expectations and outcomes.

Seth Godin criticizes "macho companies marching toward IPOs [that] pride themselves on the army of their totally committed employees, who are all too happy to endure sleepless nights and to take showers at the office."[21] If you work for (or run) that kind of company, you're definitely going to have to make some tough choices. On the other hand, more and more organizations are realizing the need for high-quality work from talented people who want to be there and need a conducive climate to do their best work.

In my experience, companies that achieve the best results from their talent have leaders who welcome honest discussions about expectations. Talk to your boss, your colleagues, your clients, and your employees. See what their expectations are about time. Share yours. If you find yourself in a clash between your company's values and your own, you'll have a choice to make. Otherwise, you'll be able to come to a mutually beneficial under-standing in which you can do your best work for the company in a way that also works well for you.

The strategies for maximizing your time can work for you. The people who use them are not all self-employed, independently wealthy, or lucky souls who get to set their own schedules. They are professionals with expectations, bosses, employees, clients, customers, targets, spouses, kids, and any number of personal challenges, and they have to negotiate the constraints on their time just like you.

Your quality of life depends on you protecting your time. So do your effec-tiveness and your ability to attain your vision. Practicing these strategies will get you there. Otherwise, you will continue giving your time away on a first-come, first-served basis, and most likely you will usually come last.

You know best how to spend your time. You know what's valuable and what will make the biggest impact. Take control of your time, and watch it grow. The goal is not just to make the best use of your time, it's to use time to get the most out of your life.

CHAPTER SUMMARY

Key Points

- We need to learn to think differently about time. We don't need to go faster from Point A to Point B. What we need is a portal. A trap door. A shortcut.
- Stress and busyness do not equal success. Goal clarity and commit-ment do.
- You can escape the rules of time if you learn to think differently. When you maximize your time, you actually do have more hours in the day.

YOUR SHORTCUTS

Now: How do you want to use your time?

Today: Which strategy will you implement first?

—Shortcut 1: Modeling	—Shortcut 6: "Unitasking"
—Shortcut 2: Define Your Time	—Shortcut 7: Power Down
—Shortcut 3: Make Appointments with Yourself	—Shortcut 8: Go to the Calendar*
—Shortcut 4: Breaking Time Rules	—Shortcut 9: The 5 Ds*
—Shortcut 5: Making Time Rules	—Shortcut 10: Project 123*

*These strategies can be found in *The Inner Edge Extension* (www.theinneredge.com).

In Two Weeks: Reflect.

1. What strategy did you implement for maximizing your time?

2. What worked and what didn't?

3. What's next?

The Seventh Practice

Build Your Team:
Who Can Support You?

Laggards work with laggards. Leaders work with leaders. It really is that simple.

—*Tom Peters, "Rule #3 Leadership Is Confusing as Hell,"*
Fast Company

THE CONTROL ROOM

One morning as the anchors of the *Today Show* discussed a breaking human-interest story, weatherman Al Roker kept throwing in impressively relevant statistics and factoids. At one point, the anchors turned to Roker and ribbed him about his superhuman knowledge. Roker turned to the audience and winked.

"We don't actually need to know anything! We just have to have a control room!"

Although Roker was joking, he made a good point. He and the *Today Show* producers whispering into his earphone know something many of us have yet to learn: No one person can know everything. Certainly no one person can run a whole show. And yet, that's exactly what many leaders try to do, day after day.

Wouldn't life be easier if we all had a control room—someone whispering in our ear what we need to know just when we need to know it? Whether it's a producer delivering the details into a reporter's ear, a coach yelling to his players on the field, the president's personal advisor helping him make world-

changing decisions, or the wise words of a mentor guiding you through a critical moment, the best leaders surround themselves with people who support
them. You will, too, by building your personal team.

You might have aspects of this team in place. Friends, colleagues, and mentors probably already support you in your personal goals and aspirations. In
this chapter, you are going to learn how to strengthen that support into a complete, custom, and comprehensive personal support team. With your personal
team in place, you will find new answers coming to you from those who want
to see you succeed as much as you do. You will no longer be one person with
big dreams going it alone. You will become a veritable force, championed by
some of the best leaders around.

THE PRACTICE OF BUILDING YOUR TEAM

> We deceive ourselves when we fancy that only weakness needs support. Strength
> needs it far more.
>
> —*Madame Anne Sophie Swetchine*

Building your team is the seventh practice of personal leadership. Building
your team means identifying the people in your life who are smart, experienced, insightful, perceptive, challenging, and inspirational, and then asking
them to support you in your success.

This team is probably not the team you already have in place. We're not
talking about your assistant, your employees, or your vendors. These people
help you get your work done; they exist for the betterment of the business.
The teams we are talking about in this chapter help you reach your vision and
goals; they exist for the betterment of *you*.

This distinction is subtle but key. Your team is made up of leadership all-
stars: your role models, mentors, and inspirations. As members of your personal support team, these people are committed to you no matter what your
vision, where you work, or what goals you choose. They will support you in a
number of ways:

- advise you
- champion you
- advance you
- elevate you

Yes, you do need team members who are committed to the work. But you also
need people who are devoted to you: to your success, your decisions, and your
vision. Some examples:

- Randy, who owns a commercial real estate firm, meets with his business partners to make decisions about the business—decisions like

where to make budget cuts and how to expand into new markets. But he also belongs to a small group of business owners like himself to address what Randy calls "the personal side of business"—topics like how the business helps him meet his personal financial goals, or how he hopes to grow as a company leader in the coming years.

- Murieta, a CFO, talks to her employees to get their input on achieving company objectives like increasing profitability and raising shareholder value. But she also confers with her role models (other CFOs) to achieve her personal leadership goals: how to be an inspirational leader and how to earn the trust of her team.
- Claire, a comedian and actress, takes guidance from the directors in her current movie about the character they want her to be. But she draws on the lessons she has learned from her heroes Lucille Ball and Carol Burnett to be the kind of actress *she* wants to be.

In all three examples, these leaders are turning to a personal support team that is different than their regular work team to explore bigger questions about what it means for them to be successful. Again, the people on your work team help you do the work. The people on your personal team support you.

An All-Star Team

The more carefully you build your team, the more powerful it will be. You don't just put people on your team because you like them. You put them on your team because they enhance you. Chris Cox, corporate trainer and founder of Amplitude (www.amplitudetraining.com), is an expert on building high-performance teams. She suggests building a "brain trust" with other leaders—a partnership in which complementary strengths are represented, bringing flexibility and balance to the team. This is important advice as you develop your personal team. You already have your own knowledge, information, and experience. Your team expands you by giving you access to what you don't know.

Lone Wolf Syndrome

Your personal team is based on a shortcut concept some leaders just don't see. *You don't have to do it alone.* Too many leaders suffer from Lone Wolf Syndrome. They do everything on their own with little support, making their attempts to excel harder than they have to be. They feel they have to work alone, either because they don't believe they need anyone else in order to be successful or because they wouldn't know who to ask for help if they did. But building your personal team stretches you in ways you cannot do for yourself. You build a team not because you cannot succeed on your own, but because you can do more with the help of others. As leadership professor and author Jim Kouzes writes in an article entitled "Getting to the Heart of Leadership,"

> We don't get extraordinary things done by working alone—with no support, encouragement, expressions of confidence, and help from others. We don't make the best decisions, get the best grades, run faster, achieve the highest levels of sales, invent breakthrough products, or live longer that way.[1]

Just as leaders need to serve and support their people, they also need to be served and supported themselves.

The Benefits of Teams

Some advantages to having your own team include:

You Find Clarity. If two heads are better than one, imagine how much better several heads are. Now imagine they're all thinking about your success. When you have help creating and achieving your vision, you don't have to figure it out. You have other creative, experienced people who can show you how to do what you have in mind.

You Achieve Many Goals at Once. Having a team expands your capacity. Other people tend to see more in us than we can see in ourselves. Your personal support team will show you what's really possible for you, encouraging you to raise the bar on your goals and achieve more of them, further and faster, with their help.

You Get Emotional Support. The need for emotional support isn't given nearly enough credence in discussions on leadership development. As corporate psychologist Dr. Kerry Sulkowicz writes in a 2005 issue of *Fast Company:*

> We all have a need for intimacy. It's hard enough to find it with people we consider our equals. The challenge for leaders at the very top is that they don't have any. Some CEOs don't like to admit how lonely they feel, but the ones who can articulate the emotional experience of being leaders—and seek help for dealing with it—tend to be more successful, especially in the long term.[2]

CEOs aren't the only ones who feel isolated. Standouts in any field sometimes have a hard time finding the emotional support they need. Your personal team provides it.

You Feel More Peaceful and Content. The teams you create when you practice personal leadership are designed around your aspirations and values. Not only will you feel connected—which for many people is an end in itself—but you will feel secure in your decisions, which leads to a spirit of relaxed progress in the direction you know is right. When people come together to focus on the same issue, problem, idea, or project, the energy created is more than the sum of the parts. By engaging other people in your vision and allowing yourself to be invested in theirs, you advance together faster than you can alone.

How to Practice

Three kinds of teams will support you in your commitment to be a better leader and lead a better life.

1. The Mastermind
2. The Dream Team
3. The Imaginary Advisory Board

One of these may suit you best, or you might decide to build all three.

THE MIND-SET FOR BUILDING YOUR TEAM

Genuine. You don't have to impress anyone with your team or pretend to be someone you're not. Be sincere and specific in what you need. It will enhance the relationship and your results.

Sensitive in the Use of Other People. With your teams, you are in a sense using people, but only in the most positive way. It's no good to be used; it is *good to be of use.* People like to be involved, they want to be needed, and they need to feel valuable. Just as they will be there for you, you will be there for them.

Generous. All highly functioning teams depend on the generosity of their members, who give of themselves to help each other. Avail yourself to other people, help them as best you can, and you will naturally be helped yourself.

THE MASTERMIND

Think about your biggest challenge. Now imagine that today you have two or three other people dedicated to helping you work it out. They listen to your questions, they offer their advice, and they help you find solutions. Then, when your problem is resolved, you turn and listen to theirs. This is the essence of a mastermind.

A *mastermind* is a small group, usually three to five people, of dedicated peers who share and support each other through the challenges of life and leadership. It provides a mutually beneficial source of inspiration, information, and collaboration for all of its members. Far more than a typical network, a mastermind is your inner circle. A personal control room. A team.

To understand what a mastermind is, we can contrast it with what it is not.

- *A mastermind is not a networking group.* You are not trying to get business from your mastermind, and they are not trying to get business from you.
- *A mastermind is not a mentorship.* Although your mastermind members share characteristics with the wise and trusted counselors we call mentors, they are not the same. Mentoring relationships tend to involve a one-way teacher-to-learner dynamic. Mastermind members are peers who see each other as equals.
- *A mastermind is not political.* You're not trying to develop any kind of power coalition in a mastermind. The purpose of a mastermind is not to join forces but to encourage the betterment of each individual member.

Networking groups, professional associations, common-interest groups—these all serve important purposes for leaders. But that's not what we are talking about here. A mastermind is a group so cohesive that the members operate as one, focusing exclusively on the needs of one member at a time, and then another, and then another.

Masterminds can be as varied and extraordinary as the leaders themselves. For example, Wendy Hunter, a 52-year-old partner in a Midwestern public relations firm, has a formal, structured mastermind with other business owners. Every month she flies to Chicago for an intense closed-door meeting with 15 of the most powerful businesswomen in her state to discuss the goals and challenges of leadership. In comparison, Joe Scarpaccio, a 49-year-old advertising executive, has a more spontaneous, informal mastermind made up of personal friends. Joe meets his buddies Matt and Paul, also executives, every Thursday for lunch. Each meeting is one man's turn in the spotlight. He throws out his biggest challenge or goal, and the three of them discuss solutions for the best possible outcome. You can see a number of other varieties in the box entitled Sample Masterminds.

SAMPLE MASTERMINDS

- Three consultants meet once a week for an hour to grow their businesses.
- Six investors meet once a month for an hour to make investment decisions.

> - Four marketing professionals meet once a month for two hours to share ideas.
> - Six small-business CEOs meet once a quarter for two hours to set goals.
> - Five executive officers meet twice a year for a full day to strategize.
> - Eight former businesswomen turned "mompreneurs" meet on an ongoing basis via phone and e-mail to answer questions and share resources.

Wendy, Joe, and many other leaders thrive with the support of their masterminds. They discuss business results, leadership challenges, goals and visions, individual and organizational strategy, and more. The support is practical, personal, and tailored to each member's unique characteristics and concerns.

But although all masterminds are different, they all share several characteristics.

- devoted
- substantive
- focused
- confidential
- self-sustaining

Leaders who belong to well-functioning masterminds defend them with fierce devotion. As busy as their lives get, many mastermind members never miss a meeting. Their gatherings are like a clandestine, customized conference to determine their next moves in the chess game of business.

Six Steps to Making a Mastermind

You will take six steps to making your mastermind. Together, these steps spell the word MASTER, because they are the steps you need to be the master behind your mastermind.

1. Mindmap It
2. Arrange It
3. Suggest It
4. Try It Out
5. Establish It
6. Regulate It

Each step is supplemented by additional resources you can find on the website (www.theinneredge.com).

1. Mindmap It. Brainstorm. What do you hope a mastermind will help you do? Provide objective advice? Be a sounding board? Hold you accountable? Having a good sense of what you want from the group will help you create it. Put your ideas onto the page in any order—in other words, make a mindmap—just to explore the possibilities.

2. Arrange It. Who will help you achieve your purpose? The most important element of a mastermind is the people. Arrange the mastermind so it's made up of the most powerful team. As you consider the possibilities, remember to look for people who are different from you. Diversity is one of the advantages of a mastermind. Your mastermind members will help best if their perspective is different than yours.

3. Suggest It. Once you have some names, extend the invitation. A phone call, an e-mail, a meeting, a conversation over lunch—however is most comfortable for you, share your idea about the mastermind and see who's interested. Not everyone understands what a mastermind is, and not everyone wants to join one. That's okay. You're not looking to strong-arm anyone. You're looking for people who are drawn to the idea. A mastermind that doesn't form naturally can be difficult to sustain. Take it easy. Float the idea. See what the response is and move forward with the partners who emerge.

4. Try It Out. Once you have found people interested in joining your mastermind, get together. Hold an informal meeting to get to know more about each other and what your mastermind could be. To get the meeting started, reiterate what a mastermind is, how you envision it unfolding, what you would hope to get out of it, and why the people you've invited seem to be a good fit. Then go around the room one person at a time and see what they think. Here are some questions to ask:

- What interests you about forming a mastermind?
- What characteristics would be important to you in this group?
- What would you be hoping to achieve?

By the end of the meeting, your goal should be to determine who, specifically, is interested in formally committing to your mastermind group at this time. Then you can set a date for your first meeting.

5. Establish It. Once you know who's on board, it's time to officially establish the mastermind. The first time your mastermind meets as a group is an important day. You will be establishing the tone for your time as a team. You will get off to a good start if you take the time in the first meeting to start well. The Mastermind Kick-Off Meeting Agenda will serve as a guide.

MASTERMIND KICK-OFF MEETING AGENDA

WELCOME

Foundational Questions

1. Who are you, what do you do, and what brought you to this group?
2. How can this group support you in the best way possible?
3. What gifts and talents do you bring to this group?
4. What ground rules would make our time together worthwhile?
5. What else do you want us to know?

Logistics

1. How often will we meet?
2. When?
3. Where?
4. What will the format be?

Closing Thoughts

Once your mastermind has discussed the needs and purpose of the members, you're ready to set up regular meetings. When, where, and how often will you meet, and how will you structure the time when you get there? The possibilities are endless. For example, a group of three could meet:

- Once a month for two hours, giving each person a turn for 40 minutes each.
- Once a week for an hour, giving each person the whole hour.
- Every other week for one hour, giving each person 10 minutes and saving time for group discussion.

Or any other configuration you can imagine. I know one group of 10 that meets twice a year at a spa in Colorado. I also know a group of five that has abandoned the idea of regular meetings and meets on an as-needed basis. You don't even have to meet in person. Many masterminds use group conference lines like All Free Conference (www.allfreeconference.com) to meet across the miles.

However you structure your meetings, make sure each member has the opportunity to discuss their following concerns:

- goals
- needs
- next steps

With these three elements, each member is sure to move swiftly in the direction of his or her vision.

6. *Regulate It.* When a mastermind group is planned thoughtfully by people who are dedicated to each other and their goals, it can be one of the most beneficial forms of support a leader can get. But masterminds can also get off track. You will protect the effectiveness of your mastermind by keeping your finger on the pulse of the value it provides each member with a little self-initiated regulation.

At the end of every mastermind—or at least occasionally—go around the table and ask this question: "On a scale of 1 to 10, 1 being low and 10 high, what was the value of today's meeting for you? Why?" Then talk about it. What would the group have to change to make it a ten? What would you personally have to change?

Assessing your mastermind this way gives members the chance to ask for what they need from the group and to take personal responsibility for anything they're doing to hold back the mastermind (and themselves). It also gives the group the chance to grow and evolve to become the best possible opportunity for all of the members to get the support they need.

One of the first masterminds I helped to set up has also been one of the most successful, meeting monthly for three years and counting. It provides a good illustration of how a mastermind gets off the ground as well as what happens in the meetings. The members include:

- Tania, the president of an engineering group
- Sydney, an information systems executive
- Denise, a business consultant

This mastermind was born when Tania complained to me in a coaching session that she didn't feel supported at work.

TANIA, SYDNEY, AND DENISE

Opening a coaching session, Tania started with a heavy sigh. "I've just been feeling really isolated. The promotion has been great. I'm adjusting to being the president, it's challenging work, but there's not as much interaction as I'd like. Mostly because it's not safe to talk to people. I mean, I'm surrounded by people all the time. If I'm not running a meeting I'm sitting in one. But there are things

I'd like to talk about that I can't really do with my direct reports and sometimes even my peers."

In the conversation that followed, I dug a little deeper and found out what she meant. A politically charged environment, a series of layoffs, a nervous and mistrustful workforce, and frankly, her success as a female leader in a male-dominated field all contributed to her feeling that she couldn't confide in her co-workers.

It occurred to me that a mastermind might help. To create the group, I led Tania through the six steps to making a mastermind. To help the mastermind get started, I attended the first meeting—a peek into which will give you a sense of how a mastermind works. In the two-hour meeting, each mastermind member had 30 minutes to present her needs for that month and get the support she needed from the group. That still left a half hour for group discussion.

Tania began. She described a particularly sticky situation she couldn't discuss with anyone at work. Then Sydney took her turn. She asked for help refining a business strategy. Half an hour later, Denise took the floor with some questions about developing her clientele. When everyone had taken a turn getting support and advice, they went around the circle one more time. Each member made a commitment about what new actions they would take in the coming month.

You can see from this description of just one meeting that a mastermind covers a wide range of topics. Over the life of the group, this band of leaders has covered everything from strategic planning to succession planning to dreams about retirement. They have helped each other resolve ethical dilemmas and make difficult decisions. They have commiserated about hard times and celebrated big wins. They have shared the names of good consultants, coaches, and vendors. When it comes to succeeding in business, these leaders are in it together.

I asked this group to tell me what they get from their mastermind. Here in their own words is what they said.

- Tania: "I get support here I can't get anyplace else. Whenever I need to make a decision or make a plan, Sydney and Denise always have good ideas. It helps to talk to people who have been in my shoes and see what worked for them and didn't work, and what advice they have."
- Sydney: "In the mastermind, I can talk about touchy issues and get concrete advice from people who want me to succeed. They don't just give me ideas but help me figure out which one is right."
- Denise: "I have other people I can go to for advice. I have a boss. I have a mentor. I have a predecessor. The difference is that if I go to them with an issue, they're going to tell me how to handle it. I feel

like I have to follow their advice. The mastermind helps me develop my own ideas."

Overall, these three leaders felt their mastermind had made them better leaders and enhanced their quality of life by making them feel connected to other leaders. Perhaps Denise summed up the conversation best of all with a comment she made at the end: "The people in my mastermind understand what it's like to be me."

Exercise

Use the "Mastermind Planning Guide" worksheet along with the agendas and templates available above and online (www.theinneredge.com), to create your mastermind.

THE DREAM TEAM

Another beneficial team I recommend for leaders who want to excel is one I fondly call *the dream team*.

A dream team is a loose collection of advisors who help you get where you want to be as a leader. You turn to them because you know that on your path to success, they are further along than you. These might include the following types of people:

- leaders you admire
- leaders who have the positions you want to hold
- leaders who have the skills you want to have
- leaders who have achieved what you want to achieve

You meet with them one by one to ask them questions, seek their guidance, and learn from their experience.

The big difference between a mastermind and a dream team is that a dream team never meets as a group. To be accurate, your dream team is more like fantasy football than a real team. You never actually assemble these people. In this respect they aren't a functioning team. However, like a real dream team, every member of this group has been hand-selected because together, they represent the best of everything you need to be the leader you aspire to be.

This strategy shares many characteristics of executive mentoring, in which "an experienced leader helps an aspiring leader by teaching specific skills, coaching the use of those skills, sharing resources, and challenging the leader to leave his or her comfort zone."[3] You can think of a dream team as a way of getting executive mentoring for yourself.

MASTERMIND PLANNING GUIDE

Mindmap It. What do you hope to achieve with your mastermind?

_____

_____

_____

_____

_____

Arrange It. What characteristics would be helpful? Consider:

__Experience	__Cultural diversity	__Knowledge of issues	__Similar goals
__Expertise	__Diversity of ideas	__Knowledge of industry	__Similar needs
__Position/Role	__Location/Proximity	__Content Knowledge	__Personality
__Other:	__Other:	__Other:	__Other:

Write down the names of potential members.

_____

_____

_____

_____

_____

Suggest It. Contact the names on your list. See the website (www.theinneredge.com) for a template you can use to form your group.

Try It Out. Meet with potential members of your mastermind to see who's interested.

Establish It. Use the first meeting with your mastermind to set up a format that will work for everyone.

Regulate It. Make sure the group continues to be worthwhile.

To set up a dream team, you brainstorm all of the people who you think would be good members of a team whose sole purpose is to help you win at the game of achieving your vision. You take some time to analyze the different ways they might be able to help, make a plan for eliciting their support, and start meeting with them one by one to see what you can learn. I suggest these steps:

1. Choose the game.
2. Pick the players.
3. Set the rules.
4. Define a win.
5. Get in the game!

1. Choose the Game

"Choose the game" means get clear on specifically why you want a dream team. What do you want to learn from meeting with your dream team members? As always, the answer should be tied to your vision. Here is a sample list of reasons leaders from my client files have developed dream teams:

- Learn how to generate passive income.
- Learn how to enjoy life more without giving up my career.
- Learn how to smoothly conduct mergers and acquisitions for business growth.
- Learn how to triple my profits.
- Learn how to be the kind of leader that balances respect for people and the results of the business, the environment as well as myself.

Notice that in each game, the focus is on *learning*. On your dream team you're the rookie, if only in this one area of your life.

2. Pick the Players

"Pick the players" means being thoughtful and strategic about who gets on the team. This is not the time to hang out with good buddies and old friends. It's a time to branch out and build new relationships with people from whom you can truly learn. Among the group, it is helpful to have these roles:

Advocates. Advocates champion you, encourage you, and contribute directly to your success, perhaps by introducing you to influential people or making you a part of their team.

Experts. Experts have information and knowledge you need to be successful. Instead of learning it all the hard way, experts help you jump to new levels of awareness by sharing their experience.

Inspirations. Inspirations are people whose accomplishments make you want to be better yourself. As you watch a person who inspires you—whether that person is your most courageous colleague, a person who has risen to the top of her field, or just someone whose approach to life you admire—you are moved to a higher level of contribution and achievement.

These roles will often cross. In fact, people who can play more than one role on your team are often your strongest supporters.

Now notice who is not on this list:

Not Friends. Friendship is not a requirement of your dream team. Chances are you will see your members as friends, and your friends may become members of your team. But you can also learn from people you hardly know and may not even enjoy.

Not Yes-Men and -Women. Do not put people on your dream team who will only tell you what you want to hear. You already have your own opinions. Your dream team is meant to supplement your ideas, not rubber-stamp them.

Not (Necessarily) Your Boss. Just because bosses manage your position doesn't mean they can help develop your gifts. They may. They may not. You decide.

The diversity of your dream team is essential. Cover as many bases as you can in terms of gender, age, race, and station in life. Your eyes will be opened to new perspectives that will enhance your learning. Look too for diversity of gifts. People who are powerful, political, compassionate, world-wise, intelligent, international, local, aggressive, spiritual, reassuring, you name it, can all add special value. So long as there's chemistry, the more wildly diverse combination of traits you can cover in your dream team, the better. Of course, you can't get all of that in one person. That's why it's a team.

3. Set the Rules

The rules of your dream team game are how you want to play. If you don't set up the process in a way you'll enjoy, you'll be less likely to see it through.

- You might look for opportunities for informal conversation when the time is right.
- You might prefer a formal introduction with a letter and a follow-up phone call.

- You might arrange meetings according to each member's choice (e.g., five minutes in the office of one, a 15-minute phone call with another, a meeting over lunch with a third).

It's a good idea to decide how you want the process to play out so you put your best foot forward and feel comfortable along the way.

4. Define a Win

Defining a win means determining the best-case scenario for your dream team.

- Are you hoping to develop long-term relationships?
- Do you just want a lot of information fast?
- Do you want complex information? Are you willing to talk to as many people as it takes to get there?

This step is important, because it respects the time of the leaders whose advice you're seeking while also meeting the goals that matter most to you. If what you want is concrete advice on how to set up a sole proprietorship, you can get it in a series of short, one-shot interviews. On the other hand, if you want to become steeped in the culture of high-quality leadership, you'll want to develop deeper, more substantial relationships with people whose work you admire.

5. Get in the Game!

"Getting in the game" means asking the people you admire to be on your team—asking them to meet with you, talking to them, and applying what you learn as you work toward your vision. If a meeting with one of your dream team members turns out to be beneficial, great. Ask them if they would mind meeting again. If not, fine. You've made a good connection. Some of these conversations will turn out to be a waste of time. Others will turn into the kinds of mentorships that last a lifetime.

Remember, the work you do with your dream team is not pandering or political maneuvering. There should be nothing in this process that smacks of manipulation. These are genuine, respectful conversations with people you admire. You are requesting the support you would be willing to give someone who asked it of you.

You'll eventually find that your dream team project becomes a practice. You will make meeting with inspirational leaders and role models a part of your own personal development, because you will see—as you saw with your mastermind—that you can achieve more, and faster, when you are supported by a strong and experienced team.

The first time I met with one of my dream team members, I suddenly felt silly. He had so much work piled on his desk, and I felt like I was stealing time from someone who had more important things to do than meet with me. But the conversation I had with that leader, who happened to be my boss's boss, became the start of a career-long relationship that has opened doors for me and helped my now-mentor impart his hopes for the business to someone who wants to help make them happen. —Nathan Rockaway, CPA, Deloitte

One leader for whom I helped build a dream team was a promising young executive named Jeff.

JEFF

Jeff was a junior vice president at the corporate offices of an investment firm. He aspired to be the president of one of the company's regional properties. Even though Jeff was pegged to be a senior leader of the company, he wanted to be sure he was prepared for every opportunity that came his way. That's when we developed his dream team.

Jeff and I brainstormed a list of leaders he wanted on his dream team to help him become a property president. Eventually we arrived at a complete roster of players. Jeff then sat down with every leader and interviewed them with a list of three to five questions that would help him grow as a leader.

With his dream team, Jeff was truly taking the lead in his career. As he put it, "No one's looking out for me." A win for Jeff would be a new professional community—one that could teach him, guide him, and support him as he sought to become a leader who was integral to his firm.

Exercise

Use the "Dream Team Planning Guide" worksheet (also available online at www.theinneredge.com) to create your dream team.

THE IMAGINARY ADVISORY BOARD

The third team that can help you reach your vision is an *imaginary advisory board*. Your imaginary advisory board is a group of people, living or otherwise, who inspire you more than anyone else. In your imagination, you can convene historical figures, spiritual guides, even celebrities or ancestors into a single group with the sole purpose of supporting you. You sit in their presence as a way of finding guidance for important actions and decisions.

DREAM TEAM PLANNING GUIDE

1. *Choose the game.* Why do you want a dream team? What do you hope to achieve?

_____
_____
_____
_____
_____

2. *Pick the players.* Brainstorm the kinds of people you'd like to have in your corner.

_____ . _____
_____ . _____
_____ . _____
_____ . _____
_____ . _____

3. *Set the rules.* Write 3–5 questions you want to ask your group or jot down some notes about how you would like the process to play out.

- _____
- _____
- _____
- _____
- _____

4. *Define a win.* What's the best result that could come from forming a dream team?

_____
_____
_____
_____
_____

5. *Get in the game!* Contact the people you'd like on your dream team and ask for help. A model introduction has been provided on the website (www.theinneredge.com).

This idea originated with author Napoleon Hill. Hill was a protégé of Andrew Carnegie and spent 20 years studying wealth creation from such masters of fortune as Henry Ford, Charles M. Schwab, John D. Rockefeller, Thomas Edison, and Alexander Graham Bell. (Talk about a dream team!) His research culminated in the 1960 classic *Think and Grow Rich.*[4] Even if your ultimate vision has nothing to do with wealth creation per se, the idea of Hill's imaginary advisory board offers an abundance of possibility.

An imaginary advisory board, like a dream team, is a group of people who can inspire and guide you toward your vision of yourself as a leader and in your life. The difference is they don't actually exist.

Actually, that's not *quite* true. They may exist or they may not, but unless you are extremely well connected or capable of time travel, the chances of sitting down with them for a conversation are slim either because you don't know them or they because they're no longer living. Your imaginary advisory board can include a variety of members:

- historical figures
- legends in their own time
- famous people in your field
- characters from fiction and nonfiction
- religious leaders
- ancestors

Your imaginary advisory board might also include people with whom you don't usually talk about your aspirations and achievements, but who represent the values you hold dear:

- spiritual guides
- your children and parents
- good friends past and present
- other people who have had a hand in shaping your life

In this way you can gather in one place the characteristics you admire most—your mother's wisdom, your bosses' clarity, your mentor's way of being direct yet empathetic—and use them to help you live and lead well.

As a brief example, here is the roll call for an imaginary advisory board from an accomplished senator. Eloise had been struggling with the issue of whether to leave politics to take care of her aging parents, which itself had become a part-time job. For guidance, she called together this imaginary advisory board:

- Former British Prime Minister Margaret Thatcher, her role model for women in politics
- A trusted high school counselor who had encouraged her to go to college
- Poet Maya Angelou

- Her Italian grandmother
- Her husband and kids

Clearly a meeting of these minds would be impossible, not to mention spectacular, but the wisdom Eloise gained from just imagining these people advising her helped her make a difficult decision. Dr. Angelou symbolized strength of character to Eloise; she inspired Eloise to dig deep into her own truth. Her husband and kids represented the practical side of life, reminding Eloise that her decisions affected the daily lives of the people she loved. Each of the members of her imaginary advisory board helped Eloise make this landmark decision in her life by reminding her to look at it from a different perspective.

Why Have an Imaginary Advisory Board?

Wisdom and Insight. The most significant reason to have an imaginary advisory board is because it brings you uncommon wisdom and insight. Our human race has produced some truly remarkable minds. These extraordinary people exemplify a certain spirit, an outlook, an attitude that is rare in the modern world. You can tap into their exceptionality when you think of them as personal advisors. Their wisdom may be strikingly relevant even if the people themselves are gone, and it can help you in the here and now.

Creativity. Your imaginary advisory board can have as many people as you like in any combination. There are no rules except that the mere thought of these people brings you back to center: true to your values, committed to your vision, and inspired to achieve.

Freedom to Think Aloud. As a leader, you don't always have the freedom you need to be yourself. Your friends and colleagues may not understand the driving force behind your aspirations, and your co-workers may not be appropriate sounding boards. Executive counselor David Nadler reveals about corporate CEOs what many leaders know to be true about themselves: "Within the company, the CEO has no true peers, no colleagues in whom he can unreservedly confide."[5] While masterminds and dream teams solve this problem to some extent, there will always be some thoughts too private to bring to light. For your innermost thoughts and concerns, your imaginary advisors may be your most trusted guides.

At first, you may feel silly and even childish meeting with your imaginary advisory board. But this team allows you to do something no other group can do: bring all of your values and aspirations into one place, each personified by a significant someone. Even though you can't be with them, you can still aspire to be like them.

Obviously the process for assembling an imaginary advisory board cuts out a few steps from the others we've explored in this chapter. No need for invitations and agendas. What you do need, however, are your questions. Who in this world do you truly admire? What would you ask them if you could? I asked these questions of one leader who was mired in some intense decisions.

MARSHALL

Marshall was a 61-year-old ex-military officer who in his civilian career was leading a Fortune 500 manufacturing company out of bankruptcy—an undertaking involving harsh budget cuts, massive layoffs, and risky business moves. It wasn't easy. Marshall was a man with deeply held ethics and tremendous conviction. Seeing him struggle to make tough decisions, I asked him who in his life he wished he could talk to for insight. These are the names he gave:

1. The founder of the company
2. His political and military hero, Winston Churchill
3. His commanding officer from his days in the Air Force
4. His father, a man of unfailing conviction
5. The children of one of the line workers
6. God
7. His 38-year-old daughter, a customer relations executive, next-generation leader, and working mom

We then discussed what each of these people might say if he asked them how to lead the company.

"The founder of the company would implore me to save it," he started, "but from my military service I know sometimes the best solution isn't always the least painful."

"What about the children of the line workers?" I prompted him. "Why did you mention them?"

"The easiest way for me to save this company is to lay people off. Thinking of those children—many of them the same age as my grandchildren—helps me remember that every job represents a mom, a dad, and a family counting on their salaries to live."

"And your daughter?" I asked.

"My daughter challenges me!" He laughed. "Sometimes I think she knows more about leadership than I do. I am learning from her all the time about what it's like to be a 'good leader,' which seems so strange since I thought I taught her everything she knows!" He laughed again, then sobered up.

"Seriously, though. With every decision I make, I'm trying to do what's best for this company, the workers, and their families, and I need to be able to see the options from every perspective. In the end I need to do what will help lead this company and keep peace in my heart."

After we had that conversation, Marshall adopted his imaginary advisory board for good. Ever since then, one way he manages to make tough decisions is to sit by himself in the conference room, filling up the chairs with the people who, if they could be there, could give him the best advice. When the chairs are filled, he asks them the questions on his mind. He sits quietly and listens to the answers he believes each of his advisors would give.

He's even been known to bring his advisors along with him to his real meetings. "In any meeting, there's always at least one empty chair," he once told me. "I put an advisor in that chair and let their presence be my guide."

Exercise

To meet with your imaginary advisory board any time you want, just use the initials I.A.B.:

I: Imagine the people you most admire. Use the graphic on the worksheet to write down the names you would like to have at the table.

A: Ask your questions. If your imaginary advisors were sitting with you now, what would you ask them? Use the "Imaginary Advisory Board Planning Guide" worksheet (also available at www.theinneredge.com) to record your ideas.

B: Be with them. Let their energy and wisdom remind you of who you are and who you want to become.

PERFECTING THE PRACTICE

From myself I am copper, through You, friend, I am gold.

—*Rumi*

When you build your personal support team, you are no longer the solitary leader trying to go it alone. You are collecting an entourage. Together with your team, you are a veritable force.

Your *Inner Edge* Coaching Assignment: Your Support Team

It's time to build your first team. Use the "Your Support Team" worksheet at the end of this chapter or get another copy online (www.theinneredge.com) if you want to build more than one.

FAQS

Q: I like the idea of a mastermind, but no one I know seems right for the group.

IMAGINARY ADVISORY BOARD PLANNING GUIDE

I: Imagine the people you most admire. Who will you imagine? (Use the graphic below to brainstorm the advisors you'd like to have around your table.)

A: Ask your questions. What will you ask?

- _____
- _____
- _____
- _____
- _____

B: Be with them. What does your imaginary advisory board tell you to do or be?

A: To form any one of your three teams, think creatively. Loyal supporters hide in the most unlikely places. You need people who challenge you as well as enrich you, understand you as well as amaze you, complement you as well as support you. Just look at the differences among these groups:

- Patricia's mastermind is a group of three best friends.
- Adam's mastermind was selected from strangers he met at a conference.
- Georgia's dream team includes several entrepreneurs even though she's a self-called corporate suit.
- Kenya's dream team lives all over the world.
- Monty's imaginary advisory board is filled with literary characters.
- Ron's imaginary advisory board consists of world and historical leaders.

When it comes to assembling the groups that will support your success, open your mind to the possibilities and allow yourself to be surprised. The "Your Team" planning guides, materials, and models on the website (www.theinneredge.com) will help.

Q: How long should my teams last?

A: As long as it's useful. Over time, you will change. Your circumstances will change. Your goals and needs will change. Most groups have a natural lifespan. If you pay attention to how much value you get from each meeting, you will be able to tell when a group has run its course. It might be three months, it might be three years. There is no one right answer about how long a group should last. It should only last as long as it helps.

Q: Every time I tell people how amazing my mastermind is, they want to join! What should I say?

A: As a rule, I prefer to be inclusive instead of exclusive most of the time. A mastermind is not one of those times. In a mastermind, it's important for the members to create deep personal connections and a detailed understanding of each other's goals and experiences. Just as importantly, each member needs plenty of time to take the floor and get the help they need. You can't get that from a big random group of acquaintances. You need a very small, dedicated group of partners. A new member can upset the delicate balance of a group's dynamics, especially if that group is established and functioning well.

The first time I learned about masterminds, I was in graduate school at the University of Washington. I was desperate for camaraderie and would have loved some sympathetic support at a time of great intellectual challenge. A friend told me she had a mastermind, and my ears perked up. I asked if I could join her group, even for a visit. What she said was a generous gift.

"Our group has been together a long time. We need to keep it small so we can give each other plenty of time. What I suggest is that you form your own group."

That was ten in the morning. I had formed my first mastermind by lunch.

From the start, we paid forward the benefits we received from each other. We limited the membership to just the four of us, and whenever someone else wanted to join, we encouraged the person instead to start his or her own. We shared our process and answered any questions they had, with the intent of getting the person the kind of help they needed without jeopardizing the integrity of our mastermind. There's more than one way to share the wealth.

On the other hand, if you're absolutely sure you've found an essential new member for your mastermind, check with the other members. If you all agree unanimously to open your doors, it could be someone new will breathe in new life.

Of course, none of this applies to your dream team or your imaginary advisory board. Because those groups don't meet all at once, dynamics aren't an issue. In those groups, the more the merrier. Let them in!

It doesn't have to be lonely at the top. You can collect an entourage of your very own. As with so many other ideas in this book, you choose how you experience success—and how you attain it.

The notion of building your team far exceeds traditional concepts of networking and professional associations. Certainly those strategies have something to offer, including business connections, advice, and information. But for people who are not just following in others' footsteps but taking the lead on their path to success, a personal team is even more powerful. A mastermind, a dream team, and an imaginary advisory board all offer ways to expand your capacity, giving you more opportunities to learn, ask questions, and lead. Just as you are doing what you do best, allow others to do what they do best to support you.

CHAPTER SUMMARY

Key Points

- Your personal support team is made of up leaders you admire who advance you, elevate you, and make it possible for you to do more/better/faster than you can do on your own.

- This team is probably not the team you already have in place. Your work team (e.g., assistants, employees, vendors) exists for the betterment of the business. Your personal support team (advocates, champions, and inspirations) exists for the betterment of *you*.
- Just as leaders need to serve and support their people, they also need to be served and supported themselves.

YOUR SUPPORT TEAM

What kind of a team do you want to create?

_____ Mastermind _____ Dream Team _____ Imaginary Advisory Board

Who will you ask to join? Use the space below to map out the members.

What will you ask?

- _____
- _____
- _____
- _____
- _____

Notes

The Eighth Practice

Keep Learning: *What Do You Most Need to Know?*

Good leaders are, by definition, voracious learners.

—*Jack Welch*

ANNETTE

Now this is living, Annette thought as she turned her face to the sun. It was a glorious spring morning. It was nine in the morning, and her day was just getting started. Annette had already taken a swim and even spent some time in the sauna. With the time she had left, she'd sat on the back deck with a cup of coffee and turned a few pages of a business journal. Relaxed and inspired, she stretched and decided to get going. She gathered her books and breakfast and headed to her brand-new office, newly redecorated and waiting for her expectantly . . . right down the hall.

How fabulous, she thought.

Annette had always dreamed of a home office: wearing jeans all day, slippers if she wanted, on no one's schedule but her own. She loved it. Today she would be developing a proposal for a new contract. Tomorrow she was going to meet with clients. Maybe she'd take the next day off. The whole lifestyle was better than she'd ever imagined. She had her own business, her own clients, her own profits, and her own ideas about how to spend each and every day. She was free.

Annette sighed and opened her eyes. Back in her top-story office, Annette stood up from her chair. She had been envisioning her future. But on this day she was still running the corporate offices of a global pharmaceutical company.

She turned back to the work that was waiting. *Someday,* she thought. *Someday that will be my life.*

As she imagined her future vision, Annette wasn't just daydreaming. She was developing a clearer vision of the new life she wanted to lead. She had a vision, focus areas, and an action plan. She knew her strengths, she'd identified her values, and she was maximizing her time. She had created a mastermind, started a dream team, and had imaginary advisors. Every step brought her closer to her vision. But some days, her dreams seemed awfully far away. Before she could make the move from where she was to where she wanted to be, she had a lot to learn.

Whether your vision is to make a big change like Annette or to excel as a leader right where you are, positive change almost always requires new learning. In this chapter, you will find powerful techniques to keep learning, but they're not the usual fare. I won't be encouraging you to find an online class or read more books. You already know how to do that.

You need learning that's more customized. Targeted. You need learning that's specifically designed for you—strategies befitting an advanced level of leadership and your deep commitment to the overall success of your life, so that you can achieve any goal you set your mind to in the shortest possible time.

THE PRACTICE OF LEARNING

Life never becomes a habit to me. It's always a marvel.

—*Katherine Mansfield*

As a coach, I believe that when it comes to what's best for you, you have your own answers. My goal in this book is to help you find them. Many of the practices of personal leadership are designed to draw out this knowledge so you can make your own decisions about how to be a better leader and lead a better life. But just as we can all be strengthened by discovering the answers we do have, we can also be stretched far beyond our capacity by seeking the answers we don't. In other words, we need to keep learning. *Learning* is the eighth practice of personal leadership.

The value of learning is well-known in business. Perhaps that's why corporate training is a booming industry. In 2000, *Leader to Leader* magazine reported the training industry overall to represent a staggering $740 billion.[1] Whole departments are set up for professional development, and every major company has a plan for employee education. Seminars, conferences, guest speakers, leadership series—they all have the shared goal of helping leaders keep learning. But they're not always practical, and unfortunately, they're not very efficient—especially when you consider that you can learn on your own. The question is whether you're learning by chance or by choice.

Learning by Chance

Leaders are indeed encouraged to learn on the job. The problem is that many of us don't. Either because we're too busy, we forget, we don't know what we need to learn, or we don't have the resources we think we need, we end up learning by *chance* or *command*. Neither one is very powerful.

Learning by chance means you take opportunities to learn whenever they show up, but you don't necessarily go looking for more. A conference brochure arrives—it seems interesting, so you go. A friend recommends a book—it looks good, so you read it. You take opportunities to learn as they come to you—in other words, when it's convenient.

Learning by command means you learn when someone else demands it. When your colleagues tell you that you need to learn to be more decisive, or when your profession requires that you get an advanced certification, or when your boss sends you through a program to learn specific skills, you are learning by command.

There's nothing inherently wrong with these approaches to learning. Any learning that advances your expertise and builds your capacity may be worth your time.

Or it may not, and that's the problem. You have so much potential, there are so many opportunities to learn, and there is so much to be gained by learning that it simply doesn't make sense to relegate your learning to the whims of chance and command. You need to learn by choice.

Learning by Choice

Learning by choice means carefully setting up your own learning opportunities based solely on what you need in order to get better results. It is based on a number of assumptions.

Learning Is Leadership. Learning is an essential component of leadership. Some experts go so far as to say learning *is* leadership—a leader's constant quest for the improvement of the business, people, and results.[2]

Learning Is Innovation and Change. The soul of business is innovation; the soul of personal leadership is the innovation of the self. You can't have one without the other. If you want to have, run, or be part of a business that succeeds in times of change, you need to be willing to change, as well.

Learning Is Life. In addition to learning for all of the practical and rational reasons that contribute to your effectiveness as a leader, there's one more. Learning is part of the fun of life. When was the last time you picked up a new sport, game, or hobby? We learn these things not because we have to, but because we want to. I have a son, Morgan, who is two years old. Watching him, I get to see firsthand the joy of learning something for the first time ever. His face shines as he rides around on his miniature scooter or announces he put the ball in the basket ("I did that!"). As adults, when we keep learning we get to experience that same zest for life. Your vision and goals will be infused with a new sense of exuberance when you commit to learning what you need to learn in order to achieve. You can do anything you want to as long as you know how to learn.

If you really want to lead well and live well, you must learn to learn well, too.

THE MIND-SET FOR LEARNING

Curious. What is there to learn?
Open. What ideas and perspectives do you need to change?
Enthusiastic. What's possible?

The Benefits of Learning

When you practice learning as an element of personal leadership, you get better results for yourself and for your work.

You Feel Powerful. By learning, you empower yourself to have, do, and be whatever you choose.

You Feel Certain of Yourself. With empowerment comes confidence. You don't second-guess yourself or worry you'll fail, because you know if you get it wrong, you'll be able to figure out how to get it right.

Learning is a key advantage in your leadership and your life. Not everyone uses it. You can.

How to Practice

Below you'll find some of the key learning strategies I recommend for every leader. One of these techniques is a process of independent study to find the most timely, relevant information you need to succeed now. Another is a process of finding coaches and mentors to sharpen and advance your skills. The third is a process of reflection to glean insight from your experiences and accelerate your growth. Strategies like these are convenient, practical, efficient, and best of all, 100 percent designed around what you need to know to reach your goals.

You do not want to be average. You do not want the status quo. You want more. You can be more. And you will be, if you're willing to learn.

A CLASS OF YOUR OWN

ANNETTE

When you met Annette earlier in this chapter, she was immersed in a vision of her future. That evening, after a long day at work, she put on her pajamas and a sweater, took a journal, and went out into the yard. She sat down to think about her life.

Annette was a 46-year-old executive at the company where she had worked for 15 years. For most of that time, her life had been subsumed by, well, life: raising kids, running a home, attending holidays and birthdays and barbecues, and gradually working her way up the company ladder.

But lately, things had quieted down. Her kids, now in their late teens, had more independent lives. Her marriage, her home life, her social life—everything felt more settled. Now as a senior vice president, she was even established in her job. The last two years had been downright comfortable. Almost too comfortable. Annette was busy enough, she was engaged, and she wasn't burned out or depressed. She wasn't even unfulfilled. She just needed a change. Too young to retire and too talented to coast, she wanted to try something new. Something for her. She decided that becoming a consultant was it.

She flipped open her journal and found her CATA list. "Learn how to become a consultant," it read. *Ha!* she laughed to herself. *If only it were that easy!*

Annette told me this story the next day when we met. She had hired me several months prior when she first started thinking about going out on her own. When she got to the punch line, she laughed and repeated it twice. "Learn to be a consultant!" she laughed as if to say, "Can you imagine? How simplistic!" I also laughed, but not because I thought the idea was so outrageous. I was smiling because I knew something she didn't.

"But Annette," I interjected when she took a breath, "it really is that easy."

She was about to learn how to make her vision a reality. She was entering a class of her own.

Being in a class of your own means *you choose* what you want to learn. To do that, you don't have to go back to school. But you do get to use a powerful concept from your school days that will help you reach your goals: the independent study.

The Independent Study

In school, an *independent study* is a way for students to learn what they want to learn even if it isn't in the course catalog. Done well, it can be the launching pad to a student's true calling, because for once the student gets to choose the content and explore what's available in an area that piques his or her interest. And even though independent study students are pursuing their own interests, they get credit for the effort. What a deal.

In your independent study, you get to be a student again in the best sense of the word. No course requirements, no class schedules, and no exams—just the chance to be new and green, seeing what there is to learn about something you want to know.

You do your independent study in three steps, each of which starts with the letter *A*—the grade you're going to earn in this class of your own.

1. Assess your options.
2. Adopt a topic.
3. Activate the learning.

An "A" in Assessing Your Options

Assessing your options means brainstorming and collecting your thoughts. To find the topic for your independent study, ask yourself some questions.

- What do you need to know that will help you achieve your vision?
- What specific skills do you need to learn?
- What practices do you need to put into place?
- What behaviors will be instrumental in helping you succeed?

We live in a fascinating world. Think about what would be fun, intriguing, and ultimately extremely powerful to learn. Then move to the second step.

An "A" in Adopting a Topic

Adopting a topic means choosing one thing to learn at a time. There are so many possibilities for learning you could easily become overwhelmed or distracted if you tackled all the options at once. To counteract the tendency to be unfocused in the midst of too much information, leadership expert and executive coach Marshall Goldsmith recommends that leaders stay focused on changing their behaviors one or two at a time.[3] The same principle applies to all of your learning. Be intentional. Really make an impact in one area.

To be strategic, make sure whatever you choose to study will get you the *one big hit* that will break you through to the win. Sure, you can probably learn lots of things that will be helpful . . . but what *one* thing can you learn that is going to send you over the top? To find the answer, I find it helpful to consider three zones for learning.

1. *Knowledge.* Is there content or information you need to know? Maybe you need to understand more about your vision, your field, or a related topic that will shed light on your ability to succeed.
2. *Skills.* Are there certain skills you need to learn? For instance, you might need to learn how to be a more effective communicator, how to inspire an entire organization to a new vision, or how to delegate and manage new responsibilities.
3. *Behaviors.* Are there characteristics and habits you need to change or develop? It might benefit you to start being more creative, to stop criticizing new ideas, or to practice being more trusting.

Whether it's knowledge, skills, or behaviors you need to learn, choosing one thing will help you truly master something that is key to your success. Even better: You get to choose what that something will be. Once you have it, you can move to the next step.

An "A" in Activating the Learning

What will you do to master the topic of your independent study? Will you read? Ask questions? Take on a new challenge? Practice? Find an internship? What are the most efficient, effective ways you can think of to learn what you need to learn? When you have some ideas, activate the learning by making a commitment. What will you do and when will you do it? How will you know when you're done? Then put the plan into motion. After your independent study, you will emerge a better leader than you were before.

When you feel you've mastered one aspect of learning, start over with a new topic. Set the intention to be committed to your learning, always having one thing that you are focusing on right now. Annette, the corporate executive and would-be entrepreneur, started with learning what it would be like to be out on her own—the challenges, the advantages, and the possibilities. Later, she moved to learning about how to build a business from scratch—things like corporate entity creation and tax implications. Later still, she sought to learn the skills of contracting. Whether you focus on your topic for a day, a week, or a month, you will get more out of your independent study if you master one topic at a time.

Exercise

Use the worksheet "A Guide to Your Independent Study" (also available at www.theinneredge.com) to set up a new learning process.

A GUIDE TO YOUR INDEPENDENT STUDY

Assess Your Options

What knowledge, skills, and behaviors do you need to achieve your vision?

_____

_____

_____

Adopt a Topic

What *one thing* will you focus on learning now?

_____

_____

_____

What difference will it make to have learned this?

_____

_____

_____

Activate the Learning

How will you go about your learning? What will you do?

_____

_____

_____

When will you do it?

_____

_____

_____

How will you know when you're done?

_____

_____

_____

"EXCELERATION"

ANNETTE

From her independent study of consulting, Annette was stocked with knowledge. Almost too much knowledge. She was having trouble taking it all in.

"It's just like you say about your strengths and your values," she quoted me.
" 'It's not enough to have the information. You have to know what to do with it.'
I'm not sure I know what to do with all of this."

"Then you'll need to make some decisions," I suggested. "This would be a
great time to get a mentor."

"A mentor?" she asked. "Usually that's my job." Annette was a senior leader
in the company, after all, and she had mentored many a new executive. But she'd
never been a consultant, I argued, and I encouraged her to find a role model.
"But why do I need a mentor?" she pressed me. "I already have a coach."

"Annette, you are well on your way to achieving your vision. You've made
some big decisions and you're moving in the right direction. How would you
like to find an inside track?"

"That would be great!" she exclaimed eagerly.

"Great," I agreed. "Your coach and your mentor will show you where it is."

If you are really serious about rising above the fray of an average life, you
need to move way past the ego that tells you "you can do it" and find the people
who already have, and then ask for their help. You need to find the masters
who are going to teach you what they know and help you find your own path
to greatness. Not just acceleration, but *excel*-eration.

Exceleration is the result when you achieve your vision faster, better, and
with more success by working with others than you would working on your
own. In my view, there is no single strategy that will do more for your overall success than exceleration through coaching and mentoring. Yes, your
coaches and mentors give you an edge simply by being sounding boards with
good ideas. But they also bring you perspective, knowledge, and opportunities. You get more than learning when you meet with those who support you
in this way.

Think of the traditions of coaching and mentoring. A *coach* is the champion
in your corner urging you on, reminding you how great you are, and jump-
ing up and down to get you to win. *Mentor* was the name of the counselor to
the mythological hero Odysseus—a sage so full of wisdom that a warrior as
strong, brave, and victorious as Odysseus turned to *him* for advice. Imagine.
You can have that, too.

The roles of coaching and mentoring often cross, but for the sake of understanding everything these two forms of learning have to offer, we'll look at them separately. We'll start with coaching first.

Coaching

Coaching is a highly customized, deeply personal process of learning and development specifically designed for one person: you. When you have a coach, you meet with someone on a regular basis to take targeted action toward your vision—someone whose expertise is in getting you to succeed.

Even if you've never had a coach, you are familiar with the process of coaching just by reading this book. This book mirrors the coaching process, which involves many of the practices of personal leadership:

- get clarity
- find focus
- take action
- tap into your brilliance
- feel fulfillment
- maximize your time
- build your team

The only difference is that as you read this book, you're going through the process on your own, whereas with a coach you have someone who knows your goals helping you apply the practices in context and in the most powerful ways for you.

You can get a sense of coaching by contrasting it with what it's not:

- *Coaching is not consulting.* Consultants advise you on what to do. Coaches help you do it.
- *Coaching is not counseling.* Counselors help you understand yourself. Coaches help you use that understanding to meet your goals.
- *Coaching is not (usually) mentoring.* Mentors tend to be in the same profession as you, which makes them invaluable for showing you the ropes. Some mentors are excellent coaches, but coaches are not usually your mentors. You are the one responsible for getting the best results out of your business, whereas your coach is responsible for helping get the best results out of *you.*

---

*I think the most valuable thing you can get from coaching is the
ability to step away and see yourself from an outsider's
perspective. It leads you to be able to think outside the box.*
—Saly Glassman, Senior Vice President–Investments, Merrill Lynch

---

As you lead your life, a coach brings important advantages to your learning.

- *Perspective.* In some ways, a coach knows you better than you know yourself. Your coach mirrors you back to yourself. He or she also provides multiple perspectives so you can see a situation from different angles and make better, more informed decisions.
- *Focus and continuity.* Your coach's job is to know what you want and be sure you're working toward it, making progress and achieving your goals.
- *Critique.* Your coach can give you the kind of feedback everyone needs but few can give: respectful and honest.
- *Questions.* Coaches believe you have your own answers. A good coach provides the right questions.
- *Accountability.* No matter how badly you may want to do something, sometimes you just don't. Coaches hold you accountable to concrete, measurable action.
- *Safety and confidentiality.* Coaching is the one place you can get every complicated thought out in the open and make sense of your ideas with the help of someone who will keep the conversation confidential and help you find solutions.

Before you rush out to find a coach, however, it's also important to consider a mentor, who will also help you excelerate your success.

Mentoring

Margaret Heffernan and Saj-Nicole Joni, in their *Fast Company* article "Of Proteges and Pitfalls," summarize the research on mentoring: "Since the 1970s, studies have repeatedly demonstrated that mentoring is the single most valuable ingredient in a successful career for both men and women."[4]

There is a significant difference between a coach and a mentor. Coaches don't need to be more experienced than you. They need to be experienced differently. Your mentor, on the other hand, usually does have more experience than you. Thus he or she can offer you several advantages:

- experiential knowledge
- good examples
- inside advice
- cautionary tales
- opportunities

To clarify further the unique role of mentoring, think about its defining characteristics.

Mentoring Is Focused on the Task. When you are being mentored, you are learning to do something well from someone who already can. If you want to learn to drive a racecar, your mentor should be a racer. If you want to learn to lead, your mentor should be a leader. You may have many different mentors, all teaching you different things.

Mentoring Is a Cross between Teaching and Coaching. The goal of mentoring is to help you learn. It's not training. Your mentor's job is not to teach you so much as to help you practice what you've learned. Neither is mentoring the same as coaching. Your coach helps you learn from your own experience; your mentors help you benefit from *theirs.*

Mentoring Is Skill Oriented. Unlike a coach, a mentor's job is not necessarily to walk you through the process of getting from where you are to where you want to be. A mentor's job is to show you how he or she does something well and to help you in any way possible to do it yourself.

Mentoring Can Get You the Answers You Don't Have. Your mentors understand your challenges. They've been there. They know what it's like. They can share what they've learned, head off your mistakes, help you untangle the messes, and make the right moves.

Mentoring Can Help with Career Advancement. Mentors don't just offer information and advice. They can help you see what your next career move should be, and in some cases, may even help you make it.

Mentors aren't just for novices. Many successful icons hold their mentors dear. Businessman Richard Branson's mentor was Freddie Laker. Alexander the Great's was Aristotle. The late Heath Ledger's was Mel Gibson, and jazz pianist Peter Cincotti's was Harry Connick, Jr. The lessons mentors leave as their legacies live on long after the mentorship has ended. To not have a mentor is to miss out on a valuable gift for both the giver and the receiver—the chance to share in another's success.

My own mentor, world-renowned executive coach Howard Morgan, author of *The Art and Practice of Leadership Coaching,*[5] once said something to which I try to aspire. His goal, he told me, was to be "one of the few people about whom people will say at the end of their life, *He made the biggest difference."* Howard has done that for me, and the right mentor will do that for you.

They say, "When the student is ready, the teacher will appear." And if not, you can go seek one out. Just follow the directions for finding a coach or a mentor on the worksheet, "A Guide to Exceleration."

Exercise

Which would be more helpful to you now, a coach, a mentor, or both? Is there someone who could fill both roles?

A GUIDE TO EXCELERATION

Directions for Finding a Coach

1. Identify what, specifically, you want a coach to help you do.
   - What do you expect to be the main focus of your coaching?
   - What outcomes do you hope to achieve?
   - How will a coach make a difference in your ability to achieve your vision?

2. Identify what, specifically, you want in a coach.
   - What characteristics are important to you in a coach?
   - What background, education, or experience do you want your coach to have?

3. Use the following resources to help you find names of three good coaches:
   - *References*: Ask around. See what response you get to the question, "Do you know a good leadership coach?"
   - *The International Coach Federation*: This professional association www.coachfed eration.org) provides a survey to help you identify the right kind of coach, then sends you appropriate names.
   - *Contact us.* We are happy to help you connect with the right coach. E-mail us at info@theinneredge.com.

4. Interview each of the three coaches.
   - Let them coach you a bit. Notice the impact. Does this feel like a good fit?
   - Ask about their background, education, and experience. Compare it to your needs.
   - Get logistical details about the coaching process and cost.

5. Choose a coach.

Directions for Finding a Mentor

1. Identify specifically why you want a mentor:
   - Why do you want a mentor?
   - What do you hope a mentor will help you learn and do?

2. Identify what, specifically, you want in a mentor.
   - What kind of mentoring do you hope this person will provide?
   - What do you hope your mentoring will look like?
   - What background, education, or experience do you want your mentor to have?

3. Use your personal and professional contacts to help you find a mentor.
   - Be thorough and creative. Ask everyone from your best friend to your human resources department to the author who wrote your favorite book.

4. Ask questions.
   - Call your prospective mentors, introduce yourself, and ask them one or two questions. That will help you move forward on your vision even if this mentor isn't a good fit.

5. Explore the possibilities.
   - If you get a positive response, ask your prospective mentor if he or she would be willing to be a resource for you as you continue your learning.

If you take these steps consistently with a variety of people, the right mentor will emerge and you will end up naturally developing a longer term mentoring relationship.

THE COURSE OF YOUR LIFE

ANNETTE

With a coach and a mentor in her corner, Annette was well on her way to her new career in consulting. It was autumn, and there were only three months before her contract at her company would run out. Soon she'd be out on her own. Fortunately, she had learned what she had to do and had the help to do it. What else could there be? It was at this time I got very explicit with Annette to teach her one of the secrets of coaching—one of our own industry shortcuts.

I taught her the art of reflection.

Reflection

Reflection is a way of learning from your mistakes and your successes in the course of your life. It means looking at your experiences to make informed decisions about what to do, when to do it, and why it should be done. Stepping back. Taking it all in. Looking ahead.

If coaching and mentoring are about exceleration, reflection is about *extraction*. You are extracting knowledge and learning right out of your life experiences, squeezing daily events for every ounce of learning they have to offer. Studying your own experiences by reflecting on them allows you to move faster toward your goals instead of having to try, try, try again until you get it right.

To some degree, reflection happens naturally, but you are far more powerful as a leader if you understand how to steer your reflection purposefully to make the most of your talent and experiences. When you do, you'll get quite an education, right there in the course of your life.

Self-reflection is important, even if it's not always easy.
People have a tendency to delude themselves.
—Wendy Nutt, VP Labor Relations, MGM Mirage

To practice reflection, you choose an event that encapsulates an important concept or skill you want to develop, then think about the event in advance, become conscious about the experience in the moment, and debrief the event afterwards to see what there is to learn and to prepare for an even more successful experience next time. In this manner, your learning curve should not be a curve at all but a continuously moving cycle of thinking-and-acting-and-thinking-and-acting-and-thinking-and-acting. That's how we learn. Researchers describe the processes like this:

- *Reflection* for *action*, or thinking before you act.
- *Reflection* in *action*, or noticing your thoughts and feelings right in the middle of the action.
- *Reflection* on *action*, or the process of looking back at your experiences to see what there is to learn so you can apply it in the future.[6]

Let's say, for instance, you want to learn the skill of encouraging other people—a leadership skill that will add meaning and richness to any endeavor. To learn this skill through reflection, you would choose an event in which you have the opportunity to encourage other people. This could be a staff meeting, a meeting with a colleague, your first meeting with your coach or mentor, or even an interaction with a loved one. Then engage in each of the processes:

1. *Reflect* for *action*. Think about the event ahead of time. Decide how you want to practice the skill of encouraging other people in this particular interaction. Envision it going well.
2. *Reflect* in *action*. Right in the middle of the event, stay cognizant of your intention to encourage other people. Like a jazz musician, play off the events of the moment, improvising as you perform. Practice the skill.
3. *Reflect* on *action*. After the interaction, ask yourself: How did it go?

   - What went well?
   - What didn't go as well?
   - What would you do differently next time?

Repeating this pattern again and again will eventually help you learn what you need to achieve your vision.

KIRK

One leader I know, Kirk, used reflection especially effectively.

Kirk was a corporate human resources officer for an international consultancy. He often met with employees who had complaints about their work. Kirk wanted to become, in his words, more "generationally savvy." To him, this meant being able to understand the varying and sometimes even contradictory motivators of employees from different generations—millennials versus baby boomers, for instance, or baby boomers compared to generation X.

Every time he sat down to meet with someone, he started by reflecting for action. He thought ahead of time about what kind of interaction he wanted to have and how he could make it as successful as possible, regardless of the generational perspective of the employee. As he held one-on-one conversations, he reflected in action. He listened intently to what was being said and changed his strategy moment to moment to accommodate the speaker's needs and requests. Later, following the conversation, he would reflect on action to see what there was to learn from the interaction and how he could be more effective in his role. Ultimately by taking this approach, Kirk became one of the most beloved leaders in his company because it seemed no matter what the problem or who complained, Kirk's employees always felt deeply understood.

Practicing this strategy will far exceed the kind of learning that would happen naturally if you just lived through the same experiences without taking the time to reflect.

"But how does reflection help?" you want to know. "How does it actually help me be a better leader and lead a better life?"

You Avoid Mistakes. Reflective leaders are rarely blindsided. You give yourself the chance to weigh options and consider consequences before making a big decision.

You Fill in the Gaps. Through your reflection, you will discover not just what you need to do, but also what you already know and what you don't yet know. Once you can see what's missing to help you be successful, be it information, education, resources, funding, or connections, you can go out and get it.

You Are Lighter on Your Feet. Many times I have seen a leader struggle with a decision. Should I or shouldn't I? Which way is best? What do I do? Reflection is a big stop sign to keep you from running in circles. The more reflective you are, the faster you can see how each and every alternative does or does not advance your goals. You make a decision and get back into action while everyone else chews on the options.

You Learn by Leaps and Bounds. Reflection is a way of learning that cuts out wasted time and unnecessary action. If you rely on learning by doing, you have to *do* a lot before you can *learn* a lot. If you couple learning by doing with reflection, however, your learning is more condensed, and therefore quicker.

You Deepen the Learning. Deepening the learning means that instead of getting a little insight or a bit of new knowledge, you come to understand something deeply. Surface learning has to happen over and over. Deep learning only has to happen once.

A GUIDE FOR REFLECTION

1. Choose the one thing you've decided to learn first. What will be the topic of your reflection? _____

_____

_____

_____

2. Choose an event. What is the next time you would be able to use or see this topic in action?_____

_____

_____

_____

3. Use the strategies to reflect on your chosen topic before, during, and after the event.

   Before: What do you want to see or have happen? How can you plan for success? _____

   _____

   _____

   _____

   During: Notice what's happening. Stay focused and aware.

   After: Think back on how the event played out. What went well? _____

   _____

   _____

   _____

4. What didn't go as well?_____

   _____

   _____

   _____

5. What would you do differently next time?_____

   _____

   _____

   _____

Exercise

To use reflection as a technique for learning what you need to learn to achieve your vision, take steps described in the worksheet, "A Guide for Reflection."

PERFECTING THE PRACTICE

People say that what we're all seeking is the meaning of life . . .I think that what we're really seeking is the experience of being alive.

—*Rudyard Kipling*

ANNETTE

Annette turned her face up to the sun. It was another gorgeous day. Her trees were blooming again. It was nine in the morning, and her day was just getting started.

That morning, Annette had already taken a swim and even spent some time in the spa. With the time she had left, she'd sat on the back deck with a cup of coffee and turned a few pages of a book on customer service. Relaxed and inspired, she stretched and decided to get going.

She gathered her books and breakfast and headed to her brand-new office, newly redecorated and waiting for her expectantly . . . right down the hall.

How fabulous, she thought. *And this time, it's real.*

The results when you take charge of your own learning are astounding. Coaching is reported to show a remarkable return on investment.[7] Mentors have such an impact that they are often on the short list of people who have helped make the world's best leaders who they are today. As for the rest, it is through reflection, study, and persistence that people become what they call self-made. To get these kinds of results, you don't have to get an advanced degree. You don't have to spend a fortune or sit all day in overrated seminars filling up on psychic junk food.[8] You can succeed beyond your expectations by peacefully, diligently practicing what the Japanese call *kaizen:* continuous improvement throughout your life.

Your *Inner Edge* Coaching Assignment: Your Personal University

Too many leaders learn the hard way that they simply will not succeed until they take ownership of their own development. By then they're already behind. Stay ahead of the curve by making a commitment now about how you plan to keep learning. Use the worksheet, "Your Personal University," at the end of the chapter or on the website at www.theinneredge.com.

FAQS

Q: I can see the value of the independent study idea, as well as the coaching and mentoring. But I'm not sure about the reflection. Isn't that an awful lot of work?

A: As a coach (as well as a former teacher), I'm always concerned when learning feels like work. One way you can tell if your learning is in line with your vision, strengths, and values is to notice how much or little effort it takes. If you're forcing yourself to do exercises, read books, and talk to boring people in either a half-hearted or an overwhelming way, it sounds like this: "Ugh. I have other things to do. As if I don't have enough to do to fulfill my obligations for my current life, now I have *new* stuff to do to create my *new* life! Sometimes I wonder if it's worth it." On the other hand, if you're learning what you want and need to learn to make your vision come alive, it will feel like this: "Wow! I can't believe this is possible! I'd never thought about that before. How do I find out more?"

You don't always need to be reflecting on your actual *experience*. You can reflect on your goals, your achievements, and your obstacles. You can reflect on the way you're spending your time, your strengths, and your struggles. You can reflect on the conversation you just had with your mother, the way you're going about building your team, whether or not you're being the kind of husband or wife you want to be, how to best gain market share, or why you don't seem to be able to lock in the Jamison deal. There are no limits whatsoever to what you can reflect on. But your thinking will be much more robust and complete if you zero in on one topic at a time.

Always remember to tie your learning to your vision so you see the results right away and are excited by the possibilities. Then reflection—and all of the strategies you use to keep learning—won't *feel like* work but they *will work*.

Q: I'm a self-motivated learner and love the idea of leading my learning. What else can I do to take charge of my own success?

A: You're smart. Since one of the "seven habits of *un*successful executives" is "they think they have all the answers,"[9] it bodes well for your success that you value learning so highly.

I'm often surprised at how little leaders actually do to keep learning. Many of them think of themselves as learners ("I'm learning every day!") but are hard-pressed to put their finger on the actual activities they've undertaken to do that. The reason? They're not always learning as much as they think. And as they say, in this age of change if you're not learning you're not just standing still. . . . You're getting further and further behind.

Here's a quick punch list of learning activities to get you where you want to be, always staying focused on your one chosen topic.

- interview the people you admire
- shadow your mentors
- read
- listen to audio programs
- ask questions
- go to conferences
- visit websites
- peruse newsletters
- do some research
- watch your role models

If you choose well, the learning you do to increase your success will also enrich your life.

When it comes to learning and leadership, research conducted by the Leadership Research Institute (LRI) in San Diego is conclusive: "The highest predictor of perceived leadership effectiveness is a commitment to self-improvement." That result is based on over 4.5 million data points from surveys conducted with leaders around the world. Howard Morgan, one of the managing partners of LRI, has met with some of the leaders personally to discover more about what the finding meant. Here is what he learned, in his own words:

A key characteristic that makes top performers excel is their commitment to self-improvement. They get better because they want to. They are not satisfied with simply being good at what they do. They want to be great.[10]

You want to be great. If you keep improving yourself, the whole world will learn how great you really are.

CHAPTER SUMMARY

Key Points

- Positive change almost always requires new learning.
- The soul of business is innovation; the soul of personal leadership is the innovation of the self.
- Learning is profit and competitive edge. It's also part of the fun of life.

YOUR PERSONAL UNIVERSITY

What strategy suits you best?

_____An Independent Study

_____Coaching and/or Mentoring

_____Reflection

What do you want or need to learn?

Knowledge_____

_____

_____

_____

Skills_____

_____

_____

_____

Behaviors_____

_____

_____

_____

What *one topic* deserves your attention now? What will be most worth it to learn?

_____

_____

_____

What will be your first step?

_____

_____

_____

What will you do, and when will you do it?

_____

_____

_____

The Ninth Practice

See Possibility: *How Can You Invite Success to You?*

Celebrate the wisdom of uncertainty.

—*Deepak Chopra*

PARIS

Paris was gray, cold, and damp. So was I. It had taken a full day, two buses, a ferry, and eight hours to get there from London. When I learned I would have to negotiate the metro system and then walk three blocks just to get something to eat, I could have cried. Tired and miserable, my traveling companions and I wedged ourselves in silence between the commuters on the train. When we emerged from the tunnel, it was raining. Perfect.

We rushed under a rooftop and looked around. Every café was either wet or closed. We spied a lone crepe stand open for business. Dinner. We raced through the rain and hunched under the umbrella. With much apprehension, I asked in my very best French, "May I please have one crepe?"

The vendor raised his eyebrows in confusion. He hadn't understood a word I'd said. This was going to be a very long trip.

Since the man only sold one thing—crepes—we managed to get our point across and sat down to eat on the driest chairs we could find. I just wanted to get into bed. Begrudgingly, my friends pulled out the map and we tried to orient ourselves back toward the subway. Heads down, we shuffled our way out of the alley.

As we rounded the corner, I heard my friend gasp. She pointed and grabbed my arm.

"Joelle! Look!"

There before us in all its glory rose Notre Dame Cathedral, pink in the light of the setting sun and framed by the sparkling Seine. Out here in the open sprawled a panorama of Paris at dusk. Pink and orange clouds were clearing to reveal a crystal blue sky. We gazed up at the majestic stone masterpiece, as glorious as it was promised to be.

Seeing Notre Dame that evening made an unforgettable impression on me. It wasn't just because of the extraordinary architecture, the breathtaking view, or the shock of standing before one of the most famous buildings in the world. It was because that moment revealed *possibility*. Without our knowing it, this surprise hid around the corner, just waiting to be found. That moment taught me about the wonder and magnificence that's available to all of us, if only we're willing to see.

Staying open to possibility is as important in day-to-day life as it is during a vacation in Paris. In rare but pivotal moments, we realize life is so much bigger than us. Beyond our efforts lie answers, ideas, and solutions we could never come up with on our own. They present themselves to us, if we let them. But most of the time we don't. Like tired tourists, we soldier on to finish the tasks before us. Eat . . . subway . . . bed. Finish the meeting . . . get through the e-mail . . . make it through the day. This chapter is meant to show you how to see possibility—to find new ways of looking at things, to look up and around at what's bigger and better than what you normally see. You will discover ways to break free from narrow limitations and discover the extraordinary.

In your vision, focus areas, action plans, and even as you've designed your talents, teams, and time, you have been taking your turn speaking about what you want. Now it's time to listen. In the words of Parker Palmer, author of *Let Your Life Speak,* "Before you tell your life what you intend to do with it, listen for what it intends to do with you."[1]

THE PRACTICE OF SEEING POSSIBILITY

Luck is what happens when preparation meets opportunity.

—Seneca

Seeing possibility is the ninth practice of personal leadership. Perhaps the most conceptual of the practices, seeing possibility means being open to surprising opportunities. To succeed with this practice, we have to consider the idea that sometimes success comes to us instead of us having to create it for ourselves.

Have you ever had one of these experiences?

- You're surprised by sudden great news.
- You're offered an unbelievable opportunity.
- Everything falls perfectly into place.
- Things turn out better than you could have imagined.
- You're in the right place at the right time.

Experiences like these can be secret passageways to phenomenal "good luck." And yet, we can't control them. We can't make them happen. What we can do is learn to create the conditions in which they appear. We can take a break from making things happen and just *let* them happen on their own.

Making It Happen versus Letting It Happen

Shakti Gawain, the author of *Creating True Prosperity*, explains that we can choose between two paths to our vision: making it happen and letting it happen.

Making it happen is the active mode. Gawain writes, "The active mode is to go after it; make it happen. The active mode requires focus, aggressiveness, confidence, persistence, the ability to do, and the willingness to risk."[2] Making it happen is our business-oriented, typically Western approach. This path is defined by a particular mind-set:

- rational
- strategic
- concrete
- action oriented
- goal driven
- aimed at results

Achieving our goals is about making things happen. Forcing them if we must. Making it happen is the default mode for many leaders.

In contrast, *letting it happen* is the receptive mode. "The receptive mode requires openness, vulnerability, trust, the ability to be and to wait, and the willingness to have and accept."[3] Letting it happen is the approach of possibility. It, too, reflects a particular frame of mind:

- intuitive
- trusting
- insightful
- knowing
- optimistic
- open to possibility

Making It Happen	Letting It Happen
• Rational	• Intuitive
• Strategic	• Trusting
• Concrete	• Insightful
• Action oriented	• Knowing
• Goal driven	• Optimistic
• Aimed at results	• Open to possibility

When we let things happen instead of making them happen, we experience circumstances that are almost too good to be true, because we have finally gotten out of the way and let a greater wisdom take over. Events like these are available to us more often than we think. We just need to open our minds.

The two paths of making it happen and letting it happen lead to the same place. You can switch back and forth between them, choosing whichever path seems shortest, easiest, or most appealing at the moment. Gawain explains:

> If we operate mainly in the active mode, we may accomplish a great deal but are likely to find it a struggle and exhaust ourselves in the process. If we operate mainly in the receptive mode, we may attract many people and opportunities but have difficulty following through with the action that's called for. . . . Most truly successful and prosperous people have a balance of both.[4]

If you want the balanced benefits of a well-rounded quest for opportunity, you can't keep powering your way through to results. You've got to see other possibilities.

Seeing possibility looks like this:

- You're in the shower and suddenly the answer to your toughest question flashes into your mind.
- You're driving along the freeway and suddenly the solution to a sticky problem becomes instantly obvious.
- You're thinking about an old friend and suddenly the phone rings. It's him.

You've had these experiences. We all have. We marvel at them and are delighted when they appear. We don't understand them, so we shake our heads, tell our friends ("Isn't that *weird?*"), and enjoy the happy circumstance.

Now imagine your vision of your life as a leader appears in the same way.

- You want a specific opportunity, and suddenly that opportunity arrives.
- You need a certain kind of mentor, and suddenly that mentor shows up.
- You want to make a certain kind of impact, and suddenly you realize *you do.*

Every time something like this happens, you are experiencing the rewards of seeing possibility.

Seeing possibility is not wishful thinking. It is not luck. It comes from expressing what you want as clearly as you can and being open to receiving it. When you move beyond your own limitations and embrace other possibilities, sometimes it seems things happen like magic.

In *The 80/20 Principle: The Secret to Success by Achieving More with Less,* author Richard Koch offers this analogy: "Think of Archimedes in his bath or Newton sitting under a tree being struck by an apple."[5] Voila! Sudden understanding of the laws of the universe. Civilization was changed forever in an instant because these men were open to seeing possibility.

In a sense, the answers just came to them. But it's important to note that Archimedes and Newton—just like you—had to create a certain set of conditions for insight to strike. Koch points out,

> The[se] immensely important insights . . . wouldn't have happened if Archimedes had not been thinking about displacement or Newton not been thinking about gravity. But also neither would have happened if Archimedes had been chained to his desk or Newton had been frenetically directing teams of scientists.[6]

Eureka moments, ahas, epiphanies—they're not scrunched into our inboxes. We can't force them to show up by working harder. Flashes of insight occur when we are relaxed, open, and alert. By knowing that we have infinite capacity and trusting that we have everything we need, we can lead a life far beyond anything we could force into being with hard work.

The Spirit of Possibility

Here in the real world, where our work is driven by metrics, deliverables, and results, it can be challenging to trust in possibility. We just need to get things done.

But the truth is, more is possible for you. You have more wisdom, more potential, and more possibility than people typically see in you—possibly more than you've ever seen in yourself.

Compared to the other practices of personal leadership, seeing possibility requires a different energy. I can't promise you that it will always be comfortable or concrete. I can promise you that if you approach it with openness, curiosity, and a willingness to experiment with a new way of being a leader, you are going to see the possibilities.

Being able to trust in possibility takes a measure of faith—an almost spiritual dimension that's sometimes lacking in our efforts to achieve. By spiritual I do not mean religious. I simply mean that grounded and trusting sense that sometimes guides us without our understanding how or why. Author William Bloom, a meditation master and expert in the field of holistic development, offers a helpful definition of spirituality as "that whole reality and dimension which is bigger, more creative, more loving, more powerful, more visionary, more wise, more mysterious—than materialistic daily human existence."[7] We can access that wisdom by tapping into this spiritual side of ourselves with faith—whether you put your faith in a higher power, the ways of the universe, or your own birthright potential.

The Benefits of Possibility

You will experience benefits when you can see possibility:

You Trust Your Instincts. Over time, you learn what it feels like when your intuition is right. You not only exude confidence, you *feel* it. Good instincts translate into stronger thinking, stronger work, and stronger results.

You Experience Everyday Miracles. As a leader, you are committed to achieving success. In the small things, in the big things, you work hard and get results. Seeing possibility is about *not* working as hard so you can get *even better* results. If day-to-day work is like pounding nails with all your might, being open to possibilities is sitting quietly watching the stars come out. It's a very calming way of being. No pressure. Just everyday miracles.

You Become Brilliant. As with all of the ideas in this book, the strategies for seeing possibility are not just meant to improve your quality of life. They also help you get better results from your leadership. The insights we get when we open up to possibility don't just make it easier to come up with ideas. It's not just a faster route to results. The real mystery of seeing possibility is that the insights are so *right*. Brilliant. Genius, even.

Seeing possibility is a path out of hard work, frustration, and confusion. You can let go of some of the struggle and relax instead into a calmer, easier way to your vision. Even though this approach feels slow at first, you will discover that it leads directly, sometimes instantly, to the delivery of your vision.

THE MIND-SET FOR SEEING POSSIBILITY

Patient. Possibility can't be rushed. It's already there.

Hopeful. I'm all for critical thinking, but you won't see something if you don't believe you will.

Trusting. Relax. Know that the answers will come.

How to Practice

Below follow several strategies for seeing possibility. I call these invitations as a reminder to you that your job is not to chase after the result but to let the opportunities come to you. These are long-term strategies that take time, and it would be too much to try them all at once. Just read through the suggestions and pay attention to which strategies appeal to you most. Later, when you have a sense of all five strategies, choose one as a place to start.

INVITATION 1: LET IT BE EASY

Letting it be easy is the first strategy for seeing possibility. My friend and mentor, Dr. Heidi McKenna, once taught me this:

If things are going your way, go that way.
If things aren't going your way, don't go that way.

To put this suggestion into effect, you have to notice what's working and do more of it. Notice what's not working and do less of it. Easy. This strategy is especially helpful for making difficult decisions or finding your way through confusion.

Take the complexity out. Make it simple.
—Howard Putnam, former CEO, Southwest Airlines

One leader I know—another coach and friend of mine named Jenn—used this strategy when her professional life got overwhelming.

JENN

One year near the beginning of her practice, executive coach Jenn was recreating her coaching business to incorporate new services. At first it was exciting, but when she was deep into the change she suddenly felt completely besieged. Speaking, writing, coaching, developing products, leading a team—what should take priority? What should come first, second, third, and fourth? The order of her opportunities was becoming a huge issue, because Jenn couldn't organize her thoughts or time. So I suggested Heidi's approach.

I asked Jenn, "What's going your way?" Jenn noticed that the coaching was really easy. Leaders who inspired and moved her appeared out of nowhere, just when they were ready for some help. Coaching fulfilled her sense of purpose. It made her happy. Coaching was definitely going her way.

I asked Jenn, "What's not going your way?" At the time, developing products like audio programs and workbooks felt halting and hard to Jenn, and it took way too much time. The speaking was stressing her out, and there wasn't any action on the team front. These things weren't going her way.

Jenn knew at that point that her primary work was to coach. She stopped everything else and just focused on that. She put the plans for the product away, unfinished. She committed to booking no more speeches for the time being. She stopped trying to redesign her practice. She just coached. She let it be easy.

A few weeks later, feeling much calmer, Jenn was sitting through a presentation for a board of directors of which we're members. The speaker was walking us through a strategic-planning process. Jenn looked down at a one-page chart meant to help develop a strategic plan for the board, and she suddenly saw the strategic plan for her business. As if written in invisible ink, the aspects of her coaching practice appeared and sorted themselves into priority order. I saw her write the answers in the margin. Coaching first. Writing second. Speaking third. Products fourth. Developing a team last. Jenn had the answers she needed.

And it had been easy.

Letting it be easy is an approach that helped Jenn see new possibilities. She was able to work smart and let the current of her life carry her in the direction it wanted to go. You, too, can put down some of the weight of success by noticing which direction seems easy and right. Take a step back every once in awhile. Notice where you're struggling. Notice where it's easy. Even if just for a while, try going the easy way. It may be the path of success. The Chinese philosopher Chuang Tzu put it simply: Easy is right.

LEADERS LETTING IT BE EASY

- "I let it be easy to choose a new assistant. I had planned to consider five or six candidates, including a background check, interviews, and references for each one. The first one seemed like such a natural fit, I just hired her. I let it be easy."

> - "I needed a publicist to generate enthusiasm and visibility for my new business. I started asking around for some names, and one of my friends offered to do my publicity for me. He was a stay-at-home dad who had been an account executive for years, and he knew what he was doing. So I let him. He did an amazing job. I let it be easy."
> - "My new client was giving me heartburn. He seemed so difficult, and I kept trying to change his behavior. Finally I gave up and focused on understanding him instead of changing him. Our relationship improved almost immediately. I let it be easy."

Exercise

Keeping your vision in mind, ask yourself these questions:

- What's going your way?
- What's not going your way?
- What do your answers suggest about what to do next? How can you let it be easy?

INVITATION 2: GIVE YOUR INTUITION SPACE

The second strategy in seeing possibility is to *give your intuition space*. Let your mind become still. Then the possibilities you need—answers to tough questions, ideas you've been seeking, solutions you need—will emerge, as if from deep in your soul.

Intuition speaks in a whisper. It needs space to be heard. It cannot be heard over the ruckus of nonstop thinking. It will not compete with frenzied action, and it is far too expansive to squeeze into an overcrowded mind. In order to hear it, you need to listen. Palmer explains why we need to be so still to hear this voice.

> The soul is like a wild animal—tough, resilient, savvy, self-sufficient, and yet exceedingly shy. If we want to see a wild animal, the last thing we should do is go crashing through the woods, shouting for the creature to come out. But if we are willing to walk quietly into the woods and sit silently for an hour or two at the base of a tree, the creature we are waiting for may well emerge, and out of the corner of an eye we will catch a glimpse of the precious wildness we seek.[8]

Somewhere in our souls are the answers we need, but we can't get them by poking, prodding, chasing, yelling, moping, throwing things, or working nonstop. To get the answers we need when they escape us, we need a softer approach.

You can give your intuition space right where you're sitting. Just stop thinking for a moment and take two breaths. Wait. Ask a question to which you need an answer, and see if one appears. It may.

Giving your intuition space takes some discipline. You may feel anxious about stopping the action when you really feel you just need to get something done. Giving your intuition space at first will feel very slow. But you're going slow to go fast, and when you see how much more easily and clearly the ideas show up when you give them the chance, you will soon find yourself taking this route to achievement more often.

DILLON

Dillon was a CEO who used this strategy of giving his intuition space one day when he was agonizing over a decision about whether to go on a business trip.

Dillon was supposed to go to an invitational conference with some clients. He had been planning to leave in about an hour, but his 8- and 10-year-old daughters had really been upset when they found out he'd be away for the weekend. He couldn't concentrate on his work. He was distracted by the possibility of calling off the trip, even though he knew he shouldn't.

Dillon was telling me all of this on the phone, and I could hear the tension in his voice. I suggested he stop talking for a moment so we could give his intuition space.

He stopped.

"Dillon, what's the bottom-line question you need to answer?"

"Should I go or not?" He replied.

I repeated the question and asked Dillon to take a deep breath.

He sucked in half a pant and said, "Okay."

Ah, I thought. *Let's do this again.*

This time I walked him through two long, slow breaths. I even asked him to close his eyes as I talked, slowing the pace and describing the airflow. Good, clean, fresh, clear air flowing in; old, cloudy air and tension flowing out. I could almost feel him settling down, as the pace of his breaths eased with every inhalation. We took an extra moment of silence for good measure. After pausing for a moment in silence, I asked him again.

"Should you go or not?"

"Yes. I really have to go." After giving his intuition space, Dillon had a clear answer to his dilemma. That degree of certainty allowed him to stop deliberating and move on to more productive questions. We spent the next half hour discussing how he could manage his business travel better in keeping with his values, and how he could maximize his time at home better so he could spend more quality time with his girls. All that from just two breaths.

The next time you find yourself having trouble thinking clearly, try giving your intuition space.

I'm not a head thinker. I'm a gut thinker.
—Kirstin Schaeffer Kent, Attorney, KPMG

Exercise

1. Name a situation in which you need some kind of answer or idea.
2. Rephrase the issue into the form of a question. What do you need to know?
3. Take two long slow breaths, letting the air clear your mind.
   Be sure you take two *full* breaths. Breathe in a long, slow breath that fills your body with air—first your stomach as you let it expand, then your ribs, then your lungs all the way to capacity. Hold it for a moment. Breathe out a slow, long exhalation that releases the air in a stream from your lungs, your ribs, and finally your stomach, pulling your belly in to help squeeze out every last drop of air. Then breathe again in the same manner a second time.
4. Sit quietly and ask the question again. What ideas did you get?

INVITATION 3: PRACTICE NOT-DOING

The third strategy for seeing possibility is to *practice not-doing*. To understand what it means to practice not-doing, let's break the phrase into its parts.

Doing. Think of all the doing in your life. Getting to work. Organizing your thoughts. Making calls. Attending meetings. Talking with people. The activity goes on and on, all day long, and so do you.

Not-doing. Now stop. Not-doing is the absence of all that. Not-doing is a verb. It's resisting the need for action.

Practice Not-doing. Try it. For the next five minutes, practice not-doing. Sit back, put your hands behind your head, and breathe. Listen to a song. Walk around the block. Clear your mind. Practice *not-doing* all the things you would normally be doing in those five minutes.

Practicing not-doing is repeating this process as often as you can, stretching out the length of time you can do it until little by little, your life slows down.

Not-doing gives your mind the space and rest it needs to function at its best. Studies of meditation, which is one common way of not-doing, show documented positive changes in brain function.[9] Doing nothing at all is also known to provide several benefits:

- strengthening the brain
- increasing circulation
- raising energy levels
- reducing stress
- sharpening the senses[10]

When you practice not-doing—just as when you give your intuition space—you gain a clearer mind with clearer thoughts. You will feel better in a number of ways:

- less stressed, more rested
- less anxious, more relaxed
- less distracted, more effective
- less frenzied, more efficient

You get better ideas. You feel centered.

Leadership advisor Robert Cooper comments, "Most exceptional individuals and leaders know how to do nothing, and do it really well."[11] If you want to be exceptional, you need to be able to "do nothing" well, too. When you do this, you will see new possibilities. As the ancient Chinese text, the Tao Te Ching (the "Book of the Way") reads, "Practice not-doing, and everything will fall into place."[12]

Mindful Activity

The strategy of not-doing is slightly deceiving in that you're not actually doing *nothing*. Rather, what you are doing is giving up the energy of non-stop action to engage in peaceful activity and relax your mind. The activities you choose should be restful, but active. Engaging, but relaxing. Mindful, not mindless.

Take for instance listening to music. You can practice not-doing by listening to music that you love. But you don't just hear it; you immerse yourself in it, letting your spirit be moved and your mind be at rest. This kind of mindful listening is not the same as driving along listening half-heartedly to whatever's on the radio—what one author calls "chewing gum for the ears." Similarly, watching TV, chatting with friends, doing chores, hanging out with your kids—these are all fine things to do and they can give you a break from your work, but they don't necessarily give your *mind* a rest.

Here are some other activities that tend to lend themselves to mindfulness and not-doing.

Listening to Classical Music	Watching the Waves	Walking through a Park	Yoga	Swimming
Jogging	Riding a bike	Driving through the country	Meditating	Preparing a meal
Painting	Drawing, sketching, or doodling	Working on a hobby	Browsing a museum	Getting a massage
Gardening	Singing a few upbeat songs	Playing fetch with the dog	Reading something inspirational	Hitting a bucket of golf balls

Engaging in activities like these prevents your mind from wandering back to stress, worry, and action. In other words, it gives you something to do while you're practicing not-doing. This gives your intuition even more of the space it needs to deliver bursts of inspiration.

If you haven't been in the practice of not-doing, you may not trust this process until you experience it. It's a practice. You don't have to jump in all of a sudden, taking three days off to meditate. Start slow and increase your effort every day. Yoga teachers call this "stretching into it"—moving into progress little by little, gently, until you find yourself far exceeding your former ability. When you stretch into not-doing, habits you once would have found difficult become easy, even routine.

The Breakout Sequence

The effects of not-doing are especially potent when juxtaposed with periods of intense activity. In a summary of the research, mind/body researcher Dr. Herbert Benson explains:

> By bringing the brain to the height of activity and then suddenly moving it into a passive, relaxed state, it's possible to stimulate much higher neurological performance than would otherwise be the case. Over time, subjects who learn to do this as a matter of course perform at consistently higher levels.[13]

Dr. Benson, who in addition to teaching medicine at Harvard Medical School has been researching neuroscience and stress for over 35 years, calls this a "breakout" sequence.

Here's how it works. You work for a while on a problem, then you take a break from the problem and engage in a mindful activity. You then return to the problem refreshed and renewed. Here are a few examples.

- You are on a tight deadline and under a lot of pressure. Instead of drilling into the work to get it done, you lie down and close your eyes and listen to classical music for 20 minutes. When you emerge you are more at peace and your ideas flow easily, fueled by inspiration instead of perspiration.
- You're about to go into a high-stakes meeting with a new prospect. Instead of pacing about and worrying how it's going to go, you close the door and meditate for half an hour. When it's time you head for the meeting with a clear head and a calm heart.
- You've got a team of Little Leaguers to coach after work, but your inbox is overflowing. You're distracted and irritable. Instead of cramming to get it all done, you put on your running shoes and jog for 40 minutes through the park. When you return your inbox somehow looks less menacing. You fly through the one or two items that need attention now and head off for a night of baseball.

You do these things not because you are running away or trying to escape, but because you know that the break will release your best ideas. Solutions and strategies will appear to you instead of you having to chase after them. Somehow *not-doing* will allow you to get everything done.

LEADERS NOT-DOING

Brandon Tenor, a principal at an international design firm, on writing acceptance speeches for awards:

I used to: Sit at my desk banging my head against the computer. Eventually, I would finish the speech.

Now I: Sit on the deck, watch the sunrise, and wait for inspiration to strike. The speech arrives in my mind fully formed.

Margaret Wong, consultant, on writing a business proposal:

I used to: Stay up all night working and sleep on the couch in my office to get a proposal done by 8:00 A.M.

Now I: Go home, get a great night's sleep, and wake up refreshed. I get up a little early to finish the proposal before breakfast. Invariably, my thinking is much sharper and I can whip out the proposal in no time.

> Paolo Ciri, company president, on preparing for a media interview:
> *I used to:* Worry about my sound bites and practice saying them over and over. In the interview, the words would come out correct but somewhat forced.
> *Now I:* Look over my sound bites for a few minutes. Then I go for a swim and take a hot shower. In the interview, the words still come out correct, but naturally.

Exercise

1. Choose a mindful activity to practice while you're not-doing.
2. How long will you practice, and when?
3. Each time you practice, ask yourself:

    - How did you feel as you practiced not-doing?
    - How did you feel afterwards?
    - What impact did not-doing have?

4. Keep practicing, stretching the time you engage in the activity longer and longer. Notice the impact.

INVITATION 4: SIT WITH THE QUESTION

The fourth strategy to see possibility is getting very clear about what you want and then asking for it even if there's no one to answer. It's called *sitting with the question.*

This strategy is called "sitting with a question" because you don't actually go out to seek the answers. You just identify the question you have as clearly and succinctly as possible. Then you sit with it, ponder it, maybe ask around for input, and wait for the answer to emerge.

To do this, take three steps.

First, put your concern into the form of a question. Keeping in mind what you want, ask yourself, "What is my *question?*" You may have to tinker with the words a bit until you get it right. Here are some of the questions I've heard leaders ask.

- How can I find peace again?
- How can I build my confidence?
- Is this the job I'm supposed to have?
- Am I happy?
- Is this right?
- How can I configure the drawings of this house to meet the customer's specifications within his budget?

- What would be the most exciting way to do this?
- How can we really make a splash?
- What role can I give my employee while he struggles to manage his health?
- What's going to make this product really stand out?
- What would make me feel better?
- Am I ready for this change?

Know that it may take a little while to find your questions. That's okay. Eventually the right question will come to you.

Second, ask. Once you've framed your challenge in the form of a question, ask. One leader I met called this "putting in your order." As if the universe were a short-order cook, she would write down her requests and put them in her out basket. It allowed her to forget about them and go back to other things. Other people I know have a running wish list or a prescription pad. I have a big green jar in my office. When I have a request—some dilemma I need to solve or question I can't seem to answer—I jot it down and put it in the jar. Find a way to pose your question, even if there's no one specific to pose it *to*. This might mean simply saying it out loud or just thinking it clearly in silence.

Third, let it go. After you've made your request, allow your subconscious to work on your question for you while you go about doing other things. Write it down and take it with you. Revisit it now and again. Ask people your question if you can, or just hold onto it until you feel more creative and can come back to it with a fresh perspective. This is the essence of sitting with a question. You're not actively doing anything with your question. You're just keeping it close.

When you sit with a question, you can let go of the effort without letting go of the issue itself. In the advice of poet Rainer Maria Rilke,

> Be patient toward all that is unsolved in your heart and try to love the questions themselves. Do not now seek the answers, which cannot be given you because you would not be able to live them. And the point is to live everything. Live the questions.[14]

This strategy of sitting with a question isn't scientific, but neither is it naive. It's just a light and easy way to acknowledge what you need and put it aside until you get it. And it works. Maybe it's because when you can finally articulate a question, you have become clear enough to actually hear the answer. Maybe it's because the act of writing or speaking your request makes it real. In any case, your answers will come to you naturally and easily—and probably when you least expect them—if you are not trying to force an answer. Just wait. Be patient, secure in the knowledge that your answer will arrive. It will. When it does, you'll be ready to receive it.

"If you want something, ask for it nicely." How simple. How easy to forget.

Exercise

1. Put your concern into the form of a question.
2. Ask.
3. Let it go.

INVITATION 5: ALLOW YOURSELF TO BE SURPRISED

The fifth strategy for seeing possibility is to *allow yourself to be surprised*, or be open to the gifts that show up unexpectedly. Here are a few examples.

Uri was happily employed as an engineer when his mentor, the CEO of another firm, announced his retirement and offered Uri the job—a dream job he never thought he'd get.

Kelly was doing research for an article on innovative approaches to information technology. When the article was published, she was invited to run the IT department for the biggest corporation in her state.

Isaiah was bored with his job. His friend mentioned this fact to a random associate at a cocktail party, who in turn tracked down Isaiah and involved him in a start-up project that became Isaiah's new vocation.

Dorothy, a talent scout, got her big break sitting next to her cousin's houseguest at Thanksgiving dinner.

Frank hired a consultant to help him get more clients and was stunned when the consultant hired him instead, filling his schedule to the top in one fell swoop.

In each of these situations, something in line with what these leaders wanted—but so much better—was delivered to them as they unsuspectingly went about their lives. The surprises they received were so big, so perfect, so unbelievable that they hadn't had the courage or imagination to ask for them. Exactly what they needed, and so much more, fell into their laps when they weren't remotely looking for it.

Maybe you can't actually create these experiences, but you can train yourself to notice them. In each of the examples above, leaders who allowed themselves to be surprised didn't ask questions. They didn't delay. They took advantage of the opportunity before them and used it to swing effortlessly from where they were to where they wanted to be. You can take advantage of these kinds of surprises in your own life. The key is to keep your eyes open and be ready to act when your good fortune shows up.

THE AIR SHOW

Where I live in Nevada, we have a spectacular air show. One year when my son Jackson was three, his grandfather (my dad) took him to see the planes. As they drove along the highway, the famed Blue Angels raced overhead. My dad couldn't believe it—they were missing them!

"Jackson! Here come the Blue Angels! Look out the window! Can you see them?" Three-year-old Jackson craned his neck. "Where? Where?" Wedged into his car seat in the back of the Jeep, he couldn't see a thing. Grandpa drove on.

They got closer to the event and saw cars everywhere. The noise of the planes overhead was deafening, even scary, to a toddler. Clearly they couldn't go in. He pulled over to the side of the road, and they got out.

"Maybe we can just see the planes from here!" he announced hopefully. "Jackson, do you see any?" They scoured the sky for a moment, then suddenly Jackson cried out in delight.

"Grandpa! Look!"

My dad's head zipped around, searching the skies for stunt planes. "Where? Where?"

"Look, Grandpa, look! Down here! Ants!"

If my father had been fixated on seeing planes that day, he would have been sorely disappointed that he never got Jackson to the air races. But what he really wanted was to spend a great day with his grandson. They could do that just as easily with ants as with airplanes. When you stop frantically searching for what you think you're looking for and allow yourself to be surprised, you may discover you already have what you want.

> *I worked really hard for a long time to be successful, but my big breaks came after I made up my mind to stop suffering. Then I came to the magical part that you can't explain, including a book deal that I didn't even ask for and an appearance on* Oprah. *Life tells you when to leap.*
> —Laura Berman Fortgang, personal coach and bestselling author
> of *Take Yourself to the Top* and *The Little Book on Meaning*

Exercise

Look for a surprise in your life. See if you can find one *today*. Slow down. Stay alert. Know what you want. When opportunities arise, notice the feelings of delight and amazement. Then ask yourself: could this be the moment I've been waiting for? How would you act if it were?

PERFECTING THE PRACTICE

Stand ready to participate, willing to be moved and inspired.

—*Benjamin and Rosamund Zander, The Art of Possibility*

There are things we know without knowing how we know them. There are things we can do without understanding them. There are forces at work around us that we cannot identify or explain. There's a spiritual element to it, although it need not be religious. There's a mystical quality about it, although it need not be weird or naive. Opening up to the inexplicable and yet favorable ways of the universe is a way into wisdom, insight, and ease. Learn to tap in, and you will discover an entirely new way of being your best—and that your best is even better than you knew.

But first you have to extend the invitation.

Your *Inner Edge* Coaching Assignment: Your Invitation

Use the "Your Invitation" worksheet at the end of the chapter or online (www.theinneredge.com) to master the strategies that will invite opportunities to come to you. You will find many more invitations online.

FAQS

Q: I'm skeptical. All of this seems a little New Agey to me, like you don't have to work for anything, it will just happen.

A: This chapter is about doing things differently. The point of seeing possibility is not to advocate a laissez-faire approach to living and leading well. Rather, the point is to show you that *you do not have to have all the answers*. You do not have to know it all, do it all, and be responsible for coming up with every idea, solution, or product with your personal time, talent, and toil. You can let go. Open up to another way of doing things. See the possibility.

It's okay to be skeptical. Don't do anything that makes you uncomfortable or that seems foolish or ill-advised. You must have your own ways of opening up your mind and seeing new possibilities. Just know that you don't have to do things the same old way every time. The world is bigger than that.

Q: I've tried many of these strategies and I'm amazed at what's happening. I've heard about manifesting. Is that what this process really is?

A: When you start to experience the breakthroughs and the brilliance that come from inviting opportunity, you're bound to wonder why it works. That question is akin to asking the very meaning of life. Is it spirituality at work? Is it God? Is it some kind of miracle? Is it science? Is it natural law? Is it voodoo? Is it some kind of new wave alternative hocus-pocus? You will find the answers to these questions everywhere from ancient traditions to the world's religions to the Internet's latest blog. And while it may be an interesting philosophical debate, what really matters is that you find your own way of understanding why and how it seems to be that the universe is conspiring for your success.

In her novel *The Hundred Secret Senses*, author Amy Tan captures the idea that there is more to know than we concretely experience. As humans, we usually think of ourselves as limited to our five senses. But in nature, other secret senses abound. The sense that tells a caterpillar it's time to wrap up into a cocoon. The sense that tells geese to fly south. The sense that tells a hibernating bear to emerge.

When you open up to possibility, you, too, are using your hundred secret senses. You will know when to let things happen and when to make them happen. You will sense the opportunities around you.

But those senses have to be developed. Too many of us have ignored them for so long we barely know how they feel. Practicing seeing possibility will sharpen your senses. Then you can stop chasing success and invite success to come to you.

CHAPTER SUMMARY

Key Points

- Sometimes success comes to us instead of us having to create it for ourselves.
- We can take a break from making things happen and just *let* them happen on their own.
- Eureka moments, ahas, epiphanies—they're not scrunched into our inboxes. We can't force them to show up by working harder. Flashes of insight occur when we are relaxed, open, and alert.
- The key to seeing possibility is to keep your eyes open and be ready to act when your good fortune shows up.

YOUR INVITATION

Part I: Choose an Invitation

Which one of the strategies (the "invitations") appeals to you most? Rank them in preferential order.

_____Invitation 1: Let It Be Easy

_____Invitation 2: Give Your Intuition Space

_____Invitation 3: Practice Not-Doing

_____Invitation 4: Sit with the Question

_____Invitation 5: Allow Yourself to Be Surprised

_____Invitation 6: Tune into the Message*

_____Invitation 7: Look for the Perfect*

*These strategies can be found in *The Inner Edge Extension* (www.theinneredge.com).

Part II: Extend the Invitation

What difference could it make for you to apply this strategy for seeing possibility?

What will you do and when will you do it?

Part III: Rsvp (Results, S'il Vous Plait)

How did it go?

What worked? What didn't work?

What will you do next?

The Tenth Practice

All . . . All at Once: *How Do You Move from Excellent to Extraordinary?*

I am the captain of my ship. I am the master of my soul.

—*William Ernest Henley, "Invictus"*

DANIEL

Dear Joelle,

When I first met you, I was subsumed with work. We had just completed a merger, and I was taking on twice the responsibility with twice the staff. I thought I needed coaching to get myself organized—restructuring the department, getting on top of the workload, and the like. It turned out what I really needed was to get a new vision of myself as a leader.

Back then, I wasn't the person I wanted to be. I was stressed and busy. I didn't make time for the important people in my life at work or at home. It was all about me. Now, I have a sense of purpose. I feel very clear about the kind of leader I want to be, and I've arranged my schedule to be more effective everyday. I'm proud to say our profits are reaching all-time highs.

But it's not just business that's better. I'm happier, too. The stress is down tremendously. I am working less, getting more done, and feeling much stronger and more confident. I really am a better leader, and I'm leading a better life.

Sincerely,

Daniel Woods

WHITNEY

Dear Joelle,

What a difference! My life has changed so much since the first time we spoke. No more 16-hour days! No more sleepless nights! No more "running on fumes!" I used to think the only way I could get any kind of "balance" in my life was to retire, quit my job, or scale way back. I haven't done any of those. I can actually take care of myself and still be a super achiever. You once told me that it was possible to be relaxed, happy, and successful all at once. I didn't believe you then, but now . . . I am!

Sincerely,

Whitney Hanover

When I receive letters like these from clients, I'm filled with a sense of amazement—not at anything I've done but at the power in every leader to live the life they want.

Daniel was a no-nonsense sales executive who led through fear when I met him. He barked orders and threatened to fire people over minor mistakes. Now he actually listens to his staff, sitting with them to define their strengths and priorities so together they get better results. As a result of his commitment to personal leadership, Daniel changed from a brutal boss to a compassionate and collaborative leader. He became a happier man, and his company profited from the change.

Whitney was a leading journalist who used to travel constantly, work nonstop, and feel bitter and jaded. But instead of burning out, she took charge of her life. She negotiated with her organization to make some changes (like a flexible schedule and more choice in her projects) to accommodate her personal needs. With just a few adjustments, she was able to make time for herself. She now spends time with family. She gets enough sleep. Her work feels less like a burden and more like a joy. She got to keep the job that she loves, and her company got to keep her talent and skills. As Whitney once described it, "For everyone involved, this really is great news."

With thought, effort, and time, Daniel and Whitney both made a commitment to themselves as leaders.

I share their stories here to give you a sense of what's ahead for you. I hope as you read their letters and see the changes they've made that you'll catch a glimpse of the exuberance and relief you're going to feel when you wake up one day and discover the vision you once had for yourself has now become your life.

In this chapter, you will be combining all of the other nine practices of personal leadership to see how they work together. You are going to discover the power behind the practices when you see what happens when you adopt them all . . . all at once.

THE PRACTICE OF ALL . . . ALL AT ONCE

> You are what your deep, driving desire is.
>
> As your desire is, so is your will.
>
> As your will is, so is your deed.
>
> As your deed is, so is your destiny.
>
> —*Brihadaranyaka Upanishad IV.4.5*

The tenth practice of personal leadership is called *all . . . all at once*. It involves bringing all of the previous nine practices of personal leadership together into a unified whole.

For an example, think about two practices of personal leadership, Tapping into Your Brilliance and Feeling Fulfillment. You know how powerful you are when you capitalize on your strengths. You know how fulfilled you feel when you live your values. Now imagine what will happen when *the thing you value most* is also *the thing you do best*. That's not just effective, it's exceptional.

For another example, choose two more practices, Taking Action and Maximizing Time. Think about how much more efficient you are when you have a sound action plan. Then think about how empowering it is to maximize every moment of your time. Now imagine what it will be like when you use the *time you save* for what you *most want to do*. That's not just good; it's spectacular.

By combining the practices of personal leadership this way, you create new possibilities. You will get exponentially more out of your efforts at personal leadership if you align and integrate the concepts all at once.

Integrative Thinking

"All at once" is a state of mind that allows you to combine different ideas and think about them at the same time. In an article called "How Successful Leaders Think,"[1] Roger Martin, the dean of the Rotterman School of Management at the University of Toronto, calls this idea "integrative thinking": a conscious way of synthesizing two or more ideas to come up with one new and superior idea. When you use integrative thinking, you hold in your mind several complex and possibly competing concepts at the same time so they come together into one complete idea.

Dr. Martin calls integrative thinking the mark of an exceptional leader. After interviewing over 50 leaders up to eight hours each, he writes, "It is this discipline—not superior strategy or faultless execution—that is a defining characteristic of most exceptional businesses and the people who run them."[2] Integrative thinking is also a defining characteristic of personal leadership.

Everything is Everything

Mathematicians have a symbol that illustrates integrative thinking beautifully. It's called a *fractal*. A fractal (see Figure 6) is a design in which every tiny piece has the design of the whole—the same swirls or angles or zigzags repeated again and again at every level. Zoom in on a tiny chunk of the design, and you see the exact same pattern as if you zoom out. Everything is everything.

When you practice integrative thinking, you approach your life as if it were a fractal. The you in your personal life is the you in your professional life. The ideas that apply over here also work over there. You are who you are wherever you are. You are true to yourself.

In our culture, we don't do that very well. We separate our work and our life into boxes. We *compartmentalize*. And while compartmentalizing may work pretty well in a storage room where you can have matching plastic bins with labels and lids, it's no way to live a life.

You are not a storage shed, some kind of staging area where your work goals can go on one shelf and your personal goals can go on another. Your head does not go in this bin and your heart in that bin over there. You are whole. How you feel affects how you act; how you act affects how you work; how you work affects your results; your results affect the way you live. It's all connected. *You* are connected; you are *one*.

FIGURE 6   A fractal

In a landmark study of spirituality in the workplace, researchers Mitroff and Denton found that wholeness is at the core of our humanity. "People do not want to compartmentalize or fragment their lives," they write. They also assert that that "the search for meaning, purpose, wholeness, and integration" is part of the journey of life.[3] You *can* be a groundbreaking businessperson, an encouraging leader, and a balanced person, partner, family member, friend, or community member all at the same time. You can get your work done, be there for everyone else, and still make time for yourself. You can accomplish your short-term tasks and move toward your long-term vision at the same time. You can make a good living while you also do something meaningful with your life. You can simultaneously serve the business, the organization, the client, your colleagues, your boss, your team, your family, your own needs, and your corner of the world.

Maybe not every day. Maybe on a moment-to-moment basis you will have to sometimes compartmentalize some emotion to get a job done, or maybe you will have to shut off your work mind to enjoy your personal life. But on the whole, across your life, *more is possible*. You *can* be a successful, achieving, contributing, peaceful, joyful person all at once.

The Benefits of All . . . All at Once

This strategy offers many important benefits:

You Find the Sacred in the Ordinary. When you are thinking about everything all at once, you bring meaning to even mundane tasks. You understand your own significance.

You Have Choices. Many people give up personal time for work because they think they don't have a choice. They settle for less than they want because they can't see another choice. They feel resentful and put-upon because they don't realize *they have a choice.* You have a choice. The more you integrate your thinking, the more you will be choosing, day after day, how you want to lead and live.

You Have Sustainability. When you think and live in integrated ways, you preserve and sustain your talent. What Harvard Business School professor and author Robert Kaplan says about a business career is true for your entire life as a leader: It's "a marathon, not a sprint, and if you aren't true to yourself, eventually you're going to wear down."[4] The sooner you can integrate the different aspects of your life, the sooner you can settle into to a comfortable pace. You can stay on a road like that for all your life.

You Get Better Results. The bottom line for businesses is that integrative thinking leads to better results. Integrative thinking leads to focus and productivity. You know what you want; you go after it. You encounter difficult issues; you work them out. You care about the people *and* the business *and* the mission all at once. Now that's leadership.

How to Practice

In order to have that kind of deep integrity throughout your life, you need the right mind-set. You need to be able to think about everything that makes you an effective leader, all at once. This chapter describes two important ways to do that: alignment and integration.

THE MIND-SET OF ALL . . . ALL AT ONCE

Abundant. Assume the best is possible. Then act as if it's true. (It usually is.)

Resourceful. Just because you haven't thought of something before doesn't mean it's not possible. Use your resources—your ideas, your creativity, the practices of personal leadership—and see how much potential you have to have, do, and be *more*.

Efficient. The better you get at integrative thinking, the better you'll be at seeing connections and making the most of your efforts.

Creative. Play! See what happens when you look for new combinations.

ALIGNMENT

Alignment is the degree to which all of your efforts lead you towards the same end.

Alignment means "positioned in a straight line" or "adjusting parts so that they are in proper relative position."[5] Applied to leadership, alignment means making sure your efforts to achieve are all lined up and aimed directly at your target vision. If they're not, you make adjustments to position them properly. Ideally, when you have alignment, every effort complements every other effort—no two goals are working against each other, and no responsibilities are competing for attention.

If you're out of alignment, your activities will feel like an obstacle course. This is true for many leaders. They shoot out of bed in the morning, ping-pong back and forth between activities all day long, dodge bullets and take detours along the way, circle back to any tasks left undone, and race down the home stretch to collapse just before bed.

Much of the craziness comes from a lack of clarity about where they're going and what they're supposed to be doing to get there.

When you practice alignment, you leave the obstacle course for a straighter path with a clear shot to your goals. There may still be barriers to progress, but the process makes more sense. Your efforts are in proper relative position. You know what's important and it shows in the decisions you make. Your actions reflect your priorities. Nothing important gets left out.

What does it look like for a leader to be in alignment versus out of alignment? Daniel, the sales executive whose letter you read above, is a great example.

DANIEL

When I first met Daniel, he exuded many of the personality characteristics of a stereotypical leader. He was charismatic and decisive, goal oriented and bold. Unfortunately, he was also a bully. He gave little credence to others' feelings and did things his way because in his mind, his way was the best way. He wanted to be a leader, but he was really just a boss. His behaviors were out of alignment with his intentions.

When Daniel's responsibilities doubled due to a merger, his bosses suggested executive coaching to "polish his leadership skills." What they meant was that he had to work better with people. Daniel had to figure out how to act in keeping with the way he wanted to be. Then his intentions and behaviors would be in alignment.

Interestingly, once I started talking to Daniel, I found that he did want to work better with people. He just didn't know how. Beneath his gruff exterior was a compassionate guy. He wanted to be a real leader. He wanted to empower people and develop them to be good contributors to the organization.

For Daniel to get in alignment, he needed to be able to see that who he wanted to be was not who he was being. If he couldn't do that, he might succeed with the numbers but he would fail as a leader.

You, too, need to be able to look across your life and gauge whether what you want is in tune with how you think, what you do, and who you are.

The Success Formulas

You can practice getting into alignment by combining a few different practices of personal leadership to see if they're adding up to the most powerful result. You can look at them as success formulas to achieve the synergy of alignment.

The Formula for Progress. Probably the most obvious and familiar place to start checking your alignment is with your vision, focus areas, and actions. The formula looks like this:

$$\text{Vision} + \text{Focus} + \text{Action} = \text{Progress}$$

It doesn't make sense to take action that doesn't align with your priorities, and what good is a vision if you don't pin it down into some goals? And yet that's what many people do every day. In fact, most people don't even *have* all three—a vision, focus areas, and an action plan. You do. Now you need to check them for alignment.

When Daniel did this, he could see immediately that he was out of alignment. His vision was to be a supportive leader, but not one of his focus areas mentioned anything about the people he was leading. They all focused on profits and systems, as if the people who generated those profits and ran those systems were irrelevant. His action plans underscored the issue. Daniel didn't even have staff meetings, much less a plan for developing the members of his team.

Getting into alignment with his goal of polishing his leadership skills didn't take much more than a change in this discrepancy. He envisioned being a supportive leader, added it as a new focus area, and built an action plan around it. This realignment made a significant impact on Daniel's ability to lead instead of just push people around. His reputation improved. His team started to gel. Daniel was making progress.

When you are in alignment in your vision, focus, and action, you are no longer wishing for your vision. You're actually working toward it.

The Formula for Quality of Life. Another area to look for alignment is between your distinct natural attributes and your values. This formula looks like this:

$$\text{Brilliance} + \text{Values} = \text{Quality of Life}$$

You work more productively, more easily, and faster when you play to your *strengths*. You feel content and complete when you live your *values*. When you couple your strengths with your values, everything you do feels right. What you care about most, you do well; what you do well contributes to what you care about most. Quality of life.

This was another place where Daniel was out of alignment.

Daniel had definite strengths in the areas of being in command and arranging systems. As a result, he often found himself bossing people around and telling them all what to do. But in his heart, Daniel had strong values about cooperation, relationships, and independence. When he connected those values to his strengths, he realized that he could be a better leader. He encouraged his team to work cooperatively and independently in creative, synergistic ways. By bringing together his strengths and his values, Daniel became a more powerful and respected leader.

When you align your strengths and your values, you are doing what you do best in the service of what you care about most.

The Formula for Transformation. I find the next four practices especially helpful for facilitating *change*. The formula looks like this:

Learning + Teams + Time + Possibility = Transformation

Change can be hard. Change takes time. And face it, change is at the core of trying to be a better leader and lead a better life.

Daniel's primary leadership challenge was to work better with people. After years of a more detached style, this was going to be a big change. He couldn't just tinker with this style. He needed a complete transformation. We looked to these four practices to help.

- *Learning*. Daniel started an independent study of connected leadership. He reflected on the learning, and he ended up with a real education about what it meant to work well with people.
- *Team*. Daniel elicited the help of a dream team of co-workers who were known for being likeable leaders. He asked them point blank, "What can I do to become more connected to my team?"
- *Time*. Daniel revamped his schedule to make time for the people and relationships that were central to his new approach to leadership.
- *Possibility*. Perhaps the biggest shift for Daniel was to see the possibilities available by connecting with his team. He practiced not doing—consciously refraining from his old tell-them-what-to-do style and stepping into the background to give others a chance to get involved.

Daniel's efforts to align these practices of personal leadership were deliberate. He and I sat in a conference room with markers and a white board and designed his approach to transformation. It worked. The four practices combined to reshape who Daniel was as a leader.

All of the practices of personal leadership will help you achieve your vision, and they are even more powerful together than they are apart. To say that you can transform your life through alignment is no overstatement.

- If you don't align your vision, focus, and action plans, you may not *achieve* your vision.
- If you don't incorporate your strengths and values, you may not *enjoy* the process.
- If you don't leverage your time, team, learning, and possibilities, you may not *have what it takes* to succeed.

The examples above put together the practices of personal leadership two, three, or four at a time. The ultimate goal is to get all nine of the other practices into alignment. Don't get carried away, though. If you tried to match up every one of the practices with every part and priority of your life, you could end up with one gigantic matrix, not to mention a terrific headache. Instead, when you set out to achieve something new, just run it through the practices to quickly check your alignment.

Got a new goal? Great. How can you use your strengths to meet that goal, and do so in a way that also honors your values?

Want to make a change? Okay. What's your vision for this change? How much time will you need, and where will you find that time?

Looking for a new opportunity? No problem. Who can help you? What do you need to learn? What are the possibilities?

This is a very conscious process. Not every leader does this—only the ones who want to excel. Your process of alignment is the detailed plan on the drafting table, the playbook, the campaign strategy. Once you know your ideas are aligned, you're ready to take a win.

You have to master the things you do. I dream of what I want my world to be like, and then I spend time visualizing it in detail. I write down what that looks like. Then I start doing the actions that need to be done to start moving toward that. I use my strengths. I have a team of people around that help me get there. It's constant alignment.
—Bonnie Hagemann, CEO, Executive Development Associates

Exercise

Quiz yourself. For each of the practices of personal leadership, ask yourself the questions in the worksheet, "Checking for Alignment." If you're in alignment, this should go fast, taking as few as five minutes to answer all of the questions. I find it helpful to do this using index cards of the 10 practices or the online version of the worksheet at www.theinneredge.com.

INTEGRATION

Alignment is one way—an important way—to think about ideas, efforts, and actions all at once. But to really experience the ease with which you can be your best you also need the skill of *integration*.

Whereas alignment is about lining things up to get them in proper relative position, integration means bringing them together into one harmonious whole.

- *Alignment* is red and blue make a red and blue checkerboard.
- *Integration* is red and blue make purple.
- *Alignment* is $1 + 1 = 2$.
- *Integration* is $1 + 1 = 11$.
- *Alignment* is like seven courses of a meal.

CHECKING FOR ALIGNMENT

Describe your vision._____

_____

_____

_____

_____

_____

Go through all 10 practices of personal leadership to see how they relate to your vision.

Practice 1	Clarity	Do you have clarity about what you want?
Practice 2	Focus	Which of your focus areas relate to this goal?
Practice 3	Action	What kind of action plan do you have? What will help you take that action?
Practice 4	Brilliance	Which of your attributes will help you achieve this goal?
Practice 5	Fulfillment	How are your values connected to this goal?
Practice 6	Time	How will you make the time to work on this goal?
Practice 7	Teams	How can your personal team help you succeed?
Practice 8	Learning	What learning strategy will improve your pace and process?
Practice 9	Possibility	What will you do to see possibility with respect to this goal?
Practice 10	All at Once	How can you align and integrate this goal with the rest of your life to meet several goals at once?

Which practices need attention for you to have alignment? What do you need to do now?

_____

_____

_____

_____

_____

_____

- *Integration* is seven ingredients combined to make one exquisite dish.
- *Alignment* means looking at the 10 practices of personal leadership as a collection.
- *Integration* means putting them together in combination to spark a new breakthrough altogether.

When you integrate your life, you pull together ideas and efforts, combining them to get more with less. To get to a state of integration, you need to move from limited *either/or* thinking to a more powerful *both/and* approach.

Either/Or

Either/or thinking means thinking in black and white.

- *Either* I can make a difference *or* I can make money.
- *Either* I can be relaxed *or* I can be accomplished.
- *Either* I can be happy now *or* I can be happy later.

Either/or thinking is an extremely restrictive, yet common, way of viewing the world.

This was the kind of thinking Whitney—the journalist whose letter you read earlier—had fallen into when I met her.

Whitney called me on the referral of a friend, not really sure what she wanted.

"I work like crazy and I'd like not to," she said, "but I hate to give up everything I've worked so hard to achieve." Either she could work a less crazy schedule or she could keep her job.

"Sometimes I think I'd like to retire, but I'm afraid I'd just be sitting around." Either she could retire or she could stay busy and active.

"I know I should take better care of myself, but there's never any time." Either she could exercise and rest or she could fulfill her responsibilities.

Perhaps you see a little of yourself in Whitney. Most of us at one time or another box ourselves into a corner believing we can *either* have this *or* that, and we force ourselves to make a choice.

Not so. You can integrate the things you want to get them all at once.

Both/And

Integrative thinking means combining ideas for a more streamlined, synergistic approach. Just look at how a simple change in wording shifts Whitney's perspective.

Either/or: Either she could work a less crazy schedule or she could keep her job.

Both/and: She could both work a less crazy schedule and also keep her job.
Either/or: Either she could retire or she could stay busy and active.
Both/and: She could both retire and also stay busy and active.
Either/or: Either she could exercise and rest or she could fulfill her responsibilities.
Both/and: She could both exercise and rest and also fulfill her responsibilities. Just reading these sentences, can you see how both/and thinking opened up the possibilities?

The main task in developing a more integrated approach to your life and leadership is to blend the practices together. You link together two things you want at the same time and ask, "How can I have *both* this *and* that?" Then try it with three things. Four. Here are a few examples.

- *Action/Focus/Fulfillment:* Go through your focus areas and your action plans. Look closely. Is each item contributing to your life or detracting from it? What would it take to make a change for the better?
- *Team/Strengths/Learning:* Look at your team. How could you implement learning opportunities to help your team make the most of its collective strengths?
- *Vision/Time/Possibility:* Think about your time. What would it be like if you thought about time not just as a resource for attaining your vision but for living that vision now, by being open to the possibility that success is not a process but a choice?

Pulling together the practices of personal leadership in this methodical, conscious way will help you start to think more creatively. Of course, the ultimate goal is not to integrate the practices of personal leadership but to integrate the different aspects of your life. To read more about how leaders integrate the different parts of their lives, take a look at the box, Leaders Discovering Integration. Then ask yourself how you can pull together the different parts of your life so you can both be a better leader and also lead a better life.

LEADERS DISCOVERING INTEGRATION

- My business partners are also my friends.
- I love my work space. It feels like home.
- I get to use my strengths in my job at least a little every day.
- I find my work extremely fulfilling. Even if I'm working hard, I don't mind because I care so much about the outcome.
- I stay open to possibilities all the time. Possibilities for the direction to take, possibilities for how to spend my time, possibilities for new connections.

- I hold meetings in my home, where we can relax and eat and be comfortable.
- I share my vision and focus areas openly with my family and my boss.
- I ask myself, "Do I *want* to do this?" I only do it if the answer is yes. Then I am using my strengths and living my values, which makes it easy to be successful.
- I envision everything. My future, my achievements, my goals. I make sure my vision incorporates everything and everyone who's important to me.
- I work long hours but I break them up. On my breaks, I jog or nap.
- I learn by reading, and I love to read. I read to discover my strengths, I read for fulfillment, I read to learn how to better manage my time.
- My wife and I go for a walk every night. We connect, we exercise, we help each other solve sticky work dilemmas. It's the whole package in 40 minutes.
- I use my strengths, and my team members use theirs. As a result, we're a closer and more productive team.

It took Whitney a long time to get the hang of integrative thinking. We had to peel off layers of limited thinking before we could get new ideas. Here's what happened.

WHITNEY

"Whitney," I started, "You're operating on the assumption that you could either work a less crazy schedule or keep your job. How might you be able to have both?"

"Oh, that would be impossible."

"Really? Why?"

She launched into a litany of reasons. Her first excuse was travel. "I'm constantly flying all over the world! You can't do what I do and not travel a lot."

I challenged the assumption: "Is traveling a lot the same thing as being crazed all the time? I know quite a few people who travel like you and have a comparatively saner life."

Her second excuse was deadlines.

"Deadlines put on way too much pressure. You're constantly under the gun in my job."

Again I challenged her: "Are deadlines really the issue? After all, you've been a journalist your whole career but you haven't always felt life was this crazy."

Her third excuse was her news organization. "The culture around here is insane. Everyone works 24/7. You never get a break."

"Have you actually looked into that? Have you talked to your boss about how insane your schedule has become?"

All of this didn't actually happen in one conversation, but gradually as Whitney and I dug around in her perceptions about her life, we found a lot of assumptions that were based on black-and-white, either/or thinking, every one of which could be challenged on the grounds that she was a leader who had influence and control over her life.

Then we asked the question again. Would there, could there, be a way that a person in Whitney's shoes could both work a more reasonable schedule and also keep her job? We explored some answers. Maybe she could lengthen her business trips—even by a day—so she could both complete her reporting and also have time to catch her breath and take some time for herself. Maybe she could get some administrative help so she could both meet deadlines and also get out from under the rest of the paperwork. Maybe she could brainstorm creative options for redesigning her schedule (redistribute the work? work from home? get an intern?) so she could both keep up with the fast-paced culture of the business and also lead the way to a higher quality of work and life.

The trick to integrative thinking is to believe both/and is possible—or at least to suspend disbelief long enough to explore some options. When you do, you'll start to see different aspects of your life overlapping to get the real synergy going. Then the momentum will take on a life of its own.

Exercise

Fill in the blanks below to practice both/and thinking in as many different ways as you can.

Start by integrating the practices of personal leadership.

How can I both_____and also_____?

(practice this)   (practice that)

How can I both_____and also_____?

(practice this)   (practice that)

How can I both_____and also_____?

(practice this)   (practice that)

Now try integrating a variety of different ideas.

How can I both_____and also_____?

(do this)   (do that)

How can I both_____and also _____?

(have this)   (have that)

How can I both_____and also _____?

(be like this)   (get that)

How can I both_____and also _____?

(focus on this)   (experience that)

How can I both_____and also _____?

(emphasize this strength)   (accept this weakness)

How can I both_____and also _____?

(honor this value)   (honor this other value)

How can I both_____and also _____?

(create this outcome)   (have this experience)

HAVING IT ALL

When you take the all at once thinking to heart, you will be living and leading with integrity. You will be who you say you want to be and doing what want to do. In the bigger picture of your life, this amounts to having it all.

At this point in the conversation, most people turn to the question, "Is that possible? Is there such a thing as having it all?" To me, it's an unhelpful question. It's distracting, for it throws you immediately out of possibility and into limitation. To me, the answer to the question, "Is it possible to have it all?" is not yes or no. It's another question: "Do you know what your all is?"

When people talk about having it all, they seem to mean getting stuff—a fine job, a great office, stock options, an enviable marriage, cute kids, and so on. That may or may not be possible. It may not even be what you want. What *is* possible is to have the kind of life you want to live. One in which nothing is missing, where you get what you need—emotionally, spiritually, financially, materially—by being clear on who you are and what you want, by being creative and strategic in having it happen, and by leading yourself wisely to the outcomes.

What does having it all mean to you? Does having it all mean some societal definition of flashy cars, tropical vacations, and a knockout spouse? Or does it mean a sense of fulfillment and satisfaction with a meaningful job and some time left over for you? Does it mean a warm and pleasant home filled with joy? A billion dollars? Your health? Making a difference in the world? Any of these definitions can work—as long it comes from you.

If you can clearly define your all in a way that is grounded, realistic, and optimistic, most likely you can have it. If you define your all as some unattainable ideal that amounts to the pot of gold at the end of the rainbow, then you might not. To find out your all, you can go back to one of the central themes of this book: You have to know what you want. You have the freedom to find out what that is, and now you have some strategies to create it. When you know what your all is, *then* you can ask the questions. Is that possible? If this is what I want, can I have it all? Can I have it all . . . all at once? You choose. Do you want to? What would it look like if you did?

Exercise

What does having it all mean to you? What would you have to

- have:
- do:
- be:

in order to feel you had it all?

KEEPING IT, TOO

You now know the 10 practices of personal leadership. You have dozens of strategies for applying them, and you have a sense of what it will mean to you to be a better leader and lead a better life. Along the way, you have discovered something profound. Something about you. Something about your future. Something about what's possible. What is it? Throughout this book, I've shared ideas that have helped other leaders. What ideas have meant the most to you? Before you set off on the journey to pursue your vision, pack your bags with the most important ideas you want to remember. Then you can not just have it all, but you can keep it all, too.

Below you'll find some questions that will help anchor the insights you've had about yourself as a leader and your life so that they will continue to inform and guide you in the years to come. I ask you these questions because the point of this book is not to memorize whatever I've said but to discover what's most powerful for *you*. Your ideas. Your insights. Your results.

It's critical that you ask yourself these questions now, while you're thinking about personal leadership. You have a lot of other things to do when you close this book. Your vision, your goals, your business, and your personal life await. Your task now is to lock in a strategy for continuing the good work you've started as you've read this book and extend it into your life in a self-sustaining way.

When I talk about continuing the good work you've started with personal leadership, I'm talking about making it a habit. Like taking care of your health or monitoring your investments or maintaining your yard, personal leadership—if you let it—will become part of the fabric of your life. Ultimately you will get the result: an independent, self-driven, highly accomplished version of the success you want, along with a relaxed, fulfilling quality of life. Leading well and living well. All . . . all at once.

Exercise

1. What's the most important thing you've learned about yourself?
2. What tools and strategies are you taking with you?
3. What new perspectives or concepts have made the most impact?
4. What old perspectives or assumptions have you changed?
5. What one key takeaway do you want to remember, and how will you remember it?
6. What will it look like for you to continue practicing personal leadership?

PERFECTING THE PRACTICE

> I picked the rose in a hurry. I was afraid of the Gardener. Then I heard the soft voice of Him, "What's the value of one rose? I give you the whole garden."
>
> —*Rumi*

The processes of alignment and integration have the power to transform your life. You can stop segmenting yourself. You can stop sacrificing. You can finally have it all.

Your *Inner Edge* Coaching Assignment: Your All

A copy of the exercises for alignment and integration have been included for you at the end of this chapter on the worksheet called "Your All" (also available at www.theinneredge.com). Use this as a quick reference to snap back into integrative thinking at a glance. Use the section titled "All at Once" to make notes about what your all is.

FAQS

Q: Is having it all really possible? I buy the practices of personal leadership but sometimes it seems like the results are too fantastic.

A: To answer this question best, we need to ask leaders who believe they do have it all. You've seen many examples of these leaders throughout this book, and chances are there are others in your life. Talk to them. Do they think it's possible to have it all? It's not my job to convince you that you can create a complete and abundant life as a leader. I believe it's possible. I see it every day in the leaders I coach, and I live it myself. You have to discover it for yourself.

You now have 10 practices that will help you find out if you can have it all. My suggestion is to test them and see what's possible. Choose one small, achievable area of your vision and work on that. Then add another and another. Notice the changes and the impact. Are you getting the results you want? Is it worth it?

In my experience, healthy skepticism is a good thing. It keeps you sharp and steers you away from false hope and disillusionment. On the other hand, doubt can become an obstacle to progress. You can get in your own way. Three steps will help you keep the right mind-set:

1. Choose an inspirational and realistic goal.
2. Believe that it's possible.
3. Lead the way, using all 10 practices of personal leadership.

Q: I'm excited about personal leadership, and I want to redesign my life around being a better leader and leading a better life. How long do you think it will take?

A: Congratulations on your decision! Your enthusiasm and gusto are going to improve the answer to your question. If you go after your vision with commitment, the answer will be, "Sooner than you think."

But depending on everything from your circumstances to your belief systems, other possible answers include the following:

"It depends."

"It could take a lifetime."

"You can start seeing results today."

The results you get from personal leadership depend entirely on what you're trying to do. You really can start seeing results today in those areas where you need to change your mind, your perspective, or a key belief. You will need more time to achieve some goals and integrate the practices of personal leadership. You will need even more time when your goals and vision are far from where you are now, especially if you need to arrange the practical elements of your life to get there. Ultimately, the practices of personal leadership will no longer become an effort, however. They will become a way of thinking and a way of life.

When you picked up this book, you had a good reason in mind. Something motivated you to want to change, to improve, to excel. When you take the lead in your life by practicing personal leadership, that's exactly what you're doing. You *are* changing. You *are* improving. You *are* excelling. What are you going to do with that power? You know how to lead well and live well. Now it's time to take your new model of leadership bigger. It's time to take it out into the world.

CHAPTER SUMMARY

Key Points

- You are going to discover the power behind the practices when you see what happens when you adopt them all . . . all at once.
- Alignment is about lining things up to get them in proper relative position. Integration means bringing them together into one harmonious whole.
- How you feel affects how you act, how you act affects how you work, how you work affects your results, your results affect the way you live. It's all connected.
- You can stop sacrificing. You can finally have it all.

YOUR ALL

Alignment

Which practices are needed for you to have full alignment? What do you need to do now?

Practice 1	Clarity	Do you have clarity about what you want?
Practice 2	Focus	Which of your focus areas relate to this goal?
Practice 3	Action	What kind of action plan do you have? What will help you take that action?
Practice 4	Brilliance	Which of your attributes will help you achieve this goal?
Practice 5	Fulfillment	How are your values connected to this goal?
Practice 6	Time	How will you make the time to work on this goal?
Practice 7	Teams	How can your personal team help you succeed?
Practice 8	Learning	What learning strategy will improve your pace and process?
Practice 9	Possibilities	What will you do to see possibility with respect to this goal?
Practice 10	All at Once	How can you align and integrate this goal with the rest of your life to meet several goals at once?

Integration

How can I both_____and also _____?

How can I both_____and also _____?

How can I both_____and also _____?

All at Once

What would it mean for you to have it all?

_____

_____

_____

_____

_____

_____

Leading on the Edge: *What Kind of a Gift Do You Want To Be?*

Twenty years from now you will be more disappointed by the things that you didn't do than by the ones you did do. So throw off the bowlines. Sail away from the safe harbor. Catch the trade winds in your sails. Explore. Dream. Discover.

—*Mark Twain*

Congratulations! As we come to the end of our work together on personal leadership, you are approaching a new beginning as a leader. I want to acknowledge you for the work you've done. As a coach, I know the heart of a leader, and here's what I know about you:

YOU

You are amazing. You are dedicated, smart, and capable. When you cracked the cover of this book, you were already a leader. You are accomplished and have had many successes. You are already a masterpiece.

But you knew something deep in your heart: More is possible for you. No matter who you are—a person who is just starting to see yourself as a leader or a well-established leader with an illustrious career; a leader struggling to find your place or one who knows exactly what you want; a leader who's been too strung out or one who has been newly fired up—you have the potential to be even more. You have greatness in you.

Throughout this book, you have learned how to find it. By being the kind of leader who wants to be your best, by committing time, energy, and effort to your own self-improvement, by being thoughtful about who you are and what you do, and by bringing leadership to your life as well as your work, you show the world what's really possible. You lead by example. Your life is that example.

You have opened up your mind to new ideas, new ways of thinking, and new ways of being as a leader and in your life. My hope is that you will be rewarded for your efforts. And you will. When you practice personal leadership, you gain a greater sense of self. You achieve your vision and goals, and you do so in a way that fulfills and sustains you. You get a sense of control in this crazy world, and you gain the ability to make choices, take risks, and be the leader only you can be. You discover that leadership itself is truly a gift.

As a leader, you have many great gifts. Your talents. Your opportunities. Your drive. By seeing yourself as a leader, you have not just received those gifts, you have torn them open. You see them for the marvel they are. Now the question is, what are you going to do with those gifts? How are you going to share them with the people around you and the rest of the world? In this chapter, I want you to give some thought to these questions. Because by now you're starting to realize, the true gift you have to give . . . is you.

SHARING THE PRACTICES OF PERSONAL LEADERSHIP

When we do the best that we can, we never know what miracle is wrought in our life, or in the life of another.

—*Helen Keller*

You have already discovered what's possible for you when you practice personal leadership. Now it's time to share the wealth. How will you give your gifts to the people you lead? How will you give to your organization and the world around you? How big can you really be?

Before you go back out there to your life as a leader, I want you to consider for a moment how things will be different. Specifically, I want you to think about how you will extend personal leadership beyond the bounds of your own life. As we conclude, I want to share with you some ideas for how to give of your gifts, and in so doing, create more gifts for yourself, for others, and the world.

Because your gifts are desperately needed.

When I started this book, leadership crisis was the news of the year. Stories in business journals as well as *Time, Newsweek, 60 Minutes,* and *Good Morning America* all reported that accomplished, talented leaders were leaving their hard-won careers to find more meaningful ways to live. The people featured in these stories invariably described a choice between success and quality of life—and in many cases, it was one they didn't want to make.

Our culture, our organizations, the times we live in—they have a way of conspiring against our efforts to be our best. But better business should not come at the expense of quality of life, and quality of life should not come at the expense of business results. Work and life should be able to coexist, happily and successfully. They can and they do.

But every day, millions of people drive onto the fast-lane and race their lives away—ironically missing the fact that everything they are doing to improve their life is actually running them into the ground. Workweeks get longer, stress levels rise, and talented leaders burn out or move on.

We need a whole new paradigm for work and life, and it starts with you. My dream is that the next evolution of our ambitious, achieving society will be to learn how to get the results we crave in the easiest, most natural way—the way that feeds us personally and enhances our quality of life. But no matter how great your life becomes, no matter how well your business does, you are holding back something even greater that the world urgently needs. Part of practicing personal leadership is sharing what you've learned and empowering others, as well.

Maybe you will be the person who plants the seeds of personal leadership in the mind of the next great world leader. Maybe you will be the one to help shift your organization into a healthier, more life-affirming place. Maybe you will initiate positive changes in the world that today you can't even imagine. People like you, who see themselves as leaders, aren't just leaders in their jobs. They are leaders by definition, wherever they go. You will always be the one people look to for leadership and guidance. You will be the one who asks the questions, has the answers, or creates the opportunities for incredible things to happen. At home, at church, at work, among your friends, in your political party, when you're with your kids, when you're giving to charity, you will be seen as a leader.

What will you do with that potential?

It's an honor and a privilege to be a leader—a real gift. What kind of a gift do you want to be?

In order to answer that question, you've got to lead on every level: your inner edge, your outer edge, and your leading edge. Then you'll be truly leading on the edge.

THE INNER EDGE

To get an image of what it means to lead on the edge, we return to the symbol with which we started this book: the Möbius strip (Figure 7). As you may remember, the Möbius strip is a geometrical shape in which the inner edge

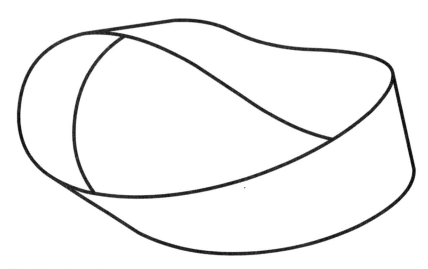

FIGURE 7   The Möbius strip

twists around to become the outer edge, and the outer edge similarly becomes the inner.

Throughout this book, we have spent our time on your *inner edge:* the work of a leader that takes place in your heart, mind, and soul. Your inner edge is the place you find clarity and motivation, conviction and strength, and it is an essential aspect of your success. But it is not the *only* side to success. In order to be a leader, you've got to bring that learning and self-awareness out to the people you lead. We call this your outer edge.

THE OUTER EDGE

Your outer edge is the part of your leadership that you present to others: the way you act and interact with the people around you. We haven't spent much time on your outer edge in this book. This was a purposeful choice on my part to show you that as a leader, your effectiveness depends as much on your inner work as the outer work of leadership.

Plus, the outer work of leadership is well-covered ground. This is where you bring your vision to others and motivate them to help you achieve it. Much has been written about this side of leadership. In my office alone, books like this on leadership literally fall off the shelf.

And yet, I worry that personal leadership is still missing on the outer edge. As you create the vision for yourself, it's essential to remember that your success as a leader depends on the commitment and well-being of other leaders just like you. Part of personal leadership is understanding how you can support others in being their best, just as you have learned to be yours.

- Can you imagine what it would be like if everyone in your company saw themselves as a leader and knew how to make the most of that opportunity?
- Can you imagine what it would be like if your employees all felt as empowered as you to create their own success?
- Can you imagine how civilization would be different if all people realized the potential they have for finding better ways of leading and living all around the world?

When I look into an ideal future, I see a world in which people know how incredible they are and how precious life is. They know what they have to offer: their vision, their strengths, their values. They connect to their sense of purpose at home and at work. They honor the work that they do, they do the work that they love, and they make the most of their lives by taking care of their health, their families, their loved ones, their friends, their co-workers, and their world.

My hope is that more and more people will excel not just because they work hard, but also because they value their own natural brilliance. They know how to tap into that brilliance to make success easy and fulfilling. They know how to make every moment count. They discover the synergy of personal support teams. They see possibility. They know what they want, and they're committed to learning how to get it in a way that serves their own needs and assists the needs of others. They don't have to be stressed and pressured all the time, because they know who they are. They're inspired to do well, and they know how to succeed in a context of ease and joy. That's what's possible when people know how to lead themselves. But it will only happen if we use leadership—personal leadership—to show others what's possible for them. This is the leader's work on the outer edge.

Management expert Tom Peters once wrote, "Leaders don't create followers, they create more leaders."[1] This idea is shared by researchers, authors, leadership professors, and leaders themselves as we move to more empowering ways of viewing the work of leadership.[2] You can create more leaders by sharing the ideas of personal leadership with others as a way of life. This isn't about creating more work for yourself. It's about knowing your power and letting it show.

Just by making the positive changes you're making for yourself, you will serve as an inspiration for other leaders. Whenever you have the chance, reveal the path that got you there. It's too easy for other people to look at healthy, balanced, centered leaders and say, "They're just lucky." That kind of thinking diminishes other peoples' ability to empower themselves. But when you make the process transparent, it becomes accessible. You show people a new possibility. You become their inspiration. That is, after all, *leadership*.

Leaders aren't just in the game for themselves. Leaders are by definition the ones who show others the way. Think of it this way. You're bright, capable, and empowered. You know you can change, and you want to make a positive difference with your life. You wouldn't see yourself as a leader if you didn't.

Not everyone has that. Just today, I've received phone calls from three leaders who are crumpling in their careers. Chris jumped out of a secure but insufferable job to reach his dream of starting his own company, but instead of flying he's flailing. Deborah is getting up at two every morning and working till ten at night, with little more than a bathroom break and a cursory kiss for her kids. Luke is being forced to take a pay cut and more responsibility at the same time as his marriage is crumbling as a direct result of his working too much.

These are real people. They are leaders who right now are grasping at straws. Yes, they have talent and potential, but today they need more than that. They need support. They need help. They need you.

As a coach, I have the privilege of sharing the principles of personal leadership one person at a time. This book is my way of widening the circle. With your help, we can widen it even more. Let others in. Help them redefine success for themselves and learn how to lead them to it. Help them discover their potential. Help them see themselves as leaders, just like you.

I challenge myself on my activities through the day. It's not just about me. What is going to affect the greater good? What is actually going to take the talent of the whole group further?
—Diane Hoskins, Global Executive Director, Gensler

Exercise

Take some time now for reflection. Write down answers to these questions.

- Who in your life is struggling?
- Who is committed to their own success?
- Who do you want to support?
- You have something to give. Who do you most hope will receive it?

Below follows a short list of ways leaders have taken personal leadership to the outer edge. Circle the ideas that appeal to you and add a few of your own.

Share:
Tell a co-worker or
    friend what you're
    doing to be a better
    leader and lead a
    better life.

Offer:
Describe one of the
    practices of personal
    leadership with
    someone you think it
    will help.

Give:
Give a copy of the book
    to someone you think
    will benefit from the
    ideas.

Lead:
Lead a study group on
    the topic of personal
    leadership.

Communicate:
Give a presentation on
    personal leadership
    to a small group with
    whom you work.

Model:
Serve as a role model
    by being open and
    forthcoming about
    your steps to improve
    as a leader.

Other: _____

_____

_____

_____

Other: _____

_____

_____

_____

Other: _____

_____

_____

_____

If you take the initiative to extend personal leadership to your outer edge, you will be an inspiration for the success of many other leaders. I encourage you in that work. But beyond the good work you do leading yourself and others exists one more dimension of leadership into which you're now ready to move. This is your leading edge.

THE LEADING EDGE

The leading edge is the shape of your leadership—the way you choose to serve the world. Some leaders are meant to develop new paradigms, some to invent new products, and some to build great companies. Some will raise incredible kids. Some leaders will improve the culture. Some will start social movements, some will feed the hungry, and some will cure cancer. *You* are meant to do something, too. You might not know what it is yet, but perhaps you have an inkling . . . a little secret wish . . . maybe a dream. To get on the leading edge is to realize your legacy will only live on if you take the lead. To think this way is to do no less than give your gifts to humanity.

Your leading edge is defined by your ideas about how the world should be, and your efforts—however small—to make it happen. Your dreams. Your discoveries. Your vision. Your cause, your calling, your purpose. Your innovations and inventions. These are the future that awaits you. Others see that future and are following you there, too.

When you practice personal leadership you make a shift from leading yourself and leading others to leading big ideas with long-term effects. Leading big ideas means developing those ideas and making them vivid, tangible, and concrete for all to see. You take the spotlight off of you, off of other people, and off of the work and shine it on the big ideas you want to champion.

For a few examples, think about the big ideas that have endured through time. Our forefathers had a big idea of "life, liberty, and the pursuit of happiness." Martin Luther King Jr. had a big idea that America would live up to its founding ideal that all men were created equal. Walt Disney had a big idea to "make children laugh." From the worldly to the whimsical, big ideas have lasting impact far beyond the leaders who launch them.

What's your big idea? Shift the focus away from yourself as a leader and think about the big ideas toward which you want to lead. What do you want to create? What big ideas do you want to support? What do you hope will happen as a result of you being here on this earth? To make that happen, you have to not just lead yourself, you have to lead the idea, too.

The same practices that helped you succeed can help your big idea succeed, too. Instead of getting clarity about your own vision, you get clarity about the vision of the big idea. Instead of creating focus areas and action plans for your life and leadership, you create focus areas and action plans to advance the big idea. Consider the strengths and weaknesses of the big idea, the values being honored by the big idea, the time spent on the big idea, the team members who can promote the big idea, the learning that needs to take place to advance the big idea, the possibilities created by the big idea, and the importance of thinking about the big idea and the rest of your ideas all at once. When you take these steps, you're not just thinking like a leader, you're truly leading on the edge.

You can see examples of this in the public sphere—leaders who are taking a risk to do something different because they believe it's important. Valuable. Needed. As I write these words, Barack Obama has just been elected the first ever African American president of the United States. Oil mogul T. Boone Pickens is lobbying for alternative sources of energy to power the future.[3] Hollywood movie stars Brad Pitt and George Clooney are receiving awards for aid work in Darfur. Bill Gates has resigned his post at Microsoft to start a movement of "creative capitalism" to transform health and education across the globe—teaching others how to "do good and do well at the same time."[4] Whatever your personal politics, you can see that these leaders are pushing the edges of what people have come to expect. They are leading on the edge. In their own ways, they are leading the world.

Leading the world may sound like an awfully lofty proposal until you consider the fact that the world is made up of people just like you and me. You don't have to be a world leader, but you can be an important leader in your world.

Start by defining your sphere of influence. My world is the world of people who see themselves as leaders and want to excel in every area of their life. My neighbor's world is the world of global supply chain management. His wife's is the world of philanthropy. Many leaders see their world as their organization, or their community, or their ethnic culture, or their family and friends. To lead the world is to recognize that in your world, you make an impact.

As a leader, whether you have the title or not, you influence the way the world works. You do this by scaling up the concepts of personal leadership and creating more (and more empowered) leaders. As you think about the ways you might take your ideas about personal leadership beyond the scope of these pages, remember: *You are a gift to this world.* What kind of a gift do you want to be?

The sooner people learn the power of investing in others,
the sooner the world around them becomes a better place.
—Rob Fazio, Cofounder and President, Hold the Door for Others

---

Exercise

1. How do you define your world? In other words, what is your immediate sphere of influence?
2. What is your big idea?
3. What specifically would you like to see implemented in your world that will make it a better place, support or expand leadership, or achieve better results?

4. How could you promote or implement that idea?

5. What resources would help? What ideas do you have for getting those resources?

YOUR OWN EXECUTIVE COACH

When you continue to develop yourself as a leader, you show yourself to be committed to your own success. I want to honor that by being committed to you. It is my intention to make sure you have everything you need to be successful with personal leadership. I've put together a number of resources you can use to serve as your own executive coach. You can find these and more at www.theinneredge.com.

The Inner Edge at a Glance. The appendix at the back of this book provides a summary of the worksheets to keep and update as you continue your practice of personal leadership. Online versions of these worksheets are available to print whenever you want.

The Inner Edge Workbook. The worksheets and processes in *The Inner Edge* are meant to be used again and again as you practice personal leadership. *The Inner Edge Workbook* includes exercises and worksheets from the book, along with a short synopsis of each practice and bonus material.

The Inner Edge Extension. The ideas and strategies presented in this book represent only a portion of the all that's available. *The Inner Edge Extension* includes articles, tools, techniques, stories, and more exercises to help you excel.

Coaching Services. On the website, you will find a list of ways you can use a coach to help with any of the 10 practices, including working with a coach, short-term or over time, to be a better leader and lead a better life.

The website. The website is constantly changing and being upgraded. Visit us to find new resources, read interviews and articles, join the *Inner Edge* community, and contribute your ideas.

Use these resources. They're there for you. I want you to have *everything you need* to succeed in your efforts to be a leader in this world. We're in this together.

A PARTING GIFT

Wherever you go, go with all your heart.

—*Confucius*

As we close, I want to acknowledge you for taking the responsibility and the opportunity to be your best as a leader. You are an inspiration. Along with the hundreds of leaders I've met who are sincere in their efforts to succeed in the way that only they can, you are a true leader. You are the one who makes a difference. You are the one who changes the world. Your vision, your potential, your efforts—they leave a mark.

My wish for you is that what you achieve will far exceed any vision you've dared to dream. I hope that you will be not just clear but also honest and courageous about what you really want for yourself, for the people around you, for your life, for your leadership, and for the world at large.

There are times you'll lose heart. You'll get busy, you'll get tired, you'll forget, you'll have setbacks, or you'll drift away. But you won't get lost. You have everything you need to succeed, right there within you. Whenever you get discouraged, I invite you to come back and reconnect. On the website (www.theinneredge.com), you will find a free three-minute audio called a "Coaching Booster"—a few words of support in my own voice to remind you how important you are and to encourage you on your way to your vision. It's not easy to be a leader. We need to support each other. This is my parting gift to you.

As you go forward into the future that awaits you, know that every step you take to improve your leadership is going to enrich your life and the lives of others. You will be the kind of leader who changes the world. The kind of leader others will follow. The kind of leader you were meant to be.

I wish you well along the way. In the words of William Shakespeare, may "health, peace, and sweet content be yours."

Joelle

CHAPTER SUMMARY

Key Points

- You are already a masterpiece.
- You lead by example. Your life is that example.
- As a leader, you have many great gifts. Now the question is, what are you going to do with those gifts? What kind of a gift do you want to be?

ONE LAST REQUEST

My inspiration comes from leaders like you. I invite you to send me your success stories—as well as your challenges and questions—about personal leadership. While I can't promise to respond to every one, I can promise that your experience will help other leaders who are trying to bring their best selves to their work . . . just like you. You can find a link to contribute your thoughts at www.theinneredge. com.

Appendix A

Your *Inner Edge* at a Glance

Throughout this book, you have been given 10 *Inner Edge* Coaching Assignments to advance your practice of personal leadership—one for every practice, found at the end of the chapters. These assignments, each in the form of a worksheet, capture your thinking and provide a resource for you to continue refining your practice. The checklist below summarizes the complete list of your assignments for easy reference. You will want to keep these pages, refer back to them, and use them as a guide as you continue improving as a leader. Collect them in a file, mark them in the book, or download electronic copies from the website (www.theinneredge.com)* to track your ideas about how to be a better leader and lead a better life.

- Your Vision
- Your Focus Areas
- Your Action Plan
- Your DNA Map
- Your Values
- Your Shortcuts
- Your Support Team
- Your Personal University
- Your Invitation
- Your All

* Worksheets, templates, and bonus material for each of these items and more are also available at www.theinneredge.com.

Appendix B

Reflective Questions

1. What is possible for you as a leader and in your life? What do you really want?
2. What are your biggest stressors? How do they affect you? What ideas do you have for alleviating them?
3. Where are your greatest joys? How do they enhance your life? What would it take to spend more time here?
4. What are your most compelling goals and future achievements? What's most important right now?
5. What are your biggest challenges at this time?
6. What keeps you from taking the action you *want* to take or know you *should* take to be more effective? What would make it easier?
7. How would others describe you? How would you describe yourself, in your best possible light?
8. Which of your values are being honored now? Which are being threatened?
9. What motivates you?
10. What strategies have helped you make the best use of your time?
11. Who helps you the most to achieve your goals? What kind of support do you wish you had?
12. How do you learn best? What do you need to learn now?
13. What do your instincts say? What do you *know*?
14. What would it mean to you to have it all?
15. How do you define personal and professional success?

Appendix C

Making Time for Personal Leadership: 10 Timesaving Techniques

In my experience, the one universal barrier to living and leading well is *time*. You need time to practice personal leadership—time to think, time to plan, time to align to your most important priorities. Here are 10 timesaving techniques to get you that time.

1. START WITH WHAT YOU WANT, NOT WHAT YOU HAVE TO DO

With all of the different formats and systems and processes out there for helping people organize their time, I have found the most effective tool to be a blank piece of paper. Every day, get out one small blank sheet. A 4×6 note card works great.

1. On the top half, write in the appointments you have today.
2. In the spaces between the appointments, schedule uninterrupted time to work on your most important priority.
3. On the bottom half, write no more than three to five actions you must accomplish—or want to accomplish—before the day is done.

Use your focus areas and action plans to do this, as well as your appointment calendar. You will start every day focused and end it having moved on your goals.

2. OPEN AND CLOSE UP SHOP

The beginning and end of the day are the most critical for saving time, because you use them to get your thoughts organized. Reserve the first and last hour of the day for yourself.

> *At the beginning of the day:* Take the time to consult your action plan, assess your schedule, and plan your day.
> *At the end of the day:* Take the time to tie up any loose ends, put away projects with a note about what to do next, revisit your action plans, schedule time in your calendar for important tasks, and ready your desk for when you return.

Back in the day before corporations and cubicles, morning and evenings were the time to open and close up shop. Even if you work odd hours and a crazy schedule, you still need that time when the doors are locked to get everything in order. You have the right to arrive and leave with a clean desk and a clear mind.

3. SET THE BOUNDARIES

To get extra hours for yourself, try these suggestions:

- *Refuse to schedule meetings when you need time for yourself.* Don't make excuses. Your time alone is just as important as your time with others. You will be more available and present for them when you return.
- *Extend your day.* If your meetings usually start at eight, your hour for yourself starts at seven. If your day usually lasts until five, the "last hour" you reserve goes from five to six.
- *Shrink your day.* If adding two high-quality hours to your day is impossible, try cutting the time you make available to others. If you need to start your day at eight and end at five, then you're available for appointments from nine to four.
- *Sweeten the deal.* Make your time for yourself nurturing. Treat yourself to a good cup of coffee and some music, or some other special indulgences, routines, or niceties to remind you that the time you save is special time for you.
- *Get out of there.* It's easier to resist temptation if temptation can't find you. Try taking your hours to yourself into private, either by closing your door or by getting away from the office.

Are there barriers that sometimes make it difficult to do this? Of course. But if you can discipline yourself to make it happen, you will learn that these hours do more to help you stay on top of your work and enjoy your life than any other hours in the day. With just a little time to get focused, you will feel complete, clear, rested, and renewed.

4. GO TO THE "LIBRARY"

When you look back on the times you've had to study—*really* study, for something important like your hardest exams—where did you go? For many of us, it was the library. You can re-create the space and silence of the library in your everyday life.

- Turn off your phone.
- Leave your PDA, Internet connection, pager, and so on behind.
- Turn off your e-mail.
- Escape to a quiet place, alone—a conference room, an empty office, a café, or your kitchen table.
- Don't tell anyone where you're going. Just slip away.

It is so hard to concentrate in our beeping, buzzing, urgent, ever-available world. But you will accomplish exponentially more if you can escape even for an hour at a time to a place where you can think and get things done.

5. GIVE YOURSELF PERMISSION

The most common words I hear when I help leaders look for time are, "I can't."

- "I can't turn off my cell phone."
- "I can't schedule time for myself during the day."
- "I can't get out of work any earlier."

Ask yourself: Whose permission do you need to do any of these things? Chances are the one who is holding you back is you.

6. GET PERMISSION

If there really *is* someone who keeps you from getting the time you need to work on your inner as well as your outer edge, ask them for time.

- Ask your boss: "I need to find at least an hour a day of uninterrupted time to concentrate on important behind-the-scenes work and stay aligned to our/my priorities. When would be the most convenient time for me to do that?"

- Ask your employees: "We could all use time to get our work done. What time of the day or week could we agree not to schedule meetings?"
- Ask your family: "I need some time for myself to work on some of my personal priorities so that I can be my best here at home and also at work. Let's make a plan for when I can have that time."

As a mother of small children, I can tell you even toddlers understand that grown-ups need some time alone. Surely reasonable people around you (who also need time for themselves) can respect your need to get time to yourself. Give them credit. Ask for their help.

7. LOP SOMETHING OFF

One reason it's hard to get big chunks of good quality time is that we're nibbling around the edges. An hour here, 15 minutes there, squeezed between a hasty lunch and the nagging to dos.

Think bigger. If your time for yourself is important, *what* is it more important *than*? Look in your life for a whole area that you can eliminate, saving you several hours in one fell swoop.

The trick is to find those activities that are less important than you really thought. You can do this both in your personal life and at work.

- Gina figured out most of her clients came from referrals. She lopped off networking events and saved several hours a month.
- Mahendra chose the most valuable of her social groups (five college friends) and lopped off book club, her parenting group, and the gourmet group and saved at least two hours a week.
- Tony realized he spent hours on yard work every weekend, and he didn't even enjoy it. He hired the neighbor kid to mow and weed, lopping off a time-consuming chore and buying him half a day every week.
- Mik recognized how tense and grumpy all his meetings were making him. He made a list of the meetings he had to attend. They tallied up to over 40 hours a week. He lopped off half of them by getting off two committees and finding more efficient ways to communicate. Then the meetings only tallied up to 20 hours.
- Brian counted up to three hours a day in traffic. He lopped off drive time by shifting his schedule for a less conventional commute, saving him over two hours a day.

Whether we want to admit it or not, we're the ones who fill up our time. Lop off a hunk of the time you spend on lesser-value activities and you'll suddenly have all the time you need.

8. BRING IT IN

Many of us drive all over town to do our errands. We drive out of our way to get to our favorite gym, then swing back across town to hit our preferred supermarket, then head all the way out the other way to meet friends for dinner. This unconscious habit eats up your time, adds to your stress, and hurts the environment. To eliminate the waste, think about the places you go and experiment with ways to bring them in closer—closer to each other, closer to home, or closer to your route to and from work.

A client of mine who was a master at this technique moved her errands pattern from all over the city into a two-mile radius. She pulled her dry cleaners, gas station, bank, drug store, doctors, mechanic, and gym all closer to home. You can do the same by filling in this sentence as many times as you can: "My _____ is too far away. How can I bring it in?" Quality services are everywhere. Give up the need to travel for miles to get them.

9. FARM IT OUT

Just as effective as bringing your community in closer is the strategy of farming things out. In your personal life, have you ever considered farming out any of these tasks?

- your cleaning
- your laundry
- your errands
- your personal accounting
- your plant care
- your cooking

In your professional life, have you ever considered farming out any of these tasks?

- your filing
- your phone calls
- your meetings
- your writing
- your sales
- your marketing
- your travel

If you have ever delegated any of these items, you know it's possible to let others do some of the work so you can get more time to yourself. Challenge yourself. What else can you farm out? Put the word out. See who's out there to help. Save yourself time.

10. DO THE HARDEST THING FIRST

It's stressful not to get to the things that matter to us, and it exacerbates our feeling that we never have enough time. Turn that situation around by doing the thing that's hardest for you first. Whether it's exercising in the morning, working on your most challenging account first thing in the day, or making the difficult decisions before doing anything else, you will feel like you've saved time because the pressure is off. You will actually have saved time because you won't waste it worrying and procrastinating.

What are your best techniques for saving time? Send them to us at www. theinneredge.com. Look for updated postings on the website to help you get the time you need for the practices of personal leadership that help you live and lead well.

Notes

THE INNER EDGE

1. Parker J. Palmer, *A Hidden Wholeness* (San Francisco: Jossey Bass, 2004), 47.

2. Rodd Wagner and James K. Harter, *12: The Elements of Great Managing* (New York: Gallup, 2006), 201.

3. For more information, see the following sources: James M. Kouzes and Barry Posner, "A Prescription for Leading in Cynical Times," *Ivey Business Journal* 68, no. 6 (2004); Bill George et al., "Discovering Your Authentic Leadership," *Harvard Business Review* 85, no. 2 (2007); and Stephen M. R. Covey, *The Speed of Trust* (New York: Free Press, 2006).

4. Tom Rath, *Strengthsfinder2.0* (New York: Gallup Press, 2007).

5. Marcus Buckingham and Donald O. Clifton, *Now, Discover Your Strengths* (New York: The Free Press, 2001), 6.

6. Marcus Buckingham, *Go Put Your Strengths to Work* (New York: The Free Press, 2007), 10.

7. Ibid., 16.

8. Daniel Pink, *Free Agent Nation: The Future of Working for Yourself* (New York: Grand Central Publishing, 2002).

9. Gary Rivlin, "In Silicon Valley, Millionaires Who Don't Live Rich," *New York Times,* August 5, 2007, http://query.nytimes.com/gst/fullpage.html?res=9C00E7D6103DF936A3575BC0A9619C8B63.

10. Tom Rath and Donald O. Clifton, *How Full Is Your Bucket?* (New York: Gallup Press, 2004), 33.

11. Joe Farcht, *Building Personal Leadership.* (New York: Morgan James, 2007).

12. Peter F. Drucker, "Managing Oneself," *Harvard Business Review* 77, no. 2 (1999).

13. John Dewey, *How We Think* (Mineola, NY: Dover, 1910).

14. W. Brian Arthur et al., "Illuminating the Blind Spot: Leadership in the Context of Emerging Worlds," Dialog on Leadership, 2000, http://www.dialogonleadership.org/WhitePaper.html.

15. Seth Godin, "There Is No Correlation at All between Success and Hours Worked," *Fast Company*, no. 47 (2001).

16. Claudia Wallis, "The New Science of Happiness," *Time*, January 17, 2005.

17. Please see the following sources: Thomas A. Kochan, "Taking the High Road," *MIT Sloan Management Review* 47, no. 4 (2006); Buckingham and Clifton, *Now, Discover Your Strengths*; Kouzes and Posner, "A Prescription for Leading"; and Robert E. Quinn, "Moments of Greatness," *Harvard Business Review* 83, no. 7/8 (2005).

18. Wagner and Harter, *12: The Elements of Great Managing*, xvi.

19. Robert Gandossey and Marc Effron, *Leading the Way* (Hoboken, NJ: Wiley, 2004).

THE FIRST PRACTICE

1. Robert Cooper, *Get Out of Your Own Way* (New York: Crown Business, 2006), 20.

2. Daniel Goleman, *Working with Emotional Intelligence* (New York: Bantam Books, 1998), 33.

3. John Hamm, "The Five Messages Leaders Must Manage," *Harvard Business Review* 84, no. 5 (2006): 116.

4. Thomas N. Gilmore and Gregory P. Shea, "Organizational Learning and the Leadership Skill of Time Travel," *Journal of Management Development* 16, no. 4 (1997).

5. "Creator of Time Warner, Steven J. Ross, Is Dead at 65," *New York Times*, December 12, 1992. Quoted in Gilmore and Shea, "Organizational Learning and the Leadership Skill of Time Travel," 303.

6. Gilmore and Shea, "Organizational Learning and the Leadership Skill of Time Travel," 310.

7. Cooper, *Get Out of Your Own Way*, 15.

THE SECOND PRACTICE

1. Robert S. Kaplan, "What to Ask the Person in the Mirror," *Harvard Business Review* 85, no. 1 (2007): 89.

2. Ibid., 90.

3. Stephen R. Covey, A. Roger Merrill, and Rebecca R. Merrill, *First Things First* (New York: Simon & Schuster, 1994), 146.

4. Peter M. Senge, "Walk into the Future," *Executive Excellence* 16, no. 4 (1999): 10.

5. Parker J. Palmer, *The Active Life* (San Francisco: Jossey Bass, 1991), 41.

THE THIRD PRACTICE

1. Rodd Wagner and James K. Harter, *12: The Elements of Great Managing* (New York: Gallup, 2006), 4.

2. Jeremy Laurance, "High Stress Jobs 'Double Chances of Developing Depression,' " *The Independent*, August 2, 2007, 8.

3. Jack Canfield, *The Success Principles: How to Get from Where You Are to Where You Want to Be* (New York: Harper Collins, 2005).

4. Robert Cooper, *Get Out of Your Own Way* (New York: Crown Business, 2006), 270.

THE FOURTH PRACTICE

1. Tom Rath, *Strengthsfinder2.0* (New York: Gallup Press, 2007), i.

2. Ibid.

3. Marcus Buckingham and Donald O. Clifton, *Now, Discover Your Strengths* (New York: The Free Press, 2001).

4. Claudia M. Shelton, *Blind Spots* (Hoboken, NJ: John Wiley & Sons, 2007), 24.

5. Marcus Buckingham, *Go Put Your Strengths to Work* (New York: The Free Press, 2007).

6. Ibid.

7. Claudia Wallis, "The New Science of Happiness," *Time*, January 17, 2005.

8. Marcus Buckingham, "Be Crystal Clear," *Executive Excellence* 21, no. 9 (2004): 10.

9. Dewitt Jones, *Celebrate What's Right with the World* (St. Paul, MN: Starthrower, 2001).

10. D. Dunning et al., "Why People Fail to Recognize Their Own Incompetence," *Current Directions in Psychological Science* 12, no. 3 (2003). Quoted in

Rodd Wagner and James K. Harter, *12: The Elements of Great Managing* (New York: Gallup, 2006), 157.

11. Daniel Goleman, *Working with Emotional Intelligence* (New York: Bantam Books, 1998), 261.

12. Buckingham and Clifton, *Now, Discover Your Strengths*, 12.

13. Buckingham, *Go Put Your Strengths to Work*, 19–20.

THE FIFTH PRACTICE

1. Parker J. Palmer, *The Courage to Teach* (San Francisco: Jossey Bass, 1998), 4.

2. Stephen R. Covey, *The Eighth Habit: From Effectiveness to Greatness* (New York: Free Press, 2004), 28.

3. Lee G. Bolman and Terrence E. Deal, *Leading with Soul: An Uncommon Journey of Spirit* (San Francisco: Jossey Bass, 2001), 11.

4. Robert H. Frank, *Luxury Fever: Why Money Fails to Satisfy in an Era of Success* (New York: Free Press, 1999).

5. Robert E. Quinn, "Moments of Greatness," *Harvard Business Review* 83, no. 7/8 (2005): 75.

6. Bill George, *Authentic Leadership: Rediscovering the Secrets to Creating Lasting Value* (San Francisco: Jossey Bass, 2003).

7. Bolman and Deal, *Leading with Soul*, 43.

8. Jeffrey N. McCollum, "The Inside-Out Proposition: Keeping (and Finding) Our Balance in Contemporary Organizations," in *Insights on Leadership*, ed. Larry C. Spears (New York: John Wiley & Sons, 1998).

9. Rebecca Ryan, *Live First, Work Second* (Madison, WI: Next Generation Consulting, 2007).

10. Alan Parker, "New Value: Urgently Wanted—Inspired Leaders," *The Edge* (Malaysia), 2007.

THE SIXTH PRACTICE

1. Jack and Suzy Welch, "Call It Work-Life Choices," *BusinessWeek*, November 27, 2006, 78.

2. Richard Koch, *The 80/20 Principle: The Secret to Success by Achieving More with Less* (Nile, IL: Nightingale Conant). Audio version. Print version published in 2001 by Nicholas Brealey Publishing.

3. Bruce Cryer, Rollin McCraty, and Doc Childre, "Pull the Plug on Stress," *Harvard Business Review* 81, no. 7 (2003).

4. Bronwyn Freyer, "Are You Working Too Hard? A Conversation with Herbert Benson, M.D.," *Harvard Business Review* 83, no. 11 (2005): 53.

5. See the following sources: Roger Eglin, "Make Your Company a Healthier Place to Work," *Sunday Times* (London), September 17, 2006; and

Wallace Immen, "A Career Killer Called Stress," *The Globe and Mail*, August 1, 2007.

6. See the following sources: Jeremy Laurance, "High Stress Jobs 'Double Chances of Developing Depression,'" *The Independent*, August 2, 2007; Rodd Wagner and James K. Harter, *12: The Elements of Great Managing* (New York: Gallup, 2006); and Tom Rath and Donald O. Clifton, *How Full Is Your Bucket?* (New York: Gallup Press, 2004).

7. Diane Fassel, "Lives in the Balance," in *Insights on Leadership*, ed. Larry C. Spears (New York: John Wiley & Sons, 1998), 219.

8. Ibid.

9. Ibid., 221.

10. Wallace Immen, "A Career Killer Called Stress," *Globe and Mail*, August 1, 2007.

11. Juliet Schorr, *The Overworked American* (New York: Basic Book, 1992).

12. Seth Godin, "There Is No Correlation at All between Success and Hours Worked," *Fast Company* 47 (2001).

13. Robert Cooper, *Get Out of Your Own Way* (New York: Crown Business, 2006), 114.

14. David H. Freedman, "Taskus Interruptus," *Inc. Magazine*, February 2007, 67–68.

15. Ibid., 68.

16. Cooper, *Get Out of Your Own Way*, 96.

17. Freedman, "Taskus Interruptus," 67.

18. See Freedman, "Taskus Interruptus," and John Blackstone, "Stress Is One of Brain's Biggest Enemies," *CBS News* (2007).

19. Ibid.

20. Stephen R. Covey, A. Roger Merrill, and Rebecca R. Merrill, *First Things First* (New York: Simon & Schuster, 1994), 31.

21. Godin, "There Is No Correlation at All between Success and Hours Worked," 78.

THE SEVENTH PRACTICE

1. James M. Kouzes, "Getting to the Heart of Leadership," *Journal for Quality and Participation* 22, no. 5 (1999): 64.

2. Kerry J. Sulkowicz, "The Corporate Shrink," *Fast Company*, September 2005, 90.

3. "Executive Update: Two Trends," *T+D* 58, no. 2 (2004): 13.

4. Napoleon Hill, *Think and Grow Rich* (New York: Fawcett Books, 1960).

5. David A. Nadler, "Confessions of a Trusted Counselor," *Harvard Business Review* 83, no. 9 (2005): 70.

THE EIGHTH PRACTICE

1. "Executive Challenges: The Seasons of CEO Effectiveness," *Leader to Leader,* 2000 no. 16 (2000): 49–51.

2. Peter F. Drucker, *A Functioning Society* (New York: Harper Collins, 2003), 55.

3. Marshall Goldsmith, "Helping Successful People Get Even Better," *Journal for Quality and Participation* 26, no. 1 (2003).

4. Margaret Heffernan and Saj-Nicole Joni, "Of Proteges and Pitfalls," *Fast Company,* (August 2005): 81–83.

5. Howard Morgan, Phil Harkins, and Marshall Goldsmith, eds., *The Art and Practice of Leadership Coaching* (Hoboken, NJ: John Wiley and Sons, 2005).

6. Joelle K. Jay, *Quality Teaching: Reflection as the Heart of Practice* (Oxford: Scarecrow Education, 2003).

7. Merrill C. Anderson, Pamela Brill, and Jessica Lynch, "The Utilization and Impact of Leadership Coaching in Organizations: Results from the Second Annual Benchmark Study ," 24: MetrixGlobal, LLC and Linkage Inc., 2007.

8. Parker J. Palmer, *The Active Life* (San Francisco: Jossey Bass, 1991), 61.

9. Sidney Finkelstein, *The Seven Habits of Spectacularly Unsuccessful Executives* (Farmington Hills, MI: Thomson Gale, 2004), 87.

10. Personal correspondence with Howard Morgan, May 5, 2009.

THE NINTH PRACTICE

1. Parker J. Palmer, *Let Your Life Speak* (San Francisco: Jossey Bass, 2000), 3.

2. Shakti Gawain, *Creating True Prosperity* (Novato, CA: New World Library, 1997), 58.

3. Ibid.

4. Ibid., 60.

5. Richard Koch, *The 80/20 Principle: The Secret to Success by Achieving More with Less* (Nile, IL: Nightingale Conant1999). Audio version. Printed version published in 2001 by Nicholas Brealey Publishing.

6. Ibid.

7. William Bloom, *The Endorphin Effect* (London, United Kingdom: Judy Piatkus Publishers Ltd., 2001), 12. Quoted in Stephen R. Covey, *The Eighth Habit: From Effectiveness to Greatness* (New York: Free Press, 2004), 55.

8. Parker J. Palmer, *A Hidden Wholeness* (San Francisco: Jossey Bass, 2004), 59.

9. Joel Stein, "Just Say Om," *Time,* August 4, 2003, 48–56.

10. Joel Stein, "Just Say Om," *Time,* August 4, 2003.

11. Robert Cooper, *Get out of Your Own Way* (New York: Crown Business, 2006), 254.

12. *Tao Te Ching* (New York: Perennial Classics, 1988), 3.

13. Bronwyn Freyer, "Are You Working Too Hard? A Conversation with Herbert Benson, M.D.," *Harvard Business Review* 83, no. 11 (2005): 55.

14. Rainer Maria Rilke, *Letters to a Young Poet* (New York: Vintage, 1903).

THE TENTH PRACTICE

1. Roger Martin, "How Successful Leaders Think," *Harvard Business Review* 85, no. 6 (2007).

2. Ibid., 62.

3. Ian Mitroff and Elizabeth A. Denton, *A Spiritual Audit of Corporate America* (San Francisco: Jossey Bass, 1999), xv.

4. Robert S. Kaplan, "What to Ask the Person in the Mirror," *Harvard Business Review* 85, no. 1 (2007): 95.

5. "Definitions of Alignment on the Web," http://www.google.com/search?sourceid=navclient&aq=t&ie=UTF-8&rls=RNWK,RNWK:2006-04,RNWK:en&q=define%3aAlignment.

LEADING ON THE EDGE

1. Tom Peters, "Rule #3 Leadership Is Confusing as Hell," *Fast Company,* March 2001, 134.

2. See the following sources: Peter F. Drucker, "What Executives Should Remember," *Harvard Business Review* 84, no. 2 (2006); Bill George, *Authentic Leadership: Rediscovering the Secrets to Creating Lasting Value* (San Francisco: Jossey Bass, 2003); and Marshall Goldsmith and Howard Morgan, "Leadership Is a Contact Sport," *Strategy + Business* 36 (2004).

3. PickensPlan, http://www.pickensplan.com.

4. Bill Gates, "Making Capitalism More Creative," *Time,* 2008, http://www.time.com/printout/0,8816,1828069,00.html.

Index

About the Author

JOELLE K. JAY is an executive coach with a Ph.D. in learning and leadership from the University of Washington, as well as a Master Certified Coach with the International Coach Federation and an adjunct faculty member at the University of Nevada. Jay coaches leaders in companies like Microsoft, Wachovia, and AT&T, as well as small business leaders and independent professionals. She is affiliated with the Leadership Research Institute and is one of the leading executive coaches in the U.S. Jay is the author of *Baby on Board: Becoming a Mother without Losing Yourself—A Guide for Moms to Be* (Amacom, 2007); *Quality Teaching: Reflection as the Heart of Practice* (Scarecrow, 2003), winner of the Robert C. Lee award for outstanding research and used in college courses throughout the country; and over 75 articles.